MW00489963

PowerShell 3.0 Advanced Administration Handbook

A fast-paced PowerShell guide with real-world scenarios and detailed solutions

Sherif Talaat

Haijun Fu

[PACKT] PUBLISHING enterprise
professional expertise distilled

BIRMINGHAM - MUMBAI

PowerShell 3.0 Advanced Administration Handbook

Copyright © 2013 Packt Publishing

All rights reserved. No part of this book may be reproduced, stored in a retrieval system, or transmitted in any form or by any means, without the prior written permission of the publisher, except in the case of brief quotations embedded in critical articles or reviews.

Every effort has been made in the preparation of this book to ensure the accuracy of the information presented. However, the information contained in this book is sold without warranty, either express or implied. Neither the authors, nor Packt Publishing, and its dealers and distributors will be held liable for any damages caused or alleged to be caused directly or indirectly by this book.

Packt Publishing has endeavored to provide trademark information about all of the companies and products mentioned in this book by the appropriate use of capitals. However, Packt Publishing cannot guarantee the accuracy of this information.

First published: April 2013

Production Reference: 1150413

Published by Packt Publishing Ltd.
Livery Place
35 Livery Street
Birmingham B3 2PB, UK.

ISBN 978-1-84968-642-6

www.packtpub.com

Cover Image by Siddhart Ravishankar (sidd.ravishankar@gmail.com)

Credits

Authors
Sherif Talaat

Haijun Fu

Reviewers
Mark Andrews

Karim CAMMOUN

Tong Young

Acquisition Editor
Rukhsana Khambatta

Lead Technical Editor
Dayan Hyames

Technical Editors
Sharvari Baet

Prasad Dalvi

Nitee Shetty

Copy Editors
Brandt D'Mello

Insiya Morbiwala

Aditya Nair

Alfida Paiva

Project Coordinator
Arshad Sopariwala

Proofreaders
Amy Guest

Chris Smith

Indexer
Monica Ajmera Mehta

Graphics
Valentina Dsilva

Production Coordinator
Shantanu Zagade

Cover Work
Shantanu Zagade

About the Authors

Sherif Talaat is a young computer science addict. He is MCSA, MCSE, MCTS, and MCITP certified. He has been working in the ICT industry since 2005. He used to work on Microsoft core infrastructure platforms and solutions with main focus on IT process automation and scripting techniques.

He is one of the early adopters of Windows PowerShell in the region called MEA — Middle East and Africa. He speaks about Windows PowerShell in technical events and user groups' gatherings; he is the founder of the "Egypt PowerShell User Group" (http://powershellgroup.org/egypt), and is the author behind the first and only Arabic PowerShell blog (http://arabianpowershell.wordpress.com). He has been awarded the Microsoft Most Valuable Professional (MVP) award for PowerShell five times in row since 2009. You can also catch him at sheriftalaat.com.

Acknowledgement

I would like to take the chance to dedicate this book to the soul of my dad and to thank my mom for her love, encouragement, and prayers. To my sisters Shereen and Dalia, and my brother Amr, thank you so much for the usual support, feedback, guidance, and for being proud of me.

To Israa, the best wife in the world, thanks for your love, support, and patience during the long days and nights I have spent writing this book. I could not have done this without you.

To my dear son Yahia, you were the hidden source of inspiration to complete this book. Keep it up my son, I need this again in future engagements.

To Prof. Ahmed Bahaa, Refaat Issa, and Sherif Tawfik, thanks for everything you taught me for building the unique, professional, persistent, and challenging person inside me. I really can't thank you enough for the support, advice, trust, and belief you had in me.

Last but not the least, thank you Packt Publishing for giving me the chance to write this book. I'd also thank every team member who contributed to this project. Rukhsana, Arshad, Dayan, the external reviewers, and the other guys whom I didn't meet—your contributions were invaluable and this book wouldn't be what it is without you.

Haijun Fu is a computer programmer and an author living in China. He was educated at the Lanzhou University. He has been a Windows PowerShell Microsoft Most Valuable Professional (MVP) since 2011.

With a strong focus on PowerShell, cloud computing, the next generation of Internet security, Internet technology development, software testing, and database design, he has been writing many articles in order to share his experience with others on his blog. He has over 7 years of experience in software development and system architecture design. He is skilled especially at systems analysis, architecture design, and software project management.

In his spare time, he likes reading and writing. He is the author of two technical books called *Windows PowerShell 2.0 Application Programming Best*, *Practices Publishing House of Electronics Industry* in Mainland China and *350 PowerShell Utilize Example: Windows Automation Technology Manual* in Taiwan.

He can be found on the Web at `fuhaijun.com` and on Twitter as `@fuhj02`. You can also reach him by e-mail at `PowerShell@live.cn`.

Acknowledgement

First and foremost, I'd like to thank my family who have always been a source of inspiration and encouragement. Without their support, who knows where I'd be. I am very thankful to my love, Ruby Liu, who has always stood by me, helped me at all times, and has even smilingly got me cups of tea during my sleepless nights of writing!

Writing a book is an interesting journey. Now that it's completed, looking back over the last several months I'm amazed at how lucky I've been to come in contact with so many terrific people.

I would also like to express my gratitude to my friend and co-author of this book, Sherif Talaat, for giving me so many useful suggestions on this book.

I was fortunate to have three great guys as reviewers for my book, Mark Andrews, Karim CAMMOUN, and Tong Young. They spent countless hours providing feedback and examples, researching specific content, offering lots of encouragement, and engaging with me in great discussions about PowerShell.

Thanks to the editorial and project team at Packt Publishing for giving me the opportunity to write this book, and also being patient and understanding through the process of writes, re-writes, technical edits. So a really big thanks goes to them, especially Rukhsana, Dayan, Arshad, and many more.

The team at Packt Publishing, it was an honor and privilege working with you.

Last but not the least, I would like to thank my friends who helped me directly or indirectly by giving me moral support.

About the Reviewers

Mark Andrews has had a varied career in technology. Over the last 18 years he has worked in several departments ranging from customer service to quality assurance. Throughout all of these positions, the responsibility of configuration management and build management has always fallen either to him personally or to one of the groups that he managed; because of his "keeping a hand in" management style, he has been involved closely with the scripting and automation framework for this area. Creating scripted frameworks that intercommunicate across machines, operating systems or domain boundaries is a passion for him.

Karim CAMMOUN is an IT consultant based in Ecublens, Switzerland, and has been working on Microsoft products for the past 20 years. With a strong expertise on Microsoft server products, he is a key player in migration projects, analyzing customer needs, and designing and deploying AD, Exchange, Lync, and Windows. Besides, he also develops in C++, PowerShell, VBscript, and VBA.

Tong Young has been working in the IT industry since 2000, focusing on Microsoft Windows Server, Exchange, SQL, SCCM, and SCOM. He is a PowerShell enthusiast who uses PowerShell every day to automate tasks and add value to everyday tasks. He is currently working at `yellowpages.com`.

www.PacktPub.com

Support files, eBooks, discount offers and more

You might want to visit www.PacktPub.com for support files and downloads related to your book.

Did you know that Packt offers eBook versions of every book published, with PDF and ePub files available? You can upgrade to the eBook version at www.PacktPub.com and as a print book customer, you are entitled to a discount on the eBook copy. Get in touch with us at service@packtpub.com for more details.

At www.PacktPub.com, you can also read a collection of free technical articles, sign up for a range of free newsletters and receive exclusive discounts and offers on Packt books and eBooks.

http://PacktLib.PacktPub.com

Do you need instant solutions to your IT questions? PacktLib is Packt's online digital book library. Here, you can access, read and search across Packt's entire library of books.

Why Subscribe?

- Fully searchable across every book published by Packt
- Copy and paste, print and bookmark content
- On demand and accessible via web browser

Free Access for Packt account holders

If you have an account with Packt at www.PacktPub.com, you can use this to access PacktLib today and view nine entirely free books. Simply use your login credentials for immediate access.

Instant Updates on New Packt Books

Get notified! Find out when new books are published by following @PacktEnterprise on Twitter, or the *Packt Enterprise* Facebook page.

Table of Contents

Preface

PowerShell 3.0 Advanced Administration Handbook comes with a set of real-world scenarios and detailed scripts that will help you get started with PowerShell and learn what PowerShell is, how to write the syntax and build your scripts, and how to use and integrate PowerShell with different technologies, products, and tools.

This handbook starts with the essential topics of PowerShell, and then introduces the new features in PowerShell 3.0. The book then goes through building PowerShell scripts, functions, and developing extensions such as snap-ins and modules, and continues with detailed examples showing the usage of PowerShell with different technologies and products to give you an idea of PowerShell usage in the real world.

What this book covers

Chapter 1, Getting Started with PowerShell, introduces us to PowerShell, which is built based on .NET and is an object-based shell and scripting language. This chapter shows us how we can make use of PowerShell's integration with COM, WMI, and ADSI technologies alongside its tight integration with .NET. Indeed, PowerShell is the only technology that enables you to create and work with objects from these various technologies in one environment.

Chapter 2, Developing Snap-ins for PowerShell, explains the use of snap-ins that are compiled into assemblies, when released as a program for third-party users. In this chapter you will see how you can extend Windows PowerShell by writing your own snap-ins. These may contain cmdlets and providers too. The author can also encrypt based on .NET code obfuscation to protect their source code. Thus the authors of programs need not worry about their snap-ins decompiling the source code.

Chapter 3, Using PowerShell Remoting, shows us how PowerShell remoting enables management of computers from a remote location. Remoting is built based on **Windows remote management (WinRM)**. WinRM is Microsoft's implementation of the WS-Management protocol.

Chapter 4, Extending Windows PowerShell, introduces us to a very import feature in Windows PowerShell 3.0 — modules. You can load most of the existing snap-ins as a module, which means you don't need to have administrator privileges to load a new snap-in. You can simply place it in any folder, access it, and tell PowerShell where to find it.

Chapter 5, Managing Core Infrastructure with PowerShell, demonstrates how PowerShell can be used to replace the GUI to perform different administration tasks on Windows Server, especially the installation of the server core.

Chapter 6, Managing Active Directory with PowerShell, introduces us to the Active Directory module for Windows PowerShell, which consolidates a group of cmdlets. The Active Directory module for Windows PowerShell provides a centralized experience for administering your directory services. In this chapter you will look at the Active Directory-related cmdlets, the Active Directory server roles, and how you can manage the Active Directory using PowerShell.

Chapter 7, Managing the Server with PowerShell, explains how you can manage your server with great flexibility using PowerShell, which is built into Windows Server 2012. Many PowerShell cmdlets exist to let you perform several of the key administrative tasks you may need to do on a daily basis, including installing features for your Windows Server 2012, managing networking, managing Group Policy, managing IIS, managing DNS server, managing Hyper-V and AppLocker, and many others.

Chapter 8, Managing Unified Communication Environments with PowerShell, introduces us to Windows PowerShell modules for Microsoft Exchange Server, Lync Server, and Office 365, and explains how it can be utilized for a better and easier administration and management.

Chapter 9, Managing Collaboration and Data Platforms with PowerShell, provides recipes on how to deal with Microsoft SQL Server, Microsoft SharePoint Server, and SharePoint Online.

Chapter 10, Managing Microsoft Desktop Virtualization with PowerShell, provides guidance and scripts on how to build end-to-end Desktop Virtualization scenarios that are session- and virtual-machine-based, using Windows PowerShell.

Chapter 11, Managing Microsoft Cloud Platform with PowerShell, tackles the Microsoft cloud platform with Windows Azure and explains how to use Windows PowerShell to automate Windows and SQL Azure tasks. It also provides ways to overcome the technical limitations of using Windows Azure Management Portal.

Chapter 12, Integrating Windows PowerShell and System Center Orchestrator, describes how PowerShell can be used in the real world in combination with Microsoft System Center Orchestrator to build an IT Process Automation standard framework.

What you need for this book

This book requires that you have Windows PowerShell 3.0, which is available out of the box in Windows Server 2012 and Windows 8. It's also available for earlier versions of Windows as part of Microsoft's Windows Management Framework (WMF) 3.0

This book is mainly about using Windows PowerShell with different technologies and tools, so you must have the following software in order to proceed:

- Windows Server 2012
- Exchange Server 2013
- Lync Server 2013
- SQL Server 2012
- SharePoint Server 2013
- An Office 365 subscription
- A Windows Azure subscription
- System Center Orchestrator 2012
- Microsoft Visual Studio 2010

Who this book is for

This book is intended for IT administrators who wish to learn Windows PowerShell, and want to quickly discover it's capabilities with different tools and technologies.

Conventions

In this book, you will find a number of styles of text that distinguish between different kinds of information. Here are some examples of these styles, and an explanation of their meaning.

Code words in text, database table names, folder names, filenames, file extensions, pathnames, dummy URLs, user input, and Twitter handles are shown as follows: "The `Out-Host -Paging` command is a useful pipeline element."

A block of code is set as follows:

```
Function Reload-Module($ModuleName)
{
if((get-module -list | where{$_.name -eq "$ModuleName"} | measure-
object).count -gt 0)
{
  if((get-module -all | where{$_.Name -eq "$ModuleName"} |
  measure-object).count -gt 0)
  {
    Remove-Module $ModuleName
    Write-Host "Module $ModuleName Unloading"
  }
  Import-Module $ModuleName
  Write-Host "Module $ModuleName Loaded"
}
Else
{
  Write-Host "Module $ModuleName Doesn't Exist"
}
}
```

Any command-line input or output is written as follows:

```
PS> Invoke-Command {(new-object BasicTest).Multiply(5, 2)}
```

New terms and **important words** are shown in bold. Words that you see on the screen, in menus or dialog boxes for example, appear in the text like this: "Click on **Run** to execute the command with the parameters you entered."

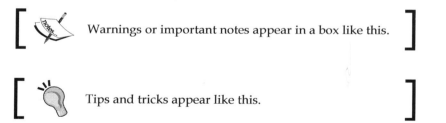

Warnings or important notes appear in a box like this.

Tips and tricks appear like this.

Reader feedback

Feedback from our readers is always welcome. Let us know what you think about this book—what you liked or may have disliked. Reader feedback is important for us to develop titles that you really get the most out of.

To send us general feedback, simply send an e-mail to feedback@packtpub.com, and mention the book title via the subject of your message.

If there is a topic that you have expertise in and you are interested in either writing or contributing to a book, see our author guide on www.packtpub.com/authors.

Customer support

Now that you are the proud owner of a Packt book, we have a number of things to help you to get the most from your purchase.

Downloading the example code

You can download the example code files for all Packt books you have purchased from your account at http://www.packtpub.com. If you purchased this book elsewhere, you can visit http://www.packtpub.com/support and register to have the files e-mailed directly to you.

Errata

Although we have taken every care to ensure the accuracy of our content, mistakes do happen. If you find a mistake in one of our books—maybe a mistake in the text or the code—we would be grateful if you would report this to us. By doing so, you can save other readers from frustration and help us improve subsequent versions of this book. If you find any errata, please report them by visiting http://www.packtpub.com/submit-errata, selecting your book, clicking on the **errata submission form** link, and entering the details of your errata. Once your errata are verified, your submission will be accepted and the errata will be uploaded on our website, or added to any list of existing errata, under the Errata section of that title. Any existing errata can be viewed by selecting your title from http://www.packtpub.com/support.

Piracy

Piracy of copyright material on the Internet is an ongoing problem across all media. At Packt, we take the protection of our copyright and licenses very seriously. If you come across any illegal copies of our works, in any form, on the Internet, please provide us with the location address or website name immediately so that we can pursue a remedy.

Please contact us at copyright@packtpub.com with a link to the suspected pirated material.

We appreciate your help in protecting our authors, and our ability to bring you valuable content.

Questions

You can contact us at questions@packtpub.com if you are having a problem with any aspect of the book, and we will do our best to address it.

1
Getting Started with PowerShell

PowerShell runs existing commands and scripts seamlessly. You can make use of PowerShell's integration with COM, WMI, and ADSI technologies along with its tight integration with .NET. Indeed, PowerShell is the only technology that enables you to create and work with objects from these various technologies in one environment.

In this chapter we will cover:

- Windows PowerShell syntax and grammar
- How to write PowerShell scripts and functions
- What is new in Windows PowerShell 3.0

In order to enable the readers to get familiar with the language environment quickly, this chapter will briefly introduce the PowerShell grammar. A key concept to grasp when starting to work in PowerShell is that everything is an object. An "object", in PowerShell, consists of properties (information we can gather) and methods (actions we can perform).

An object is something we can gather information from and/or perform an action upon. In simple terms, an object is a black box that has attributes or properties that describe it. Some of these properties are read-only. You can change or set the others. For example, consider a service that has properties such as name, display name, status, and services that it depends on.

Often, objects can also be made to do something. These actions are referred to as methods. Sometimes, the method is used to modify the object and sometimes to make an external change. A service can be stopped and started. You can also modify the service object by changing its start mode to either automatic, manual, or disabled. First of all, we will introduce the most important object in PowerShell—**pipeline**.

Working with pipelines

In a traditional command-line environment, you would have to manipulate the text to convert output from one format to another and to remove titles and column headings. A major advantage of using objects is that it is much easier to pipeline commands, that is, to pass the output of one command to another command as the input.

Windows PowerShell provides a new architecture that is based on objects rather than text. The cmdlet that receives an object can act directly on its properties and methods without any conversion or manipulation. Users can refer to properties and methods of the object by their names, rather than calculating the position of the data in the output. You do not need to manipulate strings or calculate data offsets. Pipelines act like a series of connected segments of pipe. Items moving along the pipeline pass through each segment. To create a pipeline in Windows PowerShell, you connect commands together with the pipe operator " | ". The output of each command is used as an input to the next command. A related useful characteristic of pipelines is that they operate on each item separately; thus you do not have to modify them based on each single item. Furthermore, each command in a pipeline usually passes its output to the next command in the pipeline item-by-item. This usually reduces the resource demand of complex commands and allows you to get the output immediately.

The notation used for pipelines is similar to the one used in other shells, so at first glance, it may not be apparent that Windows PowerShell introduces something new. For example, if you use the Out-Host cmdlet to force a page-by-page display of the output from another command, the output looks just like the normal text displayed on the following screen, broken up into pages:

Downloading the example code

You can download the example code files for all Packt books you have purchased from your account at http://www.packtpub.com. If you purchased this book elsewhere, you can visit http://www.packtpub.com/support and register to have the files e-mailed directly to you.

```
PS C:\> Get-ChildItem -Path C:\WINDOWS\System32 | Out-Host -Paging

    Directory: C:\WINDOWS\System32

Mode                LastWriteTime     Length Name
----                -------------     ------ ----
d----         7/26/2012     2:45 PM          0409
d----         7/26/2012     2:53 PM          AdvancedInstallers
d----         7/26/2012     2:53 PM          AppLocker
d----         7/26/2012     2:53 PM          ar-SA
d----         7/26/2012     2:53 PM          bg-BG
d----         7/26/2012     2:45 PM          Boot
d----         7/26/2012     2:53 PM          Bthprops
d----         7/26/2012     2:04 PM          catroot
d----        10/28/2012     5:37 PM          catroot2
d----        10/28/2012     5:51 PM          CodeIntegrity
d----         7/26/2012     2:45 PM          Com
d----        11/19/2012    11:23 AM          config
d----         7/26/2012     2:53 PM          cs-CZ
d----         7/26/2012     2:53 PM          da-DK
d----         7/26/2012     2:53 PM          de-DE
d----         7/26/2012     2:45 PM          Dism
d----        11/18/2012    12:52 AM          Drivers
d----        11/18/2012    12:51 AM          DriverStore
d----         7/26/2012     2:53 PM          el-GR
d----         7/26/2012     2:45 PM          en
d----         7/26/2012     2:53 PM          en-GB
d----         7/26/2012     2:49 PM          en-US
d----         7/26/2012     2:53 PM          es-ES
d----         7/26/2012     2:53 PM          et-EE
d----         7/26/2012     2:53 PM          fi-FI
d----         7/26/2012     2:53 PM          fr-FR
d----         7/26/2012     2:07 PM          FxsTmp
d----         7/26/2012     2:53 PM          GroupPolicy
<SPACE> next page; <CR> next line; Q quit
```

The Out-Host -Paging command is a useful pipeline element whenever you want to display a lengthy output slowly. It is especially useful if the operation is very CPU-intensive because processing is transferred to the Out-Host cmdlet when it has a complete page ready to display, and the cmdlets that precede it in the pipeline halt their operation until the next page of output is available. You can see this if you use the Windows Task Manager to monitor the CPU and memory consumed by Windows PowerShell. For example, run the following command:

`Get-ChildItem C:\Windows -recurse`

and command:

`Get-ChildItem C:\Windows -recurse | Out-Host -Paging`

compared the CPU and memory utilization rate..

What you see on the screen is text, but that is because it is necessary to represent objects as text in a console window. This is just a representation of what is really going on inside Windows PowerShell. For example, consider the Get-Location cmdlet. If you type Get-Location while your current location is the root of the C drive, you would see the following output:

Instead of using text to insert commands into a pipeline communication, Windows PowerShell uses objects. From the users' perspective, objects package related information into a form that makes it easier to manipulate the information as a unit, and extract specific items that you need.

The Get-Location command will not return the text that contains the current path, but returns an object called the PathInfo object, including the current path and some other information packet. Then the Out-Host cmdlet will send the PathInfo object to the screen, after which Windows PowerShell will decide what information is to be displayed and how to show it based on its format rules.

Viewing the object structure

Because objects play such an important role in Windows PowerShell, there are several native commands designed to work with arbitrary object types. The most important one is the Get-Member command.

The simplest technique for analyzing the objects that a command returns is to pipe the output of the command to the Get-Member cmdlet. The Get-Member cmdlet shows the formal name of the object type and a complete listing of its members. Sometimes the number of returned elements can be overwhelming. For example, a service object can have over 100 members.

To see all the members of a service object and page the output, please type the following:

```
PS > Get-Service | Get-Member | Out-Host -Paging
```

The output from this command will look something like this:

```
powershell                                                                    _  □  ×

PS C:\> Get-Service | Get-Member | Out-Host -Paging


    TypeName: System.ServiceProcess.ServiceController

Name                       MemberType   Definition
----                       ----------   ----------
Name                       AliasProperty Name = ServiceName
RequiredServices           AliasProperty RequiredServices = ServicesDependedOn
Disposed                   Event        System.EventHandler Disposed(System.Object, System.Event...
Close                      Method       void Close()
Continue                   Method       void Continue()
CreateObjRef               Method       System.Runtime.Remoting.ObjRef CreateObjRef(type request...
Dispose                    Method       void Dispose(), void IDisposable.Dispose()
Equals                     Method       bool Equals(System.Object obj)
ExecuteCommand             Method       void ExecuteCommand(int command)
GetHashCode                Method       int GetHashCode()
GetLifetimeService         Method       System.Object GetLifetimeService()
GetType                    Method       type GetType()
InitializeLifetimeService  Method       System.Object InitializeLifetimeService()
Pause                      Method       void Pause()
Refresh                    Method       void Refresh()
Start                      Method       void Start(), void Start(string[] args)
Stop                       Method       void Stop()
WaitForStatus              Method       void WaitForStatus(System.ServiceProcess.ServiceControll...
CanPauseAndContinue        Property     bool CanPauseAndContinue {get;}
CanShutdown                Property     bool CanShutdown {get;}
CanStop                    Property     bool CanStop {get;}
Container                  Property     System.ComponentModel.IContainer Container {get;}
DependentServices          Property     System.ServiceProcess.ServiceController[] DependentServi...
DisplayName                Property     string DisplayName {get;set;}
MachineName                Property     string MachineName {get;set;}
ServiceHandle              Property     System.Runtime.InteropServices.SafeHandle ServiceHandle ...
ServiceName                Property     string ServiceName {get;set;}
ServicesDependedOn         Property     System.ServiceProcess.ServiceController[] ServicesDepend...
ServiceType                Property     System.ServiceProcess.ServiceType ServiceType {get;}
Site                       Property     System.ComponentModel.ISite Site {get;set;}
Status                     Property     System.ServiceProcess.ServiceControllerStatus Status {get;}
<SPACE> next page; <CR> next line; Q quit
```

The `Get-Member` command lets you list only members that are properties. There are several forms of properties. The resulting list is still very long, but a bit more methodical, as shown in the following screenshot:

```
PS C:\> Get-Service | Get-Member -MemberType Properties


   TypeName: System.ServiceProcess.ServiceController

Name                  MemberType      Definition
----                  ----------      ----------
Name                  AliasProperty   Name = ServiceName
RequiredServices      AliasProperty   RequiredServices = ServicesDependedOn
CanPauseAndContinue   Property        bool CanPauseAndContinue {get;}
CanShutdown           Property        bool CanShutdown {get;}
CanStop               Property        bool CanStop {get;}
Container             Property        System.ComponentModel.IContainer Container {get;}
DependentServices     Property        System.ServiceProcess.ServiceController[] DependentServices {g...
DisplayName           Property        string DisplayName {get;set;}
MachineName           Property        string MachineName {get;set;}
ServiceHandle         Property        System.Runtime.InteropServices.SafeHandle ServiceHandle {get;}
ServiceName           Property        string ServiceName {get;set;}
ServicesDependedOn    Property        System.ServiceProcess.ServiceController[] ServicesDependedOn {...
ServiceType           Property        System.ServiceProcess.ServiceType ServiceType {get;}
Site                  Property        System.ComponentModel.ISite Site {get;set;}
Status                Property        System.ServiceProcess.ServiceControllerStatus Status {get;}


PS C:\>
```

If you need to look at the content outside of Windows PowerShell's default display format, you can do so through the use of the format cmdlets, which can format the output data.

Using format cmdlets to change the output view

Windows PowerShell's set of cmdlets allows users to control which attributes are displayed for a specific object. All cmdlet names begin with a verb form. The format cmdlets are `Format-Wide`, `Format-List`, `Format-Table`, and `Format-Custom`.

Each format cmdlet has default properties. These properties will be used if you do not specify a particular attribute to display. Each cmdlet also uses the same parameter name and attribute, but you need to specify which attribute has to appear. As the `Format-Wide` cmdlet reveals a single attribute display only, its property parameters require only a single value, but the characteristic parameters of `Format-List` and `Format-Table` will accept an attribute name list.

With the `Format-Wide` cmdlet, you can format the output as a table listing one property only. This makes it useful for displaying simple lists that show only one element per line.

The `Format-List` cmdlet is used for formatting the output as a list of properties, each on a new line. The `Format-Table` cmdlet is used for tabular output.

Using cmdlets to redirect data

Windows PowerShell provides several cmdlets that let you control the data's output directly. These cmdlets share two important characteristics that we will discuss in this section.

By default, Windows PowerShell sends data to the host window, which is just what the `Out-Host` cmdlet does. The `Out-Host` cmdlet is primarily used for paging data. For example, the following command uses `Out-Host` to page the output:

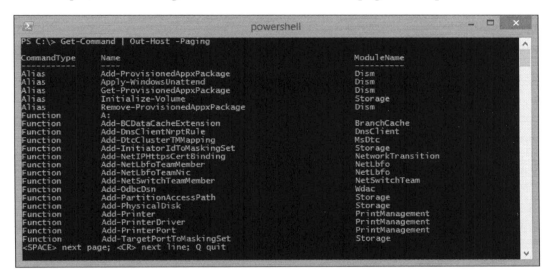

The `Out-Null` cmdlet is designed to immediately discard any input it receives. This is useful for discarding unnecessary data that you get as a side effect of running a command. When typing the following command, you will not get anything back from the command:

```
Get-Command | Out-Null
```

The `Out-Null` cmdlet does not discard an error output. For example, if you enter `Get-Command Is-NotACommand | Out-Null`, a message is displayed informing you that Windows PowerShell does not recognize `Is-NotACommand`. This is shown in the following screenshot:

You can send the output to a file instead of the console window by using the `Out-File` cmdlet. The following command line sends a list of processes to the `C:\tmp\processlist.txt` file:

```
PS > Get-Process | Out-File -FilePath C:\tmp\processlist.txt
```

Variables and objects

When you manipulate in Windows PowerShell, you are operating the .NET Framework objects. Technically, a .NET Framework object is an instance of a .NET Framework class that consists of data and the operations associated with that data. An object is a data entity that has properties.

For example, when you get a service in PowerShell, you are really getting an object that stands for the service. When you view information in it, you are viewing the properties of the service object. And, on starting a service, when you change the `Status` property of the service to `started`, you are using the `start()` method of the service object.

All objects of the same type have the same properties and methods, but each instance of an object can have different values for the properties. For example, every service object has a `Name` and `Status` property. However, each service can have a different name and a different status.

Using variables to store objects

You can store the output of a pipeline or a command in a variable for later use, or to work with it in more detail. Variables in PowerShell allow users to store the output of something that may be used later. A variable's name starts with a dollar sign ($) and can be followed by any alphanumeric character or the underscore in its name. You can create a variable and assign it a value in the same step. Windows PowerShell only creates the variable if it does not exist, otherwise it assigns the specified value to the existing variable, as shown in the following screenshot:

You can store any pipeline or command result in a variable to use it later. If that result is simple data, such as a number or a string, then the variable contains simple data. If the command generates rich text data, such as the objects that stand for system services from the `Get-Service` cmdlet, then the variable contains the list of rich data. If the command, such as a former executable, generates plain text, then the variable contains plain text.

Variables are stored in the memory; if you no longer need the variables that store a large amount of data, you should assign the `$null` value to those variables, and then PowerShell can release the memory for you.

PowerShell offers several ways to access environment variables. To list all the environment variables you can list the children of the env drive, as shown in the following screenshot:

To get an environment variable, prefix its name with $env (such as $env: variablename). An example is shown in the following screenshot:

PowerShell provides access to the environment variable through its environment provider. The provider lets you work with data storage, such as registration, environment variables, alias, and certificate, as you will visit the filesystem. Get environment variables to use their provider path; supply env: or environment:: by using the Get-ChildItem cmdlet.

Getting CIM objects

Windows Management Instrumentation (WMI) is a core technology for Windows system administration because it exposes a wide range of information in a uniform manner. As we all know, WMI is an infrastructure that supports the CIM model and Microsoft-specific extensions of CIM.

The WMI infrastructure ships in Windows 2000, which was difficult to write and use. In PowerShell 3.0, Microsoft introduced several new cmdlets, which are used for operating CIM. With these cmdlets, not only can we manage servers, but we can also manipulate all the heterogeneous devices necessary to make these servers together into a comprehensive and coherent computing platform. In today's world, cloud computing is a very important technology. Generalized cloud computing requires standard-based management. This is the reason why Microsoft paid so much attention to standard-based management in Windows Server 2012, which is expected to be a Cloud OS. We are going to discuss how to use `Get-CimClass` to access CIM objects and then how to use CIM objects to do specific things.

Listing CIM classes

The first problem of using CIM is trying to find out what can be done with CIM. CIM classes describe the resources that can be managed. There are dozens of CIM classes, some of which contain several properties.

`Get-CimClass` resolves this problem by making CIM discoverable. You can get a list of the CIM classes available on the local computer using the `-ClassName` parameter with a keyword and a wildcard character. An example is shown in the following screenshot:

`Get-CimClass` uses the `root/cimv2` namespace by default. If you want to specify another WMI namespace, use the `Namespace` parameter and specify the namespace's path, as shown in the following screenshot:

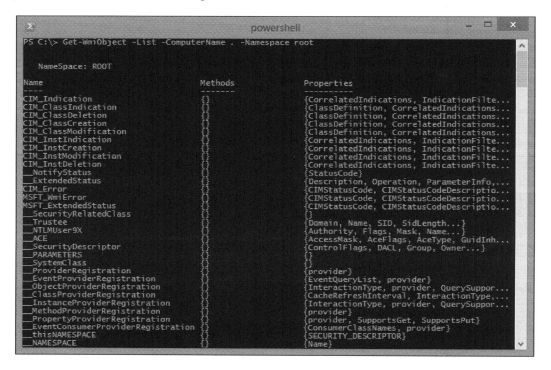

Displaying details of the CIM classes

If you are familiar with WMI cmdlets from PowerShell 2.0, you will find learning new CIM cmdlets easy. If you already know the `ClassName` value of a WMI class, you can use it to get information. For example, one of the WMI classes commonly used for searching for information about a process is `Win32_Process`. The WMI cmdlet needs to work with `ClassName` and `NameSpace`, and the CIM cmdlet follows the same pattern. Refer to the following screenshot:

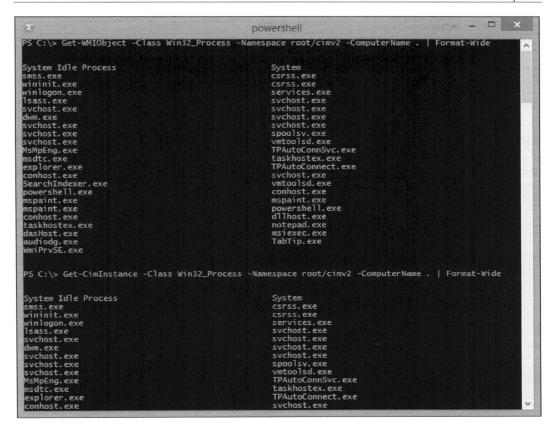

Although we are showing all of the parameters, the command can be expressed in a more succinct way. The ComputerName parameter is not necessary when connecting to the local system. We display it to demonstrate the most general case and remind you about the parameter. The Namespace parameter defaults to root/cimv2, and can be ignored as well. Finally, most cmdlets allow you to ignore the name of common parameters. With Get-WmiObject, if no name is specified for the first parameter, Windows PowerShell treats it as the Class parameter.

You will also notice that in some places, the script using the WMI cmdlet can't be simply changed to the CIM cmdlet by changing the cmdlet name. This is shown in the following example:

```
PS C:\> Invoke-WMIMethod -class Win32_Process -Name create -ArgumentList 'mspaint.exe'


__GENUS          : 2
__CLASS          : __PARAMETERS
__SUPERCLASS     :
__DYNASTY        : __PARAMETERS
__RELPATH        :
__PROPERTY_COUNT : 2
__DERIVATION     : {}
__SERVER         :
__NAMESPACE      :
__PATH           :
ProcessId        : 3528
ReturnValue      : 0
PSComputerName   :


PS C:\> Invoke-CimMethod Win32_Process -MethodName create -Arguments @{CommandLine='mspaint.exe'}

         ProcessId                    ReturnValue PSComputerName
         ---------                    ----------- --------------
               236                              0

PS C:\>
```

We can see that the parameters of the two cmdlets are completely different, and the result displayed is not the same.

Creating .NET and COM objects

There are software components with .NET Framework and COM interfaces that enable users to perform many system administration tasks. Windows PowerShell lets you use these components, so you are not limited to the tasks that can be performed by using cmdlets.

We can create an instance of an object using its default constructor. This can be done using the New-Object cmdlet with the classname as its only parameter:

```
PS C:\> $generator = New-Object System.Random
PS C:\> $generator.NextDouble()
0.473421132878131
PS C:\>
```

Many cmdlets (such as `Get-Process` and `Get-ChildItem`) generate live
.NET objects that represent tangible processes, files, and directories. However,
PowerShell supports much more of the .NET Framework than just the objects
that its cmdlets produce.

Looping and flow control

The PowerShell loop statement allows the user to execute operations without the
need to execute the command repeatedly, for example, repeating operations several
times, processing a set of items, or cycling a condition till it becomes true.

The PowerShell flow control and comparative statements let the user script adapt
to different data. They let you do this based on the value of the data by carrying out
orders, skipping some operations, and so on.

Comparison and logical operators

PowerShell allows the user to contrast data, and then make decisions with the
comparison operators. It allows making decisions based on the result of logical
operators to contrast data blocks.

Examples for comparison operators are `-eq`, `-ne`, `-ge`, `-gt`, `-lt`, `-le`, `-like`,
`-notlike`, `-match`, `-notmatch`, `-contains`, `-notcontains`, `-is`, `-isnot`, `-in`,
`-notin`, and so on.

Examples for logical operators are `-and`, `-or`, `-xor`, `-not`, `-shl`, `-shr`, and so on.

By default, the PowerShell comparison operator is not case sensitive. For all
operators that are case sensitive, the `-i` prefix makes the comparison case
insensitive, and the `-c` prefix executes case-sensitive comparisons.

Conditional statements

In PowerShell you can change the flow of execution of the script by using the
conditional statements. The following code snippet shows us an example:

```
if (condition)
{
statement block
}
elseif (condition)
{
statement block
}
```

```
else
{
statement block
}
```

If the condition calculates to $true, PowerShell implements the block you supply. Then, it continues with the rest of the if/else statement list. PowerShell needs matching parentheses in the block even if the block contains only one statement.

If the condition calculates to $false, PowerShell implements the statements under elseif until a condition matches. If there is a match, PowerShell executes the block-related conditions, and then continues to implement the rest of the if/else statement list. For example:

```
$textForMatch = Read-Host "Input some text"
$matchType = Read-Host "Supply Simple or Regex matching?"
$pattern = Read-Host "Match pattern"
if ($matchType -eq "Simple")
{
$textForMatch -like $pattern
}
elseif($matchType -eq "Regex")
{
$textForMatch -match $pattern
}
else
{
Write-Host "Match type must be Simple or Regex"
}
```

If none of the conditions calculate to $true, PowerShell executes the statement block related to the else clauses, and then continues to implement till the end of the if/else statement list.

Using switches to manage large conditional statements

A switch statement is usually used to control several conditions that have a clear value. It requires the value of the conditions to be an integer or a character. The conditions used in a switch statement are called cases. Using the value of case, the control program will jump to the matching case, and will keep running till the statement exits or meets the break statement. Usually, we can use the default clause to include other exceptions. If the conditions of the switch statement are all false, the control program will jump to execute the default clause. If the default clause is omitted, it will execute the next statement directly.

The following code snippet shows a `switch` statement:

```
switch options expression
{
comparison value { statement block }
-or
{ comparison expression } { statement block }
(...)
default { statement block }
}
```

When PowerShell evaluates a `switch` statement, it calculates the expression for the statement in the `switch` body. If the expression is a list of values, PowerShell calculates each entry against the statement in the `switch` body.

The `{comparison expression}` statement for you deals with the current input items, which are stored in the $_ variable, in any one of the script blocks. When it is dealing with a `{comparison expression}` statement, PowerShell executes a related statement block only when the `{comparison expression}` value is $true.

When dealing with a `switch` statement, PowerShell tries matching the current input object for each statement in the `switch` body even if there are already one or more matches. PowerShell exits a `switch` statement after it finds a match or if it encounters a `break` statement, which is the final statement of the block of statements.

Repeat operations with loops

A PowerShell `loop` statement lets you execute a group of statements several times.

The for statement

Consider the following code block:

```
:loop_label for(initialization; condition; increment)
{
statement block
}
```

A PowerShell `for` statement first executes the expressions given during initialization. It next assesses the condition; if the condition of the evaluation results to $true, PowerShell executes the given statement block. Then, it will execute the expressions given in increment. PowerShell continues to execute the statement block and the incremental statement as long as the condition calculates to $true.

For example:

```
for($counter = 0; $counter -lt 10; $counter++)
{
Write-Host "Processing item $counter"
}
```

The foreach statement

Consider the following code block:

```
:loop_label foreach(variable in expression)
{
statement block
}
```

When PowerShell executes a foreach statement, it implements a pipeline of the given expression. For each entry produced by the expression, it assigns an entry variable, and then executes a given statement block.

For example:

```
$handleSum = 0;
foreach($process in Get-Process |
Where-Object {$_.Handles -gt 600})
{
$handleSum += $process.Handles
}
$handleSum
```

Nested loops

Sometimes, loops may be nested within each other. However, if you are working with nested loops, how do you break and continue to work? They will always affect the inner loop, which is the loop that they were called from. However, you can also label loops and then submit the label to continue or break if you want to exit or skip the outer loops.

The next example nests two foreach loops. The first (outer) loop cycles through a field with three WMI classnames. The second (inner) loop runs through all instances of the respective WMI classes. This allows you to output all instances of all the three WMI classes. The inner loop checks whether the name of the current instance begins with "a"; if not, the inner loop will then invoke continue to skip all instances not beginning with "a". The result is a list of all services, user accounts, and running processes that begin with "a":

```
PS C:\> foreach ($wmiclass in "Win32_Service","Win32_UserAccount","Win32_Process")
>> {
>>    foreach ($instance in Get-WmiObject $wmiclass) {
>>       if (!(($instance.name.toLower()).StartsWith("a"))) {continue}
>>       "{0}: {1}" -f $instance.__CLASS, $instance.name
>>    }
>> }
>>
Win32_Service: AeLookupSvc
Win32_Service: ALG
Win32_Service: AllUserInstallAgent
Win32_Service: AppIDSvc
Win32_Service: Appinfo
Win32_Service: AppMgmt
Win32_Service: AudioEndpointBuilder
Win32_Service: Audiosrv
Win32_Service: AxInstSV
Win32_UserAccount: Administrator
PS C:\>
```

As expected, the `continue` statement in the inner loop has had an effect on the inner loop where the statement was contained. But how would you change the code if you'd like to see only the first element of all services, user accounts, and processes that begin with "a"? Actually, you would do almost the exact same thing, except that now `continue` would need to have an effect on the outer loop. Once an element was found that begins with "a", the outer loop would continue with the next WMI class:

```
PS C:\> :WMIClasses foreach ($wmiclass in "Win32_Service","Win32_UserAccount","Win32_Process") {
>>    :ExamineClasses foreach ($instance in Get-WmiObject $wmiclass) {
>>       if (($instance.name.toLower()).StartsWith("a")) {
>>          "{0}: {1}" -f $instance.__CLASS, $instance.name
>>          continue WMIClasses
>>       }
>>    }
>> }
>>
Win32_Service: AeLookupSvc
Win32_UserAccount: Administrator
PS C:\>
```

Lists, arrays, and hash tables

PowerShell makes dealing with arrays and lists similar to working with other data types: you can expediently create an array or a list, and then add or remove elements from it. You can also expediently execute sort, search, or put it in another array. When you want to store the mapping between one block of data and another, a hash table supplies a perfect solution.

For example, you can create an array and save a given set of items in it; these items should be separated by a comma, as shown in the following screenshot:

```
PS C:\> $myArray = 3,4,"Hello World"
PS C:\> $myArray
3
4
Hello World
PS C:\> _
```

You can also create an array with a specific size using the `New-Object` cmdlet. We can access a specific element of the array by using PowerShell's array access principle, as shown in the following screenshot:

```
PS C:\> $myArray = New-Object string[] 10
PS C:\> $myArray[5]="Hello PowerShell"
PS C:\> $myArray[5]
Hello PowerShell
PS C:\>
```

PowerShell's array access principle provides an easy way to visit two specific elements of an array or more combinations of the elements in the array. In PowerShell, the first item of the array is assigned index 0.

To store a command, generate a list of outputs using variable assignment, as shown in the following screenshot:

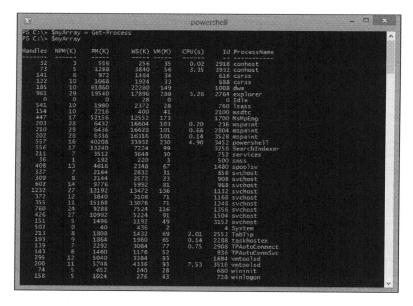

To access every item in an array, use the `Foreach-Object` cmdlet, as shown in the following screenshot:

```
PS C:\> $myArray = 1,3,5
PS C:\> $sum = 0
PS C:\> $myArray | Foreach-Object { $sum += $_ }
PS C:\> $sum
9
PS C:\>
```

To access each item in an array, use the `foreach` keyword, as shown in the following screenshot:

```
PS C:\> $myArray = 1,2,3
PS C:\> $sum = 0
PS C:\> foreach($element in $myArray) { $sum += $element }
PS C:\> $sum
6
PS C:\>
```

To access items in an array by position, use a `for` loop, as shown in the following screenshot:

```
PS C:\> $myArray = 1,2,3
PS C:\> $sum = 0
PS C:\> for($counter = 0; $counter -lt $myArray.Count; $counter++) {
>> $sum += $myArray[$counter]
>> }
>>
PS C:\> $sum
6
PS C:\>
```

PowerShell thus provides three main alternatives to deal with the elements in an array. In the `Foreach-Object` cmdlet and the `foreach` script's keywords, technology visits an element of the array and lets you use the cycle items in the array in a less structured approach.

You can use the `Sort-Object` cmdlet to sort a list of items, as shown in the following screenshot:

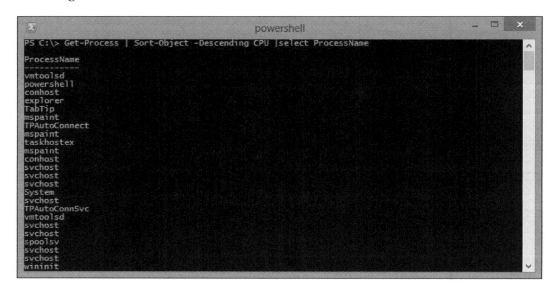

The `Sort-Object` cmdlet provides you with a convenient way to sort objects by a property that you specify. If you don't specify an attribute, the `Sort-Object` cmdlet follows the ordering rule of the objects, if they define any. In addition to sorting by a property in the ascending or descending order, the `Sort-Object` cmdlet's `-unique` `switch` operator also allows you to delete duplicates from the sorted collection.

The `-contains` operator is a useful method to determine quickly if a list contains a specific element. To search for a list item instead of matching a pattern, use the `-match` or `-like` operators. The `-eq`, `-like`, and `-match` operators are useful methods to find a matching element set for your specific condition. The `-eq` operator returns all the elements that are equal to your terms, the `-like` operator returns all the elements matched elements in the wildcard given in your pattern, and the `-match` operator returns all elements that match the regular expression given in your pattern. To delete all the elements of the array, match them to a given mode, and then you can keep all the elements that do not match the pattern.

We can use the `System.Collections.ArrayList` class to set a processing array and define it, as shown in the following screenshot:

```
PS C:\> $myArray = New-Object System.Collections.ArrayList
PS C:\> [void] $myArray.Add("Hello")
PS C:\> [void] $myArray.AddRange( ("World","Where","Are","You") )
PS C:\> $myArray
Hello
World
Where
Are
You
PS C:\> _
```

As in most languages, an array in PowerShell keeps the same length once you create them. PowerShell allows you to add an entry, delete an entry, and search for an entry in an array, but these operations may be time consuming when you are working on a large amount of data. For example, to combine two arrays, PowerShell creates a new array that is big enough to hold the contents of the two arrays, and then copies the two arrays to the destination array.

For example, if you have a collection of items, and you need to visit each item by the label that you provided, you can define a map between the label and the entry using a hash table. This is shown in the following screenshot:

```
PS C:\> $myHashtable = @{}
PS C:\> $myHashtable = @{ Key1 = "Value1"; "Key 2" = 1,2,3 }
PS C:\> $myHashtable["New Items"] = 5
PS C:\> $myHashTable

Name                           Value
----                           -----
Key 2                          {1, 2, 3}
Key1                           Value1
New Items                      5

PS C:\> _
```

Hash tables are very similar to arrays that allow you to access items by whatever label you want—not just through their index in the array. They form the keystone of a large number of scripting techniques. Since they allow you to map names to values, they form the effective basis for lookup tables such as the International Telephone Country Codes and area codes. Since they allow you to map names to fully-featured objects and script blocks, they can often take the place of custom objects. This key and value mapping also proves to be helpful in interacting with cmdlets that support advanced configuration parameters, such as the calculated property parameters available on the `Format-Table` and `Select-Object` cmdlets.

For example, consider that you have hash table keys and values, and you want column value results from the sorted key sequence. To sort a hash table, we can make use of the GetEnumerator() method in the hash table to obtain personal elements. Then, we can use the Sort-Object cmdlet, and sort by name or value, as shown in the following screenshot:

```
PS C:\> $myHashtable = @{}
PS C:\> $myHashtable = @{ Key1 = "Value1"; "Key 2" = 1,2,3 }
PS C:\> $myHashtable["New Items"] = 5
PS C:\> $myHashTable

Name                           Value
----                           -----
Key 2                          {1, 2, 3}
Key1                           Value1
New Items                      5

PS C:\> foreach($item in $myHashtable.GetEnumerator() | Sort Name)
>> {
>> $item.Value
>> }
>>
1
2
3
Value1
5
PS C:\>
```

However, the hashtable object supports the GetEnumerator() method and allows you to deal with single hash table entries that have name and value attributes. Once you have these, we can sort them easily as we can sort any other PowerShell data.

Operating script block

An elegant code block helps the process not only when controlling the collection of objects, but also in many other conditions. The most important thing is that the script block allows us to package a block of code and delay its execution. A script block holds the code snippets, and so you do not need to specify a formal name. We can dynamically create any script operation and of course, we can also perform the transfer of different parameters many times.

Defining script blocks

Defining a script piece for writing is very simple; it is just surrounding several program statements within curly brackets. This statement will not be executed immediately; on the contrary, a new script block object will be created and returned. In order to facilitate calling the script block after that, we may allocate a script block to a variable. The following screenshot shows a sample script block:

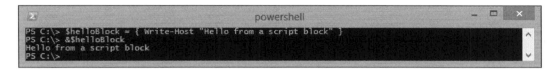

We can call a script block using the invoke operator (&). The following screenshot shows how we can use this operator with a variable when this variable contains a block:

```
PS C:\> $helloBlock = { Write-Host "Hello from a script block" }
PS C:\> &$helloBlock
Hello from a script block
PS C:\>
```

Block compile objects can be passed in and executed multiple times. They are reference objects and we can assign a variable to a block just to make the variable point to the block quoted in memory.

Passing parameters and returning values

As we have seen so far, none of the blocks have executed an action or an interaction with the outside world in complex ways. Now that I have already mentioned the expression, we can see the operation from the point of view of the block, which can be used in an expression. The operation parameters evaluate the return value. This return value from the script block simply asks you to output an object that will neither be a cmdlet nor another expression. The following is an example of a return value:

```
PS C:\> $number = { 5 }
PS C:\> &$number
5
PS C:\> 1 + (&$number)
6
PS C:\>
```

As you can see from the last command in the previous example, the return number cannot be used directly in a conditional expression; you must make use of parentheses. If you don't, the plus (+) operator will be mistaken as the right-hand operand and an error, as shown in the following screenshot, will be raised:

Note that the output of an object does not terminate the execution of the block, and the rest of the statement outputs after the object are still implemented. For example, you can print a string to the console window to return a value, and the retuning value does not contain other output statements, as shown in the following screenshot:

The `$numberPrint` block returns a value and writes a string to the console. Looking at the anonymous block invocation, you may think that the block returns or prints two variables, but this in fact is not the case. Look at the assignment operation in the following screenshot. The `$result` variable is assigned number 5; this will return the real value and the string will be printed to the console.

We can use a `return` statement to end the execution and exit the script block. It terminates the execution and gives the return value. Changing the block before using `return` will prevent the `Write-Host` command from executing:

```
PS C:\> $number = { return 5; Write-Host "generated a number" }
PS C:\> $a = &$number
PS C:\> $a
5
PS C:\>
```

You can use the `return` statement to simply quit a block and stop execution. It doesn't ask you to provide a value. If you omit the value, the script block will only exit and not return a value. In this case, the block returns a value to the caller only if there is an output before the `return` statement.

A useful scripting block will need a way to get parameters from the outside world so that it can be executed with different data. The parameters can be passed and retrieved according to their position. A piece of scripting block will always have a predefined `$args` variable through automatic settings, and it will contain a group of provided parameters. We can use it to create and output a custom message to the user giving a first name and a family name as shown in the following screenshot:

```
PS C:\> $greeter = {
>> $firstName = $args[0]
>> $lastName = $args[1]
>> Write-Host "Hello, $firstName $lastName"
>> }
>> &$greeter "Bill" "Gates"
>> &$greeter "John" "Bundy"
>>
Hello, Bill Gates
Hello, John Bundy
PS C:\>
```

Though the indexed access to parameters is a good technology, which can be used in many programming languages, unfortunately, it's too easy to make a mistake once the parameters grow in quantity. It is best to be used in a very simple scene where you cannot go wrong. In an advanced scenario, when you don't know the number of parameters while defining your script block, a mistake is likely to occur. We did not talk much about simple and advanced scenarios and in most cases we make use of named parameters. These are announced in the script block using the `param` keyword. Here is how the previous example switches to named parameters:

```
PS C:\> $greeter = {
>> param ($firstName, $lastName)
>> Write-Host "Hello, $firstName $lastName"
>> }
>> &$greeter -firstName "Bill" -lastName "Gates"
>>
Hello, Bill Gates
PS C:\>
```

Note that usually the first letter of a parameter name will suffice. In cases where multiple parameter names start with the same character sequence, you will have to provide the initial characters that uniquely identify the parameter.

We can set default parameter values, which can contain any expression. We can exploit this fact to implement mandatory parameters. Mandatory parameters are parameters that absolutely have to be provided when calling the script block. To do that, we add an expression that throws an exception when evaluated. In that way, the exception will be thrown if the caller fails to provide the parameter. Based on this consideration in the $greeting block, the $firstName parameter is essential:

```
PS C:\> $greeting = {
>> param ($firstName = $(throw "firstName required!"), $lastName)
>> Write-Host "Hello, $firstName $lastName"
>> }
>> PS > &$greeting -lastName "Gates"
>>
At line:5 char:6
+ PS > &$greeting -lastName "Gates"
+      ~
Missing file specification after redirection operator.
At line:5 char:7
+ PS > &$greeting -lastName "Gates"
+       ~
Ampersand not allowed. The & operator is reserved for future use; use "&" to pass ampersand as a string.
    + CategoryInfo          : ParserError: (:) [], ParentContainsErrorRecordException
    + FullyQualifiedErrorId : MissingFileSpecification
PS C:\>
```

Now, you can follow the $(throw "wrong information") model to realize forced parameters.

Functions

A function in PowerShell is just a subroutine having another name or a piece of code that can accept parameters, operations, and return values. A subroutine is probably the most important invention in the field of computer science programming. Subroutines allow writing code snippets that are independent of the main program, and can be called when you need them. A function is the main mechanism to construct abstraction, and produce reusable code snippets in PowerShell. By learning to structure the code and the function, you can make them more manipulative and readable.

A function is very similar to a script block in the sense that it contains executable code. The main difference is that it is a script with two anonymous parameters and it must be assigned to a variable so that it is assessed. For functions to get their name in their creation, their name must be immediately assessed. For defining a function, we must use the function keyword as shown in the following code snippet:

```
function <name>(<parameter list>)
{
<function body>
}
```

The function name should start with a letter and may contain any alphanumeric character sequence and an underscore character. This is how we define a simple function to output some text:

```
PS C:\> function Say-Hi()
>> {
>> Write-Host "Hello from a function"
>> }
>>
PS C:\> Say-Hi
Hello from a function
PS C:\>
```

Having a function to accept parameters, we can provide a list of function definitions. The following is a sample function; it accepts two numbers and writes the sum to the console:

```
PS C:\> function Write-Sum($first, $second)
>> {
>> $sum = $first + $second
>> Write-Host "Sum: $sum"
>> }
>>
PS C:\> Write-Sum 4 5
Sum: 9
PS C:\>
```

Scripts

A PowerShell command sequence can be saved as a script file and can be executed later. We need to use a script file when we want to create small scripting tools, which we can run on a regular basis. We also need to use script files in cases where we create a complex modular script to keep their code in a different file. This will facilitate function development and maintenance.

Creating scripts

The typical PowerShell script is a text file, which can be created using all kinds of tools. By default, these documents carry the `.ps1` file extension. You can create them using Notepad, but it is best if you use a more powerful tool such as a programmer's text editor with syntax highlighting and intelligent word completion, for example Notepad++, ISE, and PowerGUI.

Notepad++ is a free source code editor and is a Notepad replacement that supports several languages. With a plugin that supports PowerShell, it gives you full syntax highlighting for PowerShell.

The Windows PowerShell **Integrated Scripting Environment** (**ISE**) is a host application for Windows PowerShell. Powershell v3 comes with a pretty good ISE built-in. In Windows PowerShell ISE, you can run commands and write, test, and debug scripts in a single Windows-based graphic user interface with multiline editing, tab completion, syntax coloring, selective execution, context-sensitive help, and support for right-to-left languages.

PowerGUI is a graphical user interface and script editor for Microsoft Windows PowerShell. You can find it at `www.PowerGUI.org`. It is the freeware tool that the administrators need for speeding up PowerShell adoption, and harnessing the power of PowerShell to efficiently manage their entire Windows environment. PowerGUI simplifies management with an intuitive user console.

You can even create scripts from the PowerShell console using the string and the `Set-Content` cmdlet. The following screenshot shows how you can create your first script:

As you can see, the `hello-world.ps1` file is a pure text file; we can check its contents using the `Get-Content` cmdlet.

Invoking scripts

PowerShell finds a file to invoke just by looking at the path environment variable. It is interesting to note that the current folder is not in the system path. This means that invoking a script in the current folder will require you to prefix it with a path. Thus the command in our case becomes .\hello-world ps1. This will look familiar if you come from a Unix background as shell will not include the current folder path variable.

When in action, PowerShell's default security construction principle only allows interactive commands and will be implemented in the console input. Shell has several executive policies, configuration levels of security, and user privileges to run the script. By default, the shell will run in the restricted policy level; this means that is not allowed to run a script. We can check the executive policy by calling the Get-ExecutionPolicy cmdlet.

Passing parameters

The PowerShell script files also allow users to pass parameters for initialization. Script files have the $args variable set up with the parameters passed at the time of their invocation. The following is example code for using $args to get parameters:

```
$firstName = $args[0]
$lastName = $args[1]
Write-Host "Hello, $firstName $lastName"
```

We can save the code as Get-HelloArgs.ps1, and then execute it as follows:

Of course, we also can use the param keyword for accepting a parameter. The following is the example code:

```
param ($firstName, $lastName)
Write-Host "Hello, $firstName $lastName"
```

We can save the code as Get-HelloParam.ps1 and execute it as follows:

Return values

A parameter is, most of the time, a one-way communication mechanism, and will only transfer data from the environment of the script. We need to be able to return values from our script. PowerShell provides a good way to output the return value from a script and we should make use of this method.

An object can be bound to a variable or outputted to a pipeline for the next command. We can use it to generate a pile of objects from our script and output them. The following screenshot gives us a script that gives an output of three temporary filenames:

```
PS C:\> $code = @"
>> "File1.tmp"
>> "File2.tmp"
>> "File3.tmp"
>> "@
>>
PS C:\> Set-Content Generate-TempFiles.ps1 $code
PS C:\> $files = .\Generate-TempFiles.ps1
PS C:\> $files
File1.tmp
File2.tmp
File3.tmp
PS C:\> .\Generate-TempFiles.ps1 | foreach { "File: " + $_ }
File: File1.tmp
File: File2.tmp
File: File3.tmp
PS C:\>
```

As you can see, this value can be assigned to a variable or can be passed down the line as a `foreach` command. A `return` statement will output an object and terminate execution.

Developing and maintaining script libraries

Sooner or later, you will be responsible for creating a bigger, more complex solution using PowerShell as its implementation language. Earlier when you wrote your own code, there were cases where each piece of code was stuck in a separate file and you could not find a way through the code. This was not a pleasant situation as you must be aware that your options are separated from the script code into several files to make things easier to manage. In addition to this, fast navigation to the correct location of the correct file with less code makes it more reusable. This is a very common and useful function that lets you move out of the first client code to another file, and is then included in many documents. In practice, I usually use a folder in my system path that contains useful scripts so that I can easily include useful features in any of the scripts and start working on the production code in no time.

Script libraries are normal files that contain useful functions. They are ordinary PowerShell scripts that do not execute an action—they just define several functions and let the library client code call them to do the real job.

Including or importing a script library in a script file is similar to executing it. It is a good programming practice to ensure that the scripting library should contain any executable code function definition.

Discovering what's new in Windows PowerShell 3.0

A few months ago, Windows PowerShell 3.0 was launched as part of the Windows Server 2012 and Windows 8 RTM release. PowerShell 3.0 introduced a lot of new features, and improved some existing features in order to allow system administrators to control and manage their systems more easily and efficiently. In this section, the focus will be on the unique features of Windows PowerShell 3.0 to make sure that you gain the knowledge and the edge of using it.

Windows PowerShell Web Access (PSWA)

Windows PowerShell Web Access (PSWA) is one of the new features in Windows PowerShell 3.0 that has been introduced in Windows Server 2012. Yes, it is what you are guessing right now. PowerShell Web Access is a web-based version of the PowerShell console where you can run and execute PowerShell cmdlets from any web browser that is not only available on desktops but also on any mobile or tablet devices. PowerShell Web Access allows you to do your administration tasks smoothly anywhere and anytime using any device running a web browser regardless of it being a Microsoft or a non-Microsoft one.

How PSWA works

The Windows PowerShell Web Access gateway is the name of the server where PowerShell Web Access is installed and configured. This gateway is the bridge between the end user and the managed servers, so once you connect to the web interface of the PowerShell Web Access for writing your cmdlets and scripts, the gateway will be responsible for executing them on the right server. In the real world, the PSWA gateway is placed in the **DMZ (demilitarized zone)** and the web interface is published to the Internet so that you can easily connect to your server anytime and anywhere.

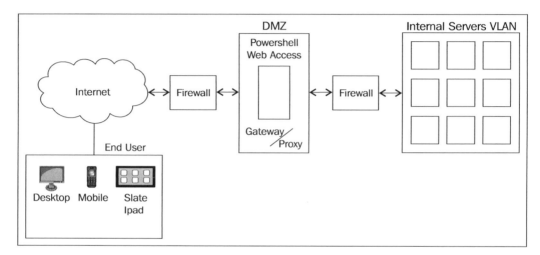

Installing and configuring Windows PowerShell Web Access

This part will show how to install and configure Windows PowerShell Web Access easily in a few steps.

Step 1 – installing the Windows PowerShell Web Access Windows feature

In this step we will add the Windows PowerShell Web Access Windows feature. There are two ways to accomplish this task; either we can use the Server Manager Wizard or Windows PowerShell. Since PowerShell is our hero in this book, let's do it in the PowerShell way, using the following steps:

1. Run the Windows PowerShell console with administrative privileges.

2. Install the Windows PowerShell Web Access feature using the `Install-WindowsFeature` cmdlets. The purpose of this is to install PowerShell Web Access and the pre-requisites, if not installed.

```
PS > Install-WindowsFeature WindowsPowerShellWebAccess -
IncludeAllSubFeature -IncludeManagementTools
```

The following screenshot shows the execution results that you should get after using this command, and also warns you that you still need to do some configuration in order to complete the PSWA installation:

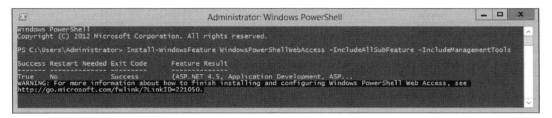

Step 2 – configuring Windows PowerShell Web Access Gateway

The gateway is the server where Windows PowerShell Web Access is installed and running. It is called a gateway because it is the gateway/proxy between the end user and the managed servers/nodes in your network. Now, after installing the PowerShell Web Access feature we will configure the gateway. In this step, we will create an IIS web application that runs PowerShell Web Access and configures the SSL certificate. There are two ways to accomplish this task; we can either do it manually or use PowerShell, and again here we are using PowerShell:

1. Run the Windows PowerShell console with administrative privileges.

2. Use the `Install-PswaWebApplication` cmdlet to install and configure `PswaWebApplication`:

```
Install-PswaWebApplication –WebSiteName "Default Web Site" -
WebApplicationName "PSWA" -UseTestCertificate
```

The following screenshot shows the execution results that you should get after installing the PSWA application, and it also shows a warning because you have to choose a `UseTestCertificate` switch:

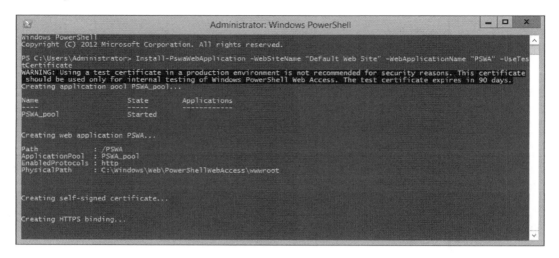

 Make use of `UseTestCertificate` for testing purposes in your private lab only. Never use it in a production environment; for your production environments use a certificate from a trusted **Certificate Authority (CA)**.

3. Open PSWA using `https://<server_name>/PSWA` to verify your installation. We should see a screen similar to the following:

The PSWA web application files are located under %windir%\Web\ PowerShellWebAccess\wwwroot.

Step 3 – configuring the PowerShell Web Access authorization rules

Now, we have PSWA up and running; however, no one will be able to sign in and use it until we create the appropriate authorization rule. The reason behind this is that it is a good practice to secure your environment by restricting the access to your network until you create the right access for the right person. The authorization rule is the access control for your PSWA that adds an additional security layer to your PSWA. It is similar to the access list on your firewall and network devices. We can configure the PSWA authorization rule using the following steps:

1. Run the Windows PowerShell console with administrative privileges.

2. Use the `Add-PswaAuthorizationRule` cmdlet to create the authorization rule with the `-UserName`, `-ComputerName`, and `-ConfigurationName` switches.

   The following screenshot shows the execution results that you should get after configuring the PSWA authorization rule:

 The PSWA authorization rule's files are located under %windir%\Web\ PowerShellWebAccess\data\AuthorizationRules.xml.

Signing in to PowerShell Web Access

Now, let's verify the installation and start using the PSWA by signing into it using the following steps:

1. Open the Internet browser.

2. Enter `https://<server_name>/PSWA`. The following screen will appear:

3. Enter the values for **User name, Password, Connection type**, and **Computer name**.

4. Click on **Sign In** to get the following screen:

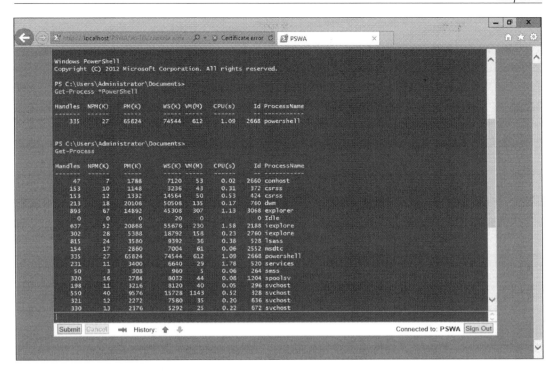

Auto-loading of modules

PowerShell 3.0 will now be able to check and load all the cmdlets and modules installed on the local computer and load them automatically while starting up so you do not have to use the `Import-Module` cmdlet to import each module that you want to use.

Online and updatable Help

In the previous version of PowerShell, we used the Get-Help cmdlet to show the Help information that comes embedded by default with the cmdlets. In PowerShell 3.0, the inline help has been replaced with a Help file hosted on the Internet. By default, the Get-Help cmdlet will not show you any Help information until you use the Update-Help cmdlet to download the help files from the Internet. If you are running the Get-Help cmdlet for the first time without using the Update-Help cmdlet, it will automatically prompt you to download the latest Help files from the Internet. The reason behind this is that in the previous versions of PowerShell, the Help information was static and sometimes there were mistakes as well as updates in the Help information. There was no available way to update the Help information even while using a Windows update. Thus Microsoft introduced a new update method using the Update-Help cmdlet, which gets the latest Help information from the Help files hosted on the Internet. Also, you can use the SAVE-HELP cmdlet to save the Help files locally or on shared folders so that every computer in your network can get them directly. Moreover, if you do not want to download the help files locally, you can use the Get-Help cmdlets with the –Online switch for redirecting you to the web pages that contain the Help information for the cmdlets, but you have to consider the Internet connectivity each time you use this parameter. The following screenshot shows the use of the Get-Help cmdlet:

Scheduled jobs

Scheduled jobs are similar to background jobs introduced in PowerShell 2.0. Both jobs run asynchronously in the background without interrupting the user interface, but the difference is that the background jobs must be started manually using the Start-Job cmdlet, and in some cases, if you want to automate this job you can use a scheduled task to create a scheduled job that triggers your script. In PowerShell 3.0, scheduled jobs are introduced to reduce the hassle of scheduling the background jobs in multiple steps. Simply, scheduled jobs can create background job and schedule it for a later execution using a set of cmdlets instead of using the **Task Scheduler** wizard. You can also get the results of running scheduled jobs and resume interrupted jobs.

In the following example, we will create a simple scheduled job that clears the event log for application, security, and system log stores every day at 02:00 am. The first thing we need to define is when the scheduled job will be executed using the `New-JobTrigger` cmdlet, then create and register the job using the `Register-ScheduleJob` cmdlet. The code snippet is as follows:

```
$trigger = New-JobTrigger -Daily -At 2am

Register-ScheduledJob -Name ClearEventLogDaily -Trigger $trigger -
ScriptBlock {Clear-EventLog -LogName Application,Security,System
```

 All PowerShell scheduled tasks are saved by selecting **Task Scheduler | Task Scheduler Library | Microsoft | Windows | PowerShell | ScheduledJobs**.

The Show-Command cmdlet

The `Show-Command` cmdlet allows you to display the command in a **Graphical User Interface (GUI)** as if you are browsing a web form or a normal Windows program. You can use `Show-Command` to compose a command in a GUI form, select the required variables and write the values, then click on **Run** to execute the command with the parameters you entered. You can also click on the **Copy** button to copy the command with the parameters and values to the clipboard so that you can paste it to the PowerShell console and save it to a script. Refer to the following screenshot:

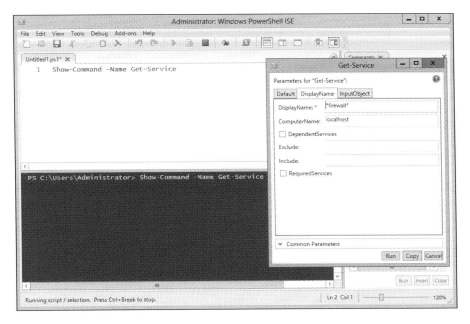

Integrated Scripting Environment (ISE)

PowerShell ISE is the GUI editor for PowerShell. It is similar to the Blue PowerShell console but with more advanced features. In the previous version of PowerShell, ISE was just a graphical editor that allowed you to write and execute the PowerShell commands and scripts in a nice user interface that highlights the syntax and with the ability to add/remove breakpoints for debugging capabilities. In PowerShell 3.0, new features have been added to ISE to give the administrator a different experience while using it. In this section we will highlight these features.

IntelliSense

IntelliSense is the name of Microsoft's implementation for the autocomplete technique. Autocomplete is one of the most famous features in today's applications, and everyone using a computer is using autocomplete. Simply, autocomplete is a feature embedded in most of the search engines that gives you a list of suggestions once you start typing on your keyboard. IntelliSense in PowerShell not only shows you a suggestion for words but also for commands, parameters, variables, and even UNC paths on your computer. The following screenshot shows us an example:

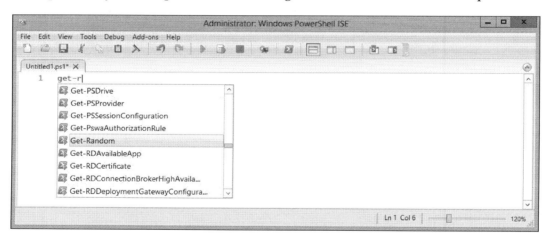

Script snippets

Code snippet is the name used to describe a piece of reusable code, and it is usually used to speed up the process of writing code especially when using a repetitive code and syntax. PowerShell 3.0 ISE introduced the snippets feature to make the script-writing process easier. By using snippets you do not have to know the syntax for each command and function. For example, the ForEach code snippet inserts the syntax of the ForEach loop and you just have to modify your variables. The following screenshot shows us a similar example:

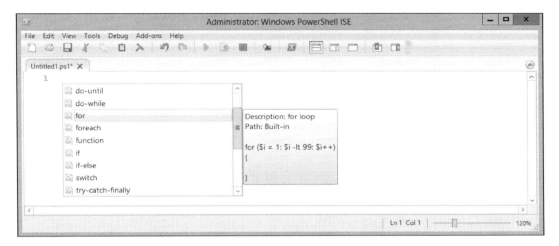

How to use snippets

You can use snippets using *Ctrl + J* or by selecting **Edit | Start Snippets**.

How to create/add new snippets

In order to create a new code snippet we use the New-IseSnippet cmdlet. In the following example we will create a new snippet to restart all SQL Server Services:

```
New-IseSnippet -Title RestartSQLServerServices -Description
"Restart all SQL Server Services" -Text "Restart-Service
-Name *SQL*"
```

In PowerShell, snippets are saved in the form of an XML file with the snippet.ps1xml file's extension under **User Profile | Windows PowerShell | Snippets**.

You can get the path of the snippets' folder using the following command:
`Join-Path (Split-Path $profile.CurrentUserCurrentHost) "Snippets"`

To display all user-defined snippets we use the `Get-IseSnippet` cmdlet. This command will show the name of each snippet and where it is located. To remove a snippet, open the folder that contains all the user-defined snippets and delete the snippet file. By default, PowerShell loads all the snippets located in the default folder automatically during startup; however, if you have saved your snippet's files in a separate folder, use `Import-IseSnippet -Path <Snippets_Folder_Path>` to load it.

Add-on tools

Add-on tools are **Windows Presentation Foundation (WPF)** controls that can be added to PowerShell ISE to add extra features and functionalities to the ISE, such as spelling checker and script-printing features. One of the most popular add-ons is **Microsoft Script Explorer**. The Microsoft Script Explorer enables you to find scripts, snippets, and modules in the script repositories such as TechNet Script Center and other community repositories such as PoshCode, and also it can search for scripts in local and network filesystems.

Autosave and restart manager

PowerShell ISE 3.0 automatically saves any runspace and script file that is open , so in case a failure happens in your ISE or your operating system restarts suddenly, ISE will restore all your runspaces once you open it again. It is similar to "restore session" in Internet Explorer.

PowerShell remoting

PowerShell remoting is one of the most impressive features that make PowerShell unique and give it a different flavor over other shells. PowerShell remoting allows IT administrators to control and execute PowerShell scripts on multiple remote computers from a local PowerShell console without moving to any place. We will talk more in depth about PowerShell remoting in the coming chapters, but let's take a sneak peak at what is new in PowerShell 3.0 from the remoting perspective.

Disconnected session

PowerShell remoting is now similar to a remote desktop session; you can disconnect your session without interrupting any running process, application, or script, and you can connect later to this session again from the same or a different computer to continue your work.

Remoting on a public network

Remoting in PowerShell 3.0 can be enabled on public networks on the client operating systems such as Windows 7 and Windows 8. In simple terms, we use the `SkipNetworkProfileCheck` switch with the `Enable-PSRemoting` or `Set-WSMANQuickConfig` cmdlets.

The custom session configuration file

The custom session configuration file is a predefined session configuration that includes information about which cmdlets, snippets, modules, and other PowerShell components should be loaded in this session and the configuration that can be used by the user, which gives another edge of security for PowerShell in general and PowerShell remoting specifically.

Windows PowerShell Workflow (PSW)

The word "workflow" represents a set of objects, tasks, and activities that are connected together and running concurrently or sequentially or both. In IT, the word workflow always links to another word automatically. For example, in Microsoft SharePoint Server we use a workflow to automate an approval process such as vacation request approval, or we can use Microsoft System Center Orchestrator to automate a process such as provisioning new users and applications.

Workflow capabilities have been introduced in Windows PowerShell 3.0, and it is designed specifically to help you perform time and effort-consuming complex tasks across multiple and different devices in different locations.

You might wonder what the real value of Windows PowerShell Workflow is, as you already use PowerShell to write different scripts and modules that allow you to perform long-running tasks, and this is the aim of scripting in general. Well, before I tell you the answer let's think about these questions together: can you write a script that restarts an operation on a device and waits for this device to boot-up to resume the rest of the commands again? Can you write a single script that runs on multiple devices concurrently? PowerShell Workflows is designed to be interruptible, stoppable, restartable, and also parallelizable, which is why it is more efficient for long-running tasks than scripts.

The script consists of a set of commands; however, workflow consists of a set of activities. Commands normally represent an action that you want to execute; however, the activities represent a task you want to perform. Moreover, commands execute sequentially and activities run sequentially and concurrently.

There are two methods to define a workflow; we can either use the PowerShell syntax or, since it is built on top of Windows Workflow Foundation (WF), you can use an XAML file designed by Visual Studio Workflow Designer.

Creating a workflow using PowerShell

Writing a PowerShell Workflow is similar to writing a PowerShell function with a little difference. The first difference is using the word "workflow" instead of "function". Also, as in functions, the same definition of parameters using `param()` can be used with `CmdletBinding` to add some advanced workflow features. `CmdletBinding` allows you to add advanced capabilities to your function and workflows, such as adding the `-Verbose`, `-Debug`, `-whatif`, and `-confirm` parameters to your workflow without implementing them manually. It also defines `HelpUri` that will be used by the `Get-Help` cmdlets to get the online help for the workflow or function. The following code snippet shows how we write a PowerShell Workflow:

```
Workflow Test-Workflow
{
 [CmdletBinding(ConfirmImpact=<String>,
 DefaultParameterSetName=<String>,
   HelpURI=<URI>,PositionalBinding=<Boolean>)]
  Param([string] <Parameter_Name>)
}
```

As mentioned earlier, PowerShell Workflows use activities that are similar to cmdlets; the PowerShell team has already implemented all PowerShell core cmdlets as activities, which makes it easier for PowerShell users to use activities and not get confused, except for a set of cmdlets that are excluded from this implementation. Does it mean that the excluded cmdlets cannot be used in a workflow?

No, PowerShell automatically executes them using a special activity called `inlineScript`. The purpose of this activity is to execute any PowerShell command that is valid in PowerShell but not supported by workflows, such as executing a `.ps1` file or calling a dynamic parameter inside a workflow.

 For the list of excluded cmdlets you can visit `http://technet.microsoft.com/en-us/library/jj574194.aspx`.

PowerShell Workflows can be executed concurrently and sequentially by using the reserved keywords such as `Parallel` and `Sequence`. The activities inside the `Parallel` block will be running concurrently, and activities inside the `Sequence` block will be running sequentially. `ForEach -parallel` is a combination of the `Sequence` and `Parallel` executions. `ForEach -parallel` will execute the activities sequentially on the items in the collection concurrently. In other words, if there is a collection of computers where a set of activities such as rename and restart computer are being executed, the activities will be executed in sequence on all computers at the same time. The following script block shows the syntax of using the `Parallel` and `Sequence` execution capabilities inside a workflow:

```
Workflow Test-Workflow
{
  Parallel
{
  <Activity_1>
  <Activity_2>
  <Activity_3>
}

Sequence
{
  <Activity_1>
  <Activity_2>
  <Activity_3>
}

ForEach -parallel ($item in $collection)
{
<Activity_1>
  <Activity_2>
  <Activity_3>
}
}
```

`Parallel` execution is useful for running independent activities concurrently, such as starting a process and restarting a service at the same time where each activity is running independently from the other one.

Sequence execution is useful for defining a set of activities to run sequentially inside a Parallel or ForEach -parallel execution.

 For more information on the different ways of creating a PowerShell Workflow refer to http://msdn.microsoft.com/en-us/library/windows/desktop/hh852738(v=vs.85).aspx.

Controlling PowerShell Workflow execution

One of the most interesting features in PowerShell Workflow, and what makes it unique compared to a normal script is the flexibility of controlling the execution; at any point you can interrupt, suspend, or resume the workflow's execution. You can even restart the computer while running the workflow and complete the execution upon startup.

You can suspend the workflow's execution using the Suspend-Workflow activity that will save the execution state, variables, and values in a checkpoint and return the job ID for the suspended workflow, so you can use the job ID as a parameter for the Resume-Job cmdlet to resume the workflow execution again.

In the following example, we will learn how to suspend and resume the workflow execution:

```
Workflow Test-Workflow
{
  <Activity_1>
  <Activity_2>
Suspend-Workflow
  <Activity_3>
}
```

You can execute this workflow using the following command:

PS C:\>Test-Workflow

The first two activities will be executed and the workflow will be suspended, and the result of suspend-workflow will be information about the workflow-executed job.

Id	Name	PSJobTypeName	State	HasMoreData	Location	Command
2	Job2	PSWorkflowJob	Suspended	True	localhost	Test-Workflow

In order to resume the workflow again, we will use the `Resume-Job` cmdlet:

```
S C:\>Resume-Job –Name Job2
```

In order to get the results of the activities executed after resuming, in our case Activity 3, we will use the `Get-Job` and `Receive-Job` cmdlets:

```
PS C:\>Get-Job –Name Job2 | Receive-Job
```

Since PowerShell Workflow is recoverable, you can restart the target computer and smoothly resume the workflow again using the `Restart-Computer` activity. Simply use the `–wait` switch with `Restart-Computer` so that the workflow will wait for the computer to restart and reconnect again before proceeding with the workflow execution.

In the following example, the workflow will restart the targeted computer after executing `Activity 1` and `Activity 2`, and then wait for the computer to boot up again to resume and execute `Activity 3`. You can also use the `-PSConnectionRetryCount` and `-PSConnectionRetryInterval` parameters to specify the connection retries and the interval between each connection retry.

```
Workflow Test-Workflow
{
  <Activity_1>
  <Activity_2>
  Restart-Computer –Wait –PSConnectionRetryInterval 4 –
  PSConnectionRetryCount 8
  <Activity_3>
}
```

In order to maintain these features of PowerShell Workflow, it is a must to implement another feature in workflows, which is "CheckPoint". Checkpoints in PowerShell Workflow take a snapshot of the current state and data, and then save it in the profile of the user who executes this workflow on the hard disk, so on resuming, the workflow will start from the last checkpoint instead of starting from the beginning. PowerShell by default adds checkpoints in the beggining and ending of the workflow. In addition, you can use the `-PSPersist` switch with any activity to take a checkpoint after completing its execution. Also, you can use the `Checkpoint-Workflow` activity at any point in your flow to take a checkpoint.

Workflows are used to execute tasks faster, so using checkpoints without any need or optimization will slow the execution and make the usage futile.

In case of using pipelines and parallel execution, checkpoints will not be taken until the completion of the pipeline or the parallel activities; however, you can use checkpoints in sequence activities to take a checkpoint after completion of every single activity.

Summary

In this chapter, we studied variables and data structures such as objects, lists, arrays, and hash tables, which are used frequently in the examples in later chapters. This chapter facilitated the explanation for the later examples.

If arithmetic is the soul of the program, then the control flow is the skeleton of PowerShell. Control flows directly determine the program operation's path. Pipelines, script blocks, functions, and script files are major program-organization tools of PowerShell.

PowerShell 3.0 introduced a lot of new features, such as PowerShell Web Access and PowerShell Workflow. PowerShell 3.0 improves some existing features such as PowerShell ISE. Since the later chapters will be based on this chapter content, readers are encouraged to review characteristics of the PowerShell language at this step.

In the next chapter we will introduce a snap-in for protecting your PowerShell code. The user can encrypt based on the .NET code obfuscator to protect the source code from getting cracked.

2
Developing Snap-ins for PowerShell

There may be times when PowerShell does not include a built-in cmdlet with the specifications you want; in such a scenario you will have to write a PowerShell snap-in to register your custom cmdlet. You will see how easy it is to actually build a custom-class library that in turn is an extension of the PowerShell console and will add a couple of extra commands according to your preference.

In this chapter we will cover:

- Creating a PowerShell snap-in
- Writing a PowerShell snap-in
- Registering and removing a PowerShell snap-in
- Listing and executing cmdlets in a PowerShell snap-in
- Debugging a PowerShell snap-in

A Windows PowerShell snap-in provides a mechanism for registering sets of cmdlets and providers with the shell, thus extending the functionality of the shell. A PowerShell snap-in can register all the cmdlets and providers in a single assembly, or it can register a specific list of cmdlets and providers.

Sometimes, when you have developed a product for which you want the source code to be kept as a secret from your client or you have written some scripts and then released them to be used by others, and you want to protect this source code against reverse engineering, cracking, and modification by others, snap-ins are the best choice. Normally, commercial PowerShell solutions use the snap-ins method to publish their own products, such as VMware vSphere PowerCLI and the Quest Active Directory series. The code will be complied into assemblies so that all security options for C# and VB.NET code can be used.

Creating a PowerShell snap-in

All Windows PowerShell snap-in classes are derived from the PSSnapIn or CustomPSSnapIn class. The default type is PSSnapIn, which registers all cmdlets and providers in a single assembly. The other type is CustomPSSnapIn, which allows users to specify the list of cmdlets and providers from either a single assembly or multiple ones. The registration mechanism adds the cmdlets, providers, or hosting applications to the current session. In this chapter, we will introduce how to create snap-ins to expand the cmdlets of PowerShell.

First of all, we need to introduce a programming environment to facilitate the description of the follow-up. We will require the following:

- Tools: Visual Studio 2010 and .NET Framework 3.5
- Environment: PowerShell 3.0 and Windows 2008

It is easy to build a custom-class library that is in turn an extension of the PowerShell console and will add a couple of extra commands according to your preference. We should download the Windows SDK in order to get the System.Management. Automation.dll file to make PowerShell easily accessible. We can download this from http://www.microsoft.com/en-us/download/details.aspx?id=8279.

Users can write some code for a snap-in and compile the code into a .NET assembly. Then you should register the assembly as a snap-in with PowerShell. Before you can use the cmdlets or providers in your snap-in, you need to load the snap-in into a PowerShell session. After the snap-in is loaded, users can use cmdlets or providers in the snap-in just like other built-in cmdlets and providers. To avoid the loading operation of your snap-in every time you want to use it, you can load a snap-in by saving it into a configuration file.

Writing a PowerShell snap-in

In this section, we will explain how to write a snap-in.

Creating a new class library project

First of all, we should create a class library project and name it MySnapIn in Visual Studio 2010 as shown in the following screenshot:

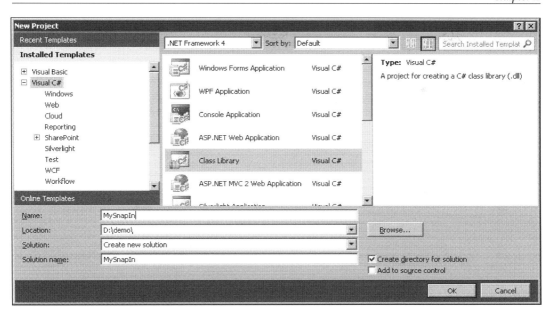

Then, add a reference to the `System.Management.Automation.dll` (found in `C:\ Windows\assembly\GAC_MSIL\System.Management.Automation\1.0.0.0__31bf 3856ad364e35`) and `System.Configuration.Install.dll` (found in `C:\Windows\ Microsoft.NET\Framework\v2.0.50727`) files. You should now have the following reference added:

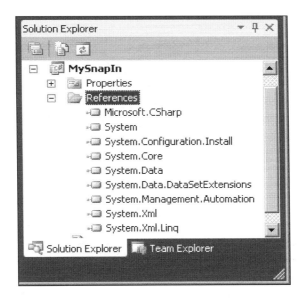

Creating a PowerShell installer class

In order for our PowerShell cmdlet to work, we have to create an `Install` class. This class looks fairly worthless, but nevertheless it is still required because this class will be invoked when you install the snap-in and provide the system with some information, such as where it comes from and what it is supposed to do.

Create a public class that derives from the `PSSnapIn` class. In this example, the class name is `MySnapInInstallclass`. First, start by adding the necessary references. Next, add the following code to that class:

```csharp
using System.Management.Automation;
using System.ComponentModel;

namespace MySnapIn
{
    [RunInstaller(true)] // snap-in installation class
    public class MySnapInInstallclass : PSSnapIn
    {
        /// <summary>
        /// Get a name for this PowerShell snap-in.
        /// This name will be used in registering
        /// this PowerShell snap-in.
        /// </summary>
        public override string Name
        {
            get
            {
                return "MySnapIn";
            }
        }
        /// <summary>
        /// Vendor information for this PowerShell snap-in.
        /// </summary>
        public override string Vendor
        {
            get
            {
                return "fuhj";
            }
        }
        /// <summary>
        /// Gets resource information for vendor. This is a string of format:
        /// resourceBaseName.resourceName.
        /// </summary>
        public override string VendorResource
        {
            get
            {
                return "MySnapIn,fuhj";
            }
        }
        /// <summary>
        /// Description of this PowerShell snap-in.
        /// </summary>
        public override string Description
        {
            get
            {
                return "This is a PowerShell Snap-In that include several Cmdlets.";
            }
        }
        public override string DescriptionResource
        {
            get
            {
                return "MySnapIn, This is a PowerShell Snap-In that include several Cmdlets.";
            }
        }
    }
}
```

The property for name, vendor, and description of the snap-in need to be emphasized. Especially the property for the name of the snap-in, as it will be used when we call `Add-PSSnapin` to register it to the PowerShell session. Meanwhile, the property for the vendor resources and description resources are optional. The public property for the name of the snap-in do not use any of these characters: #, (,), { , }, [,], $, -, /, \, ;, :, ", ', <, >, |, ?, @, `, and *. Use of any of these characters is illegal.

This essentially provides some information to the system upon installing your snap-in. In fact, the information is stored in the computer registry and the PowerShell session depends on the information found in the snap-in file storage location and the related information, for execution. We will introduce these contents later on.

Creating a class file to include several PowerShell cmdlets

We will now introduce the most important part of a snap-in. Let's create a cmdlet class file that is named `MySnapInCmdletsclass.cs`, in the project. The users can set several classes in a file and also each class in the respective file, because a snap-in only contains the `install` and `cmdlet` classes. Here, in order to make it convenient for the users' understanding, all the cmdlet classes are placed in a file and the installer class is placed in the other file. If the user's snap-in contains a lot of cmdlets, it facilitates maintenance when the user creates a class file for each cmdlet class.

Use the `[Cmdlet()]` attribute in your class to tell the system that it's going to be a cmdlet for PowerShell. Your class name comprises of two parts: verb and noun. The verb defines the action that this cmdlet will perform, and the noun defines the object on which the verb acts. The keyword `VerbsCommon.Get` means that it is a cmdlet with the built-in verb `Get`. And the keyword after the comma, with double quotation marks, is the noun of the verb-noun structure. The cmdlet, which is composed of the verb and noun, will be invoked when a snap-in is registered in a PowerShell session. The only method of the class that needs to override into the actions is `ProcessRecord()`.

The code will be as follows:

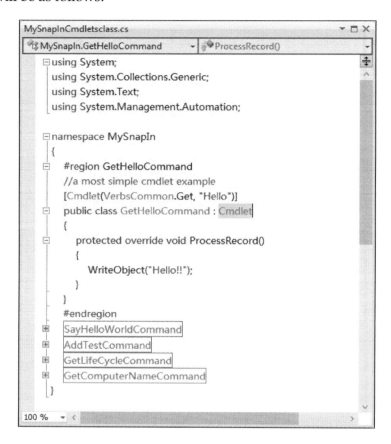

We can see that all of the cmdlet classes are derived from Cmdlet. In fact, the snap-in not only already contains the most basic function units, but can also compile successfully. The subsequent section introduces you to the registration and the call, in a way that we can use now.

Next, I want to give an example of custom verbs taking parameters and logic judgment. The code is shown in the following screenshot:

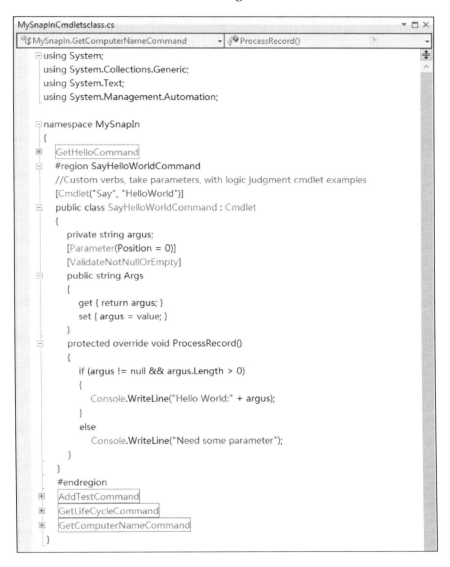

```
MySnapInCmdletsclass.cs                                    ▾ □ ×
MySnapIn.GetComputerNameCommand          ▾  ProcessRecord()         ▾
using System;
using System.Collections.Generic;
using System.Text;
using System.Management.Automation;

namespace MySnapIn
{
    GetHelloCommand
    #region SayHelloWorldCommand
    //Custom verbs, take parameters, with logic judgment cmdlet examples
    [Cmdlet("Say", "HelloWorld")]
    public class SayHelloWorldCommand : Cmdlet
    {
        private string argus;
        [Parameter(Position = 0)]
        [ValidateNotNullOrEmpty]
        public string Args
        {
            get { return argus; }
            set { argus = value; }
        }
        protected override void ProcessRecord()
        {
            if (argus != null && argus.Length > 0)
            {
                Console.WriteLine("Hello World:" + argus);
            }
            else
                Console.WriteLine("Need some parameter");
        }
    }
    #endregion
    AddTestCommand
    GetLifeCycleCommand
    GetComputerNameCommand
}
```

It is very similar to the first example that used the `[Cmdlet()]` attribute; the difference is that the parameter `VerbsCommon.Get` is replaced by a custom parameter `"Say"`, which is contained within double quotes. This is an essential attribute for cmdlet classes. In the `ProcessRecord()` method, there is an `if/else` logic judgment as well as an `argus` keyword for saving the input parameters.

In the subsequent sections, we will see the rest of the method-declaring parameters. Because the method of declaring parameters is exclusive, we can't demonstrate all methods in one example.

Declaring cmdlet parameters

Let's consider an example where we define a public property as shown in the preceding code. When we add the `Parameter` attribute and set the `Position` keyword to the argument position, the first position is indicated a value of `0`. It means that you declare a positional parameter, and then the first parameter in the pipeline will be assigned to the designated variables, as the parameters of the index starts at `0`.

If you want to declare a named parameter, you can add the `Parameter` attribute and omit the `Position` keyword from the attribute. Just as shown in following code:

```
[Parameter()]
public string PersonName
{
  get { return personName; }
  set { personName = value; }
}
private string personName;
```

If you want to declare a mandatory parameter, you should add the `Parameter` attribute and set the `Mandatory` keyword to `true`. It means the snap-in we create with this keyword will force the user to input the specified parameters, otherwise it will report an error. This is very useful when a snap-in needs an obligatory parameter. Refer to the following code:

```
[Parameter(Position = 0, Mandatory = true)]
public string PersonName
{
  get { return personName; }
  set { personName = value; }
}
private string personName;
```

If you want to declare an optional parameter, you just omit the `Mandatory` keyword when you add the `Parameter` attribute. Just as shown in following code:

```
[Parameter(Position = 0]
public string PersonName
{
  get { return personName; }
  set { personName = value; }
}
private string personName;
```

The example that we just saw introduces the method of declaring a parameter, but sometimes we need our snap-in to accept several different parameter groups. These parameter groups are optional. Once a parameter group is input, the parameters in this group must follow their own parameter rules. For example, the unique parameter of the `Get-Command` cmdlet is optional. Now we need to declare a parameter set to solve this problem; we will introduce the declared parameter set in the next section.

Declaring parameter sets

Now we will show how to define two parameter sets when you declare the parameters for a cmdlet. Each parameter set has both a unique parameter and a shared parameter that is used by both parameter sets. We will declare these parameter sets using the following steps:

1. We declare a `Mandatory` parameter, and then add the `Parameterset` keyword to the `Parameter` attribute for the unique parameter of the first parameter set.

   ```
   [Parameter(Position = 0, Mandatory = true,
   ParameterSetName = "Tests01")]
   public string PersonName
   {
     get { return personName; }
     set { personName = value; }
   }
   private string personName;
   ```

2. Add the `Parameterset` keyword to the `Parameter` attribute for the unique parameter of the second parameter set.

   ```
   [Parameter(Position = 0, Mandatory = true,
   ParameterSetName = "Tests02")]
   public string CarName
   {
   ```

```
    get { return carName; }
    set { carName = value; }
}
private string carName;
```

3. For the parameter that belongs to both of the parameter sets, add a
    `Parameter` attribute for each parameter set and then add the `Parameterset`
    keyword for the `Parameter` attribute. In each `Parameter` attribute, you can
    specify the defined parameter and share if the parameter is `Optional` or
    `Mandatory` and in which `Parameterset` set:

```
[Parameter(ParameterSetName = "Tests01")]
[Parameter(Mandatory= true,ParameterSetName = "Tests02")]
public string SharedProperty
{
    get { return sharedProperty; }
    set { sharedProperty = value; }
}
private string sharedProperty;
```

Now we show an example that defines two parameter sets in which both of them
share a property. In the `Tests02` parameter set, the parameters `CarName` and
`sharedProperty` are set to `Mandatory`, and the parameter `sharedProperty` in the
`Tests01` parameter set is set to `Optional`.

After defining the parameters for a snap-in, it is very important that we validate
whether the parameter is legal or not, such as an argument set, argument range,
argument pattern, argument length, and argument count. The normal working
of snap-in is directly related to whether the parameters are legal or not. We will
introduce how to validate the parameter input in the next section.

Validating the parameter inputs

As we enter into the program execution, the input needs to be checked. In order to
ensure that the parameters are legal, we program according to our expectations.

Validating the argument set

We can specify a validation rule that the PowerShell runtime can use to check the
parameter argument before the cmdlet is run. This validation rule provides a set of
the valid values for the parameter argument.

Add the `ValidateSet` attribute before the `Parameter` attribute as shown in the following code. This example specifies a set of three possible values for the `PersonName` parameter, and when the `IgnoreCase` keyword is specified the case of the parameter is ignored when you check the parameter.

```
[ValidateSet("Gates", "Jobs", "Ballmer" , IgnoreCase = true)]
[Parameter(Position = 0, Mandatory = true)]
public string PersonName
{
  get { return personName; }
  set { personName = value; }
}
private string personName;
```

Validating the argument range

We can specify a validation rule that the PowerShell runtime can use to check the minimum and maximum values of the parameter argument before the cmdlet is run. You set this validation rule by declaring the `ValidateRange` attribute.

Add the `ValidateRange` attribute before the `Parameter` attribute as shown in the following code. This example specifies a range of 0 to 10 for the `ReceivedData` parameter.

```
[ValidateRange(0, 10)]
[Parameter(Position = 0, Mandatory = true)]
public int ReceivedData
{
  get { return receivedData; }
  set { receivedData = value; }
}
private int receivedData;
```

Validating the argument pattern

We can specify a validation rule that the PowerShell runtime can use to check the character pattern of the parameter argument before the cmdlet is run. You set this validation rule by declaring the `ValidatePattern` attribute.

Add the `ValidatePattern` attribute as shown in the following code. This example specifies a pattern of five digits, where each digit has a value of 0 through 9 for the `ReceivedData` parameter.

```
[ValidatePattern("[0-9][0-9] [0-9] [0-9] [0-9]")]
[Parameter(Position = 0, Mandatory = true)]
public int ReceivedData
{
  get { return receivedData; }
  set { receivedData = value; }
}
private int receivedData;
```

Validating the argument length

We can specify a validation rule that the PowerShell runtime can use to check the number of characters of the parameter argument before the cmdlet is run. You set this validation rule by declaring the `ValidateLength` attribute.

Add the `ValidateLength` attribute as shown in the following code. This example specifies that the length of the argument should have a length of 0 to 5 characters for the `PersonName` parameter:

```
[ValidateLength(0, 5]
[Parameter(Position = 0, Mandatory = true)]
public string PersonName
{
  get { return personName; }
  set { personName = value; }
}
private string personName;
```

Validating the argument count

We can specify a validation rule that the PowerShell runtime can use to check the count of arguments that a parameter accepts before the cmdlet is run. You set this validation rule by declaring the `ValidateCount` attribute.

Add the `ValidateCount` attribute as shown in the following code. This example specifies that the parameter will accept one argument or as many as four arguments.

```
[ValidateCount(1, 4)]
[Parameter(Position = 0, Mandatory = true)]
public string PersonName
{
  get { return personName; }
  set { personName = value; }
}
private string personName;
```

Thus this section showed us examples of how to validate a parameter input by using various attributes to implement validation rules.

Overriding methods

In the following example, there are a couple of different methods to be used: `BeginProcessing()`, `EndProcessing()`, `ProcessRecord()`, `StopProcessing()`. The code is as shown in the following screenshot:

```csharp
using System;
using System.Collections.Generic;
using System.Text;
using System.Management.Automation;

namespace MySnapIn
{
    GetHelloCommand
    SayHelloWorldCommand
    #region AddTestCommand
    //Complete cmdlet example with BeginProcessing(),EndProcessing(),ProcessRecord(),StopProcessing() method
    [Cmdlet(VerbsCommon.Add, "Test")]
    public class AddTestCommand : Cmdlet
    {//Initialization, ready for data
        protected override void BeginProcessing()
        {
            WriteObject("BeginProcessing method - Execution has begun");
        }
        //Implement operation
        protected override void ProcessRecord()
        {
            WriteObject("ProcessRecord method - Executing the main code");
            base.ProcessRecord();
        }
        //Complete, clear scene
        protected override void EndProcessing()
        {
            WriteObject("EndProcessing method - Finalizing the execution");
            base.EndProcessing();
        }
        //Break down, rollback operation
        protected override void StopProcessing()
        {
            WriteObject("StopProcessing method - Break down, rollback operation");
            base.StopProcessing();
        }
    }
    #endregion
    GetLifeCycleCommand
    GetComputerNameCommand
}
```

We can see that all of these methods have been overridden in this example. With these methods, we can accomplish various missions whether the cmdlet executes successfully or not. The BeginProcessing() method is used for initializing parameters and getting ready for the data. The ProcessRecord() method is used for the main implementation operation. The EndProcessing() method is used for finalizing the execution. The StopProcessing() method is used for breaking down the execution and the rollback operation.

In the following example, we will introduce how to share variables between two different executions and how to use a custom-defined object. The code is as follows:

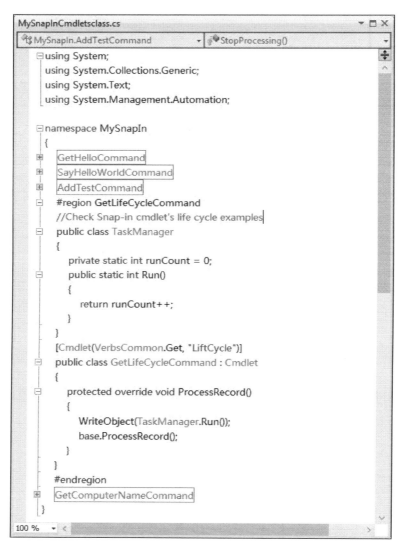

There is an object that contains a private variable and a public method in the example. When the Run() method is invoked in the ProcessRecord() method, the value of the variable runCount will be maintained in the PowerShell session.

Now, we put all the cmdlet classes merged into the code of the MySnapInCmdletsclass.cs file and compile out the assembly of our choice, which is used for the presentation of the subsequent section.

First of all, we need to use the following statement in the namespace that is used to import the class library assembly that the following code depends on:

```
using System;
using System.Collections.Generic;
using System.Text;
using System.Management.Automation;
```

We need to import some namespaces. Using other namespaces in an ordinary console program is very common, but here we need to emphasize the use of the System.Management.Automation namespace. The System.Management.Automation namespace is the root namespace for Windows PowerShell. It contains the classes, enumerations, and interfaces required to implement custom cmdlets. In particular, the Cmdlet class is the base class from which all cmdlet classes must be derived. System.Management.Automation is found under C:\Program Files\ Reference Assemblies\Microsoft\WindowsPowerShell\v1.0.

Then, we will introduce several simple cmdlet examples that contain some language characteristics that the cmdlet may mention when we are developing. The first class is GetHelloCommand; it looks as follows:

```
[Cmdlet(VerbsCommon.Get, "Hello")]
public class GetHelloCommand : Cmdlet
{
    protected override void ProcessRecord()
    {
        WriteObject("Hello!!");
    }
}
```

The statement [Cmdlet(VerbsCommon.Get, "Hello")] means that we will define a cmdlet such as Get-Hello. The VerbsCommon.Get statement means we use the built-in verb, Get. Our class GetHelloCommand inherits the Cmdlet class. And in the class, we override the ProcessRecord() method, which only contains the WriteObject method used to output a string. This simple cmdlet only outputs a string to the console.

The second class, which is named SayHelloWorldCommand, is used to demonstrate how to create a cmdlet that contains user-defined verbs and takes parameters with logical judgment. Its code looks as follows:

```
#region SayHelloWorldCommand
//Custom verbs, take parameters, with logic judgment cmdlet examples
[Cmdlet("Say", "HelloWorld")]
public class SayHelloWorldCommand : Cmdlet
{
    private string argus;
    [Parameter(Position = 0)]
    [ValidateNotNullOrEmpty]
    public string Args
    {
        get { return argus; }
        set { argus = value; }
    }
    protected override void ProcessRecord()
    {
        if (argus != null && argus.Length > 0)
        {
            Console.WriteLine("Hello World:" + argus);
        }
        else
            Console.WriteLine("Need some parameter");
    }
}
#endregion
```

The statement [Cmdlet("Say", "HelloWorld")] will create a cmdlet called "Say-HelloWorld" without using the built-in verbs or the keyword VerbsCommon. The statements [Parameter(Position = 0)] and [ValidateNotNullOrEmpty] are used to limit the received command-line parameter to the first parameter (note that the index starts from 0), and do not allow this parameter to be null or empty. In the override method of ProcessRecord(), if the parameter argus is not null or the length is greater than zero, the cmdlet will output parameters; otherwise, it will prompt the need for parameters.

In the third class, named `AddTestCommand`, is a complete cmdlet example with the `BeginProcessing()`, `ProcessRecord()`, `EndProcessing()`, and `StopProcessing()` keywords. The code for it is as follows:

```
#region AddTestCommand
//Complete cmdlet example with BeginProcessing(),EndProcessing(),ProcessRecord(),StopProcessing() method
[Cmdlet(VerbsCommon.Add, "Test")]
public class AddTestCommand : Cmdlet
{//Initialization, ready for data
    protected override void BeginProcessing()
    {
        WriteObject("BeginProcessing method - Execution has begun");
    }
    //Implement operation
    protected override void ProcessRecord()
    {
        WriteObject("ProcessRecord method - Executing the main code");
        base.ProcessRecord();
    }
    //Complete, clear scene
    protected override void EndProcessing()
    {
        WriteObject("EndProcessing method - Finalizing the execution");
        base.EndProcessing();
    }
    //Break down, rollback operation
    protected override void StopProcessing()
    {
        WriteObject("StopProcessing method - Break down, rollback operation");
        base.StopProcessing();
    }
}
#endregion
```

The `BeginProcessing()` method is used for initializing the environment and readying of data. The `ProcessRecord()` method is used for implementing the operation. The `EndProcessing()` method is used for clearing the scene when the execution completes. And the `StopProcessing()` method is used for breaking down and rolling back the operation when the execution has errors.

The following example checks the snap-in cmdlet's life cycle; the code is as shown in the following screenshot:

```csharp
#region GetLifeCycleCommand
//Check Snap-in cmdlet's life cycle examples
public class TaskManager
{
    private static int runCount = 0;
    public static int Run()
    {
        return runCount++;
    }
}
[Cmdlet(VerbsCommon.Get, "LiftCycle")]
public class GetLifeCycleCommand : Cmdlet
{
    protected override void ProcessRecord()
    {
        WriteObject(TaskManager.Run());
        base.ProcessRecord();
    }
}
#endregion
```

We defined a class named `TaskManager`, in which we declared a variable `runCount` for keeping a track of the running time of the cmdlet, and the static method `Run()` for updating the variable. In the `GetLifeCycleCommand` class, we invoke the `Run()` method of the `TaskManager` object. When we execute the `Get-LifeCycle` cmdlet, the output number will increase with the increase in the number of executions.

The last example is shown for capturing the hostname. This is the only example that is close to the real-world applications. The code is as shown in the following screenshot:

```csharp
#region GetComputerNameCommand
//The example for capture the host name
[Cmdlet(VerbsCommon.Get, "ComputerName")]
public class GetComputerNameCommand : Cmdlet
{//
    protected override void ProcessRecord()
    {
        WriteObject(System.Environment.GetEnvironmentVariable("ComputerName"));
        base.ProcessRecord();
    }
}
#endregion
```

We can see that the example uses the `System.Environment.GetEnvironmentVariable` method to get the `ComputerName` variable.

Readers can find the complete program code of this example from the Packt Publishing website at `http://www.packtpub.com/`. Our project should look something like the following:

We can see that these selected items include two `.dll` files and two class files. Now, we will compile the project to build it into a snap-in. In Visual Studio, go to **Build | Build Solution**. There is a `.dll` file in the `bin/debug` subdirectory of the code directory.

In order to use cmdlets in a snap-in, you must register it with PowerShell first. This will be described in the next section.

Registering and removing a PowerShell snap-in

In order to use a cmdlet that is contained in a snap-in, the cmdlet needs to be registered and loaded into a PowerShell session for execution. Because registering a DLL file needs administrator rights, it is required to start a PowerShell session as an administrator and invoke a statement for registering a snap-in.

Registering and removing snap-in in PowerShell 1.0

In PowerShell 1.0, we have to register a snap-in into PowerShell using `installutil.exe`, which is contained in the .NET Framework. The default installation position will be one of the following:

- `%windir%\Microsoft.NET\Framework64\v4.0.30319\` (Used for x64)
- `%windir%\Microsoft.NET\Framework\v4.0.30319\` (Used for x86)

Users must set the location of the PowerShell session to the directory that contains the assembly DLL file of the snap-in, and then use `installutil.exe` to register the DLL file. Next, we can load a snap-in into the PowerShell session using `Add-PSSnapin MySnapIn`. We can use `Get-Command -PSSnapIn MySnapIn` to get cmdlets that are registered by the `MySnapIn. All` command as shown in the following screenshot:

```
Install.ps1 X
1   #dll name
2   $FileName="MySnapIn.dll"
3   #snap-in name
4   $PSSnapinName="MySnapIn"
5   $rtd = [System.Runtime.InteropServices.RuntimeEnvironment]::GetRuntimeDirectory()
6   set-alias installutil (resolve-path (join-path $rtd installutil.exe))
7   installutil (Join-Path (Split-Path $MyInvocation.MyCommand.Path) $FileName)
8   Add-PSSnapin $PSSnapinName
9   Get-Command -PSSnapin $PSSnapinName
```

Registering and removing a snap-in in PowerShell 3.0

If you're running PowerShell 3, you don't need to install this using `PSSnapin`. You can use `Import-Module` to load it. Just as shown in the following screenshot:

```
Administrator: powershell                                              _ □ ×
PS C:\> Import-Module MySnapIn
WARNING: The names of some imported commands from the module 'MySnapIn' include unapproved verbs
that might make them less discoverable. To find the commands with unapproved verbs, run the
Import-Module command again with the Verbose parameter. For a list of approved verbs, type
Get-Verb.
PS C:\> Get-Command -module MySnapIn

CommandType     Name                                              ModuleName
-----------     ----                                              ----------
Cmdlet          Add-Test                                          MySnapIn
Cmdlet          Get-ComputerName                                  MySnapIn
Cmdlet          Get-Hello                                         MySnapIn
Cmdlet          Get-LiftCycle                                     MySnapIn
Cmdlet          Say-HelloWorld                                    MySnapIn

PS C:\>
```

When executing the statement, we need to take care that we create a snap-in and place it in its own subdirectory in the system module directory $env:PSModulePath (such as C:\Windows\System32\WindowsPowerShell\v1.0\Modules) or the user's module directory (such as C:\Users\Administrator\Documents\WindowsPowerShell).

In fact, depending on the information we implement for the snap-in installer, the following registry information will be created when we register a snap-in. A registry key with a snap-in name, in our example it is named MySnapIn, which was defined in the MySnapInInstallclass.cs class file, will be created with a key under HKLM\SOFTWARE\Microsoft\PowerShell\1\PowerShellSnapIns\. Just as shown in the following screenshot:

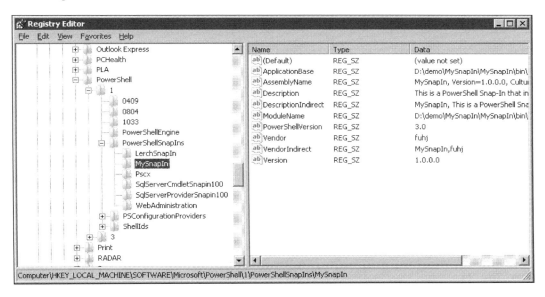

We can see that the information we registered in the installer class has been created in the registry. The system finds the snap-ins depending on the key registered in the registry.

Once you load the snap-in into PowerShell, the snap-in will always load automatically in every PowerShell session until it is removed by the Remove-Module cmdlet using the following command:

```
PS C:\> Remove-Module MySnapIn
```

In order for PowerShell 3.0 to be compatible with the earlier versions of the PowerShell runtime environment, we create a script file named `Install.ps1` and use it in different operation environments for snap-in installations. For earlier versions of PowerShell, such as PowerShell 1.0 and PowerShell 2.0, we can directly place this script file in the directory of snap-in assemblies and invoke `.\Install.ps1` for installation. For PowerShell 3.0 you only need to add `-Force` parameters for executing the registered snap-in. Just as the code shown in the following screenshot:

```
Install.ps1 X
 1   #Run mode PS> .\Install.ps1 -force
 2   #follow configuration
 3   #dll name
 4   $FileName="MySnapIn.dll"
 5   #snap-in name
 6   $PSSnapinName="MySnapIn"
 7   #follow do not modify
 8
 9   if($PSVersionTable) {
10       Write-Host "You're running PowerShell $($PSVersionTable.PSVersion),
11       so you don't need to Install this as a PSSnapin, you can use Import-Module (or Add-Module in CTP2) to load it.
12       If you still want to install it as a PSSnapin, re-run this script with -Force"
13       if($args -notcontains "-Force") {
14           return
15       }
16   }
17
18   $rtd = [System.Runtime.InteropServices.RuntimeEnvironment]::GetRuntimeDirectory()
19   set-alias installutil (resolve-path (join-path $rtd installutil.exe))
20
21   # cd C:\Users\Administrator\Projects\PowerShell\MySnapIn\bin\Debug
22   installutil (Join-Path (Split-Path $MyInvocation.MyCommand.Path) $FileName)
23
24   if($?) {
25       # Get-PSSnapin -registered
26       Add-PSSnapin $PSSnapinName
27
28       #Get-PSSnapin -registered
29
30       # get-help *-Window
31       Get-Command -PSSnapin $PSSnapinName
32
33       Write-Host "To load the Snapin in the future, you need to run:"
34       Write-Host "Add-PSSnapin $PSSnapinName" -fore Red
35       Write-Host
36       Write-Host "You can also add that line to your Profile script to load it automatically."
37   } else {
38
39       Write-Warning @"
40   `nInstallation Failed. You're probably just not running as administrator.
41   If you see a System.UnauthorizedAccessException in the log output above, with an HKEY_LOCAL_MACHINE path,
42    that's deffinitely what happened, just start an administrative console and try again.
43   "@
44   }
```

The following screenshot shows the script file for uninstalling:

```
UnInstall.ps1 X
1    #Run mode PS> .\UnInstall.ps1
2    #follow configuration
3    #dll name
4    $FileName="MySnapIn.dll"
5    #snap-in name
6    $PSSnapinName="MySnapIn"
7    #follow do not modify
8
9    Remove-PSSnapin $PSSnapinName
10
11
12   $rtd = [System.Runtime.InteropServices.RuntimeEnvironment]::GetRuntimeDirectory()
13   set-alias installutil (resolve-path (join-path $rtd installutil.exe))
14
15   installutil /u (Join-Path (Split-Path $MyInvocation.MyCommand.Path) $FileName)
```

In these two script files, users only need to replace the $FileName and $PSSnapinName values with their own snap-in assembly name and snap-in name to register their own snap-in.

Listing and executing cmdlets in a PowerShell snap-in

We can use Get-Module or Get-PSSnapin -registered to get a list of registered snap-ins in the current PowerShell session, as shown in the following screenshot:

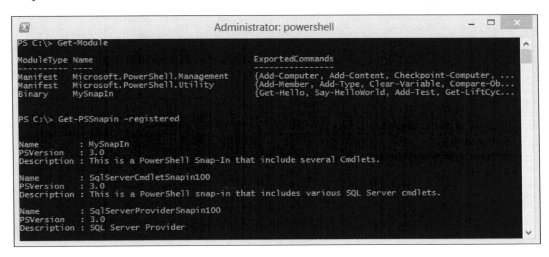

We can use `Get-Command` with the `-module` parameter for listing cmdlets in a PowerShell snap-in, as shown in the following screenshot:

We can now use the cmdlet register in our snap-in, just like a native cmdlet. All the cmdlets in our snap-in can be invoked as shown in the following screenshot:

Debugging a PowerShell snap-in

Once you have built a cmdlet, set a breakpoint in your code in Visual Studio. Once you have done that, open a new PowerShell window, switch to the compilation directory of the snap-in, and install your module or snap-in. The operation is the same when you load the cmdlet with `Add-PSSnapin` or `Import-Module`. In Visual Studio, go to **Debug | Attach to Process**. Scroll through the list and look for `PowerShell.exe`, just as shown in the following screenshot:

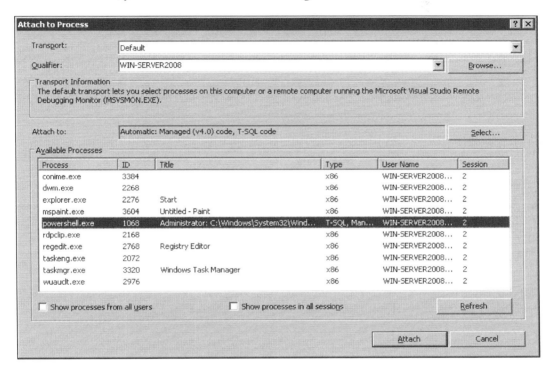

When you find the right process, select it and click on the **Attach** button. Now, go to your PowerShell window and run the command that can trigger your breakpoint. If all goes according to plan, your breakpoint will be hit and you can step through the cmdlet's code, as shown in the following screenshot:

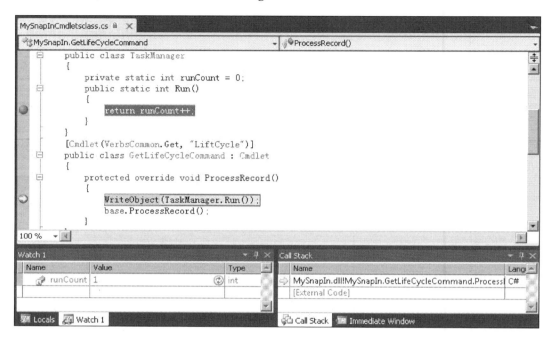

We can see in the screenshot that the breakpoints we set are hit and the variable being watched can also get a value. We can thus very conveniently debug a cmdlet registered in any snap-in.

Summary

In this chapter, we discussed how to create a snap-in and compile these class files into an assembly. Then we introduced how to register the assembly as a snap-in to a PowerShell session and debug a PowerShell snap-in.

At the end of this chapter, we believe that you have been able to attempt creating a snap-in independently. As snap-ins are a powerful support mechanism, users can easily expand any function of PowerShell according to their own needs.

The snap-in is compiled into assemblies when it is released to a program for third-party users. The author can also encrypt based on .NET code obfuscation to protect their source code. Program authors do not need to worry about their snap-in decompiling out the source code.

In the next chapter, we will discuss how to use PowerShell remoting. PowerShell remoting can manage remote computers through the network. We will learn how to enable and disable remoting, execute remote commands, enter an interactive remoting session, and save remote sessions to a disk.

3

Using PowerShell Remoting

PowerShell v2 introduced a powerful new technology, **remoting**, which was refined and expanded upon for PowerShell v3. Based primarily upon standardized protocols and techniques, remoting is possibly one of the most important aspects of PowerShell. Future Microsoft products will rely upon it almost entirely for administrative communications across the network.

In this chapter we will cover:

- PowerShell remoting system requirements
- Enabling/disabling remoting
- Executing a remote command
- Interactive remoting sessions
- Saving a remote session to a disk
- Understanding session configuration

The most important and exciting characteristic of PowerShell is its remote management ability. PowerShell remoting can control the target remote computer through the network. PowerShell remoting uses **WinRM (Windows Remote Management)**, which is based on Microsoft's WS-Management protocol. With PowerShell remoting, the administrator can execute various management operations on dozens of target computers throughout the network. In this chapter we will introduce content relevant to PowerShell remoting .

An overview of PowerShell remoting

A few cmdlets in PowerShell support accessing information on a remote computer. These cmdlets have a `ComputerName` parameter, such as `Get-WmiObject` or `Invoke-WmiMethod`. All of them get objects from remote computers by using .NET Framework methods to retrieve the object. The remoting ability of these cmdlets is dependent on PowerShell. Whether a cmdlet has this ability depends on author implementation of methods such as **Remote Procedure Call (RPC)**, to realize remote access. They do not use the Windows PowerShell remoting infrastructure.

WS-Management protocol, a SOAP-based, firewall-friendly protocol, was designed for systems to locate and exchange management information. The intent of the WS-Management protocol specification is to provide interoperability and consistency for enterprise systems that have computers running on a variety of operating systems from different vendors. To use WS-Management-based Windows PowerShell remoting, the local and remote computers must be configured for remoting, and the host application must run in elevated mode. WS-Management protocol is based on standard web service specifications such as HTTPS, SOAP over HTTP (WS-I profile), SOAP 1.2, WS-Addressing, WS-Transfer, WS-Enumeration, and WS-Eventing.

Universal Code Execution Model (UCEM) is a characteristic feature of PowerShell remoting. UCEM means that the execution can be local and in any position. PowerShell remoting can import from local threads using remote commands — this feature works as the implicit remote management, which allows the user to save and export these incoming commands to a hard disk and could be used in the future of the module. PowerShell Remote Management allows various connection modes, including interactive (1:1), fan-out (1:n), and fan-in (n:1) by using of IIS hosting model. Here we will be explaining how we can configure a host on any one of these work forms.

To enable PowerShell remoting sessions on Windows PowerShell 2.0, the local and remote computer participating in remote management must have the following:

- Windows PowerShell 2.0 or higher
- The Microsoft .NET Framework 2.0 or higher
- Windows Remote Management 2.0

To run remote sessions on Windows PowerShell 3.0, the local and remote computers must have the following:

- Windows PowerShell 3.0 or higher
- The Microsoft .NET Framework 4.0 or higher
- Windows Remote Management 3.0

You can create remote sessions between computers running Windows PowerShell 2.0 and Windows PowerShell 3.0. However, features that run only on Windows PowerShell 3.0, such as the ability to disconnect and reconnect to sessions, are available only when both computers are running Windows PowerShell 3.0. PowerShell 3.0 supports operating systems such as Windows 7 Service Pack 1, Windows Server 2008 R2 SP1, and Windows Server 2008 Service Pack 2, or higher versions. All of these operation systems should install **Windows Management Framework (WMF)** 3.0 separately, which includes PowerShell 3.0. Windows 8 and Windows Server 2012 have PowerShell built in by default. Because of PowerShell remoting, PowerShell 3.0 contains more language characteristics. The content of these chapter-related scripts and commands will be represented based on the version of Windows 8.

To be able to run scripts and commands on remote computers, the user performing remote script execution must be:

- A member of the administrators group on the remote machine
- Able to provide administrator credentials at the time of remote execution
- Able to access the PS session configuration on the remote system

Also, on client OS versions of Windows such as Windows Vista and Windows 7, network location must be set to either Home or Work. WS-Management may not function properly if the network location for any of the network adapters is set to Public.

Enabling/disabling remoting

In a workgroup, two computers need to be awarded the permissions of remote access. For security purposes, the default settings don't allow remote access. If you try to log in to the host in the workgroup, since there is no strict security requirement and infrastructure or domain setting, you will need to modify the configuration. When the host is configured, you can remotely access one from the other hosts using PowerShell remoting. The following section will show you how to configure PowerShell remoting in a domain environment.

Operating PowerShell in a no-domain environment

What needs to be stressed on here is that PowerShell remoting can't be enabled remotely in a no-domain environment. In the subsequent section, we will talk about how to configure PowerShell remoting in a domain environment. Remoting in PowerShell can be enabled by just running the following command in an interactive PowerShell prompt:

```
winrm quickconfig
```

WinRM is the Microsoft implementation of the WS-Management protocol and provides a secure way of communicating with local and remote computers using web services.

Before we execute this command, we can check the WinRM configuration by using following command:

```
winrm get winrm/config -format:pretty
```

We will get the result in the form of an error that tells us that the service of the destination computer isn't running or that it doesn't accept the request, as shown in the following screenshot:

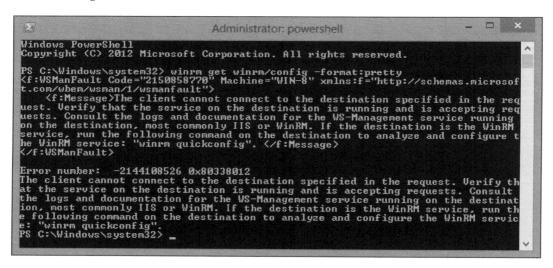

Then, we execute the previous command. You will be asked to respond to a couple of questions that are based on OS architecture. You can see this in the following screenshot:

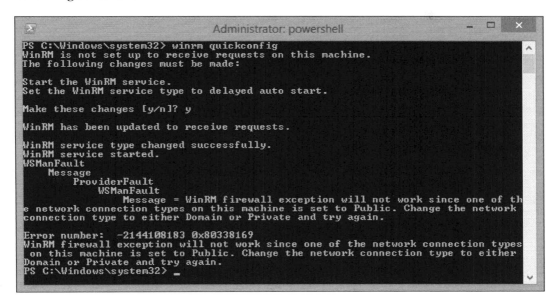

As we can see, the output has an error. The reason for the error is that the WinRM firewall exception will not work when the network connection types on this machine is set to Public.

Setting the network location to Private

The WinRM firewall exception did not work since one of the network connection type on this machine was set to Public. Change the network connection type to either Domain or Private and try again.

The network location feature was introduced in Windows Vista. It provides an easy way to customize your firewall settings based on whether or not you trust the computers around you. There are three network location types: Private, Public, and Domain. If your computer is a member of a domain, you won't be able to change the network location type. If your computer is standalone or part of a workgroup, you can choose what type of network location you want, Public or Private. Private means that you are a member of a trusted network and you can lower your network security a little bit. Public means that you have no trust in the network outside and you will not let your guard down. We can find it in **Networking and Sharing Center**, as shown in the following screenshot:

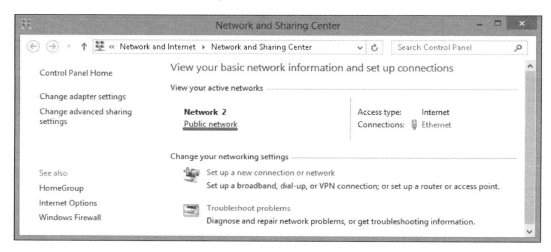

Setting the correct network location type is very important for Windows PowerShell remoting. You cannot enable Windows PowerShell remoting on your machine if your connections are set to Public. It means you won't be able to connect to this machine using Windows PowerShell remoting. Vista provides a UI dialog for setting network location, but unfortunately, there is no command-line utility for that. You can, however, do it with Windows PowerShell.

The API for setting network location type in Vista is COM-based, and the code in the following screenshot shows how to call this API with the Windows PowerShell script:

```
Set_network_location_to_Private.ps1  X
1   # Skip network location setting for pre-Vista operating systems
2   if([environment]::OSVersion.version.Major -lt 6) { return }
3   # Skip network location setting if local machine is joined to a domain.
4   if(1,3,4,5 -contains (Get-WmiObject win32_computersystem).DomainRole) { return }
5   # Get network connections
6   $networkListManager = [Activator]::CreateInstance([Type]::GetTypeFromCLSID([Guid]"{DCB00C01-570F-4A98-8D69-199FDBA57238}"))
7   $connections = $networkListManager.GetNetworkConnections()
8   # Set network location to Private for all networks
9   $connections | % {$_.GetNetwork().SetCategory(1)}
```

After the execution of the script, we will find in **Networking and Sharing Center** that network location types have been switched to Private, as shown in the following screenshot:

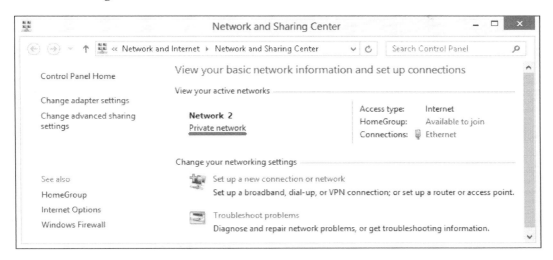

Now, we can execute the `winrm quickconfig` command again, as shown in the following screenshot:

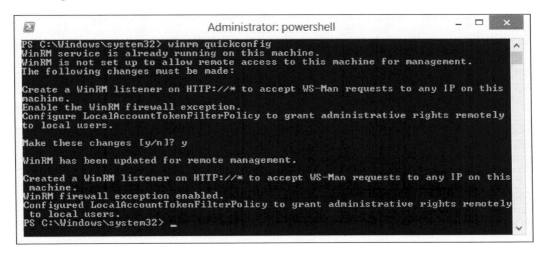

The following things happen when you run this command:

- The WinRM service gets enabled and the startup type is set to autostart.
- A WinRM listener gets created to accept remoting requests on any IP addresses assigned to a local computer.
- Windows firewall exceptions for WinRM service will be created. This is essentially the reason why the network location cannot be set to Public if you want to enable PS remoting. Windows firewall exceptions cannot be enabled if the network location is set to Public.
- All registered PS session configurations are enabled.

By default, WinRM only enables HTTP transport to accept remoting requests. You can manually enable HTTPS transport using either the `winrm` command or the `New-WSManIntance` cmdlet.

Enable PSRemoting

In fact, we can also use the `Enable-PSRemoting` cmdlet to enable PowerShell remoting, as shown in the following screenshot:

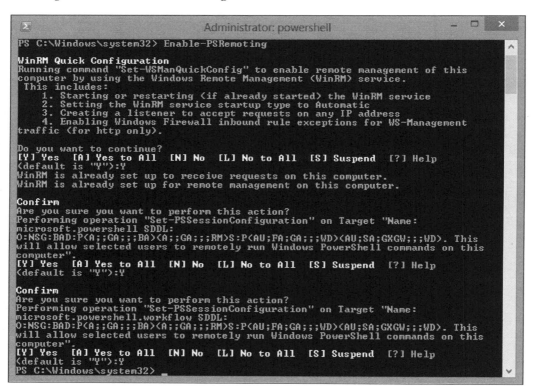

You should always use the more comprehensive `Enable-PSRemoting` cmdlet. You can use the `-force` parameter along with this cmdlet to silently enable remoting.

You can use the `Enter-PSSession` cmdlet to test whether remoting is enabled on the local machine or not.

```
Enter-PSSession -ComputerName localhost
```

If remoting is enabled and functional, you will see the prompt changing to something like this:

Next, we check the remoting configuration information, so that we can compare the results with the previous execution.

```
winrm get winrm/config -format:pretty
```

We get a result similar to the following:

```
PS C:\Windows\system32> winrm get winrm/config -format:pretty
<cfg:Config xml:lang="en-US" xmlns:cfg="http://schemas.microsoft.com/wbem/wsman/1/config">
    <cfg:MaxEnvelopeSizekb>500</cfg:MaxEnvelopeSizekb>
    <cfg:MaxTimeoutms>60000</cfg:MaxTimeoutms>
    <cfg:MaxBatchItems>32000</cfg:MaxBatchItems>
    <cfg:MaxProviderRequests>4294967295</cfg:MaxProviderRequests>
    <cfg:Client>
        <cfg:NetworkDelayms>5000</cfg:NetworkDelayms>
        <cfg:URLPrefix>wsman</cfg:URLPrefix>
        <cfg:AllowUnencrypted>false</cfg:AllowUnencrypted>
        <cfg:Auth>
            <cfg:Basic>true</cfg:Basic>
            <cfg:Digest>true</cfg:Digest>
            <cfg:Kerberos>true</cfg:Kerberos>
            <cfg:Negotiate>true</cfg:Negotiate>
            <cfg:Certificate>true</cfg:Certificate>
            <cfg:CredSSP>false</cfg:CredSSP>
        </cfg:Auth>
        <cfg:DefaultPorts>
            <cfg:HTTP>5985</cfg:HTTP>
            <cfg:HTTPS>5986</cfg:HTTPS>
        </cfg:DefaultPorts>
        <cfg:TrustedHosts></cfg:TrustedHosts>
    </cfg:Client>
    <cfg:Service>
        <cfg:RootSDDL>O:NSG:BAD:P(A;;GA;;;BA)(A;;GR;;;IU)S:P(AU;FA;GA;;;WD)(AU;SA;GXGW;;;WD)</cfg:Ro
otSDDL>
        <cfg:MaxConcurrentOperations>4294967295</cfg:MaxConcurrentOperations>
```

By default, PowerShell remoting uses port number 5985 (for HTTP) and 5986 (for HTTPS). This can be changed by modifying `wsman:\localhost\Listener\listener*\port` to a different value using the `Set-Item` cmdlet. However, beware that this will change the port number for every WinRM listener on the system.

Configuring WSMan trusted hosts

You will not be able to connect a computer that is in a workgroup just by running the `Enable-PSRemoting` cmdlet. This is because the security levels on a workgroup-joined computer are more stringent than on a domain-joined computer. So, on workgroup-joined computers, you need to do more work before you can create remoting sessions. If we execute the `Invoke-Command` cmdlet without configuring a trusted host, we will get an error message:

```
Windows PowerShell
Copyright (C) 2012 Microsoft Corporation. All rights reserved.

PS C:\Windows\system32> Invoke-Command -ComputerName 192.168.10.11 -ScriptBlock
{Get-Process}
[192.168.10.11] Connecting to remote server 192.168.10.11 failed with the
following error message : The WinRM client cannot process the request. If the
authentication scheme is different from Kerberos, or if the client computer is
not joined to a domain, then HTTPS transport must be used or the destination
machine must be added to the TrustedHosts configuration setting. Use winrm.cmd
to configure TrustedHosts. Note that computers in the TrustedHosts list might
not be authenticated. You can get more information about that by running the
following command: winrm help config. For more information, see the
about_Remote_Troubleshooting Help topic.
    + CategoryInfo          : OpenError: (192.168.10.11:String) [], PSRemoting
   TransportException
    + FullyQualifiedErrorId : ServerNotTrusted,PSSessionStateBroken
PS C:\Windows\system32> _
```

We can see that a computer that doesn't join the domain must be added to the `TrustedHosts` configuration setting or the connecting operation will be refused.

On all workgroup-joined computers, you need to add the IP address of all remoting clients to the list of trusted hosts. To do this:

```
Set-item wsman:localhost\client\trustedhosts -value *
```

Using `*` as the value will add all computers as trusted hosts. If you want to add only a specific set of computers, use the following command:

```
Set-item wsman:localhost\client\trustedhosts -value "Computer1,Computer2"
```

If you want to add all computers in a specific domain, use the following command:

```
Set-item wsman:localhost\client\trustedhosts -value "*.domain.com"
```

If you want to add an IP address of a remote computer to the trusted hosts list, use the following command:

```
Set-item wsman:localhost\client\trustedhosts -value "192.168.10.11"
```

Of course, we can also use the WinRM batch script to add a computer to the trusted hosts list by using the following command:

```
winrm set winrm/config/client `@`{TrustedHosts=`"`192.168.10.11`"`}
```

The screen will look like this:

Once these changes are made, you can use the `Enable-PSRemoting` cmdlet to enable remoting on these workgroup-joined computers.

Configuring PowerShell remoting on a domain using Group Policy

In the workgroup environment, two servers need an interactive session to enable PowerShell remoting, and then each operation on the remote computer needs to provide corresponding credentials so that the remote computer can recognize whether the operation is legal. This is appropriate for managing a small number of hosts, but for a large number of hosts the situation gets more complicated; the account may be different on different computers, and the password is also different. To manage a large number of hosts, Active Directory is a simple and fast method because a domain-joined host can realize unified login authentication throughout the domain controller. We will introduce you to configuring PowerShell remoting in a domain environment using the Group Policy in following section.

Allowing remote server management through WinRM

When we enable PowerShell remoting in a domain environment, we must create a **Group Policy Object (GPO)** for it, using the following steps:

1. Launch **Group Policy Management (GPMC)** via **Control Panel | All Control Panel Items | Administrative Tools | Group Policy Management**, and create a new GPO titled `Windows Remote Management`.

2. Right-click on **Edit** to edit the newly created GPO by using Group Policy Management Editor, and then expand it through the Computer Configuration Policy structure using **Windows Remote Management | Computer Configuration | Administrative Templates | Windows Components | Windows Remote Management (WinRM) | WinRM Service** and selecting **Allow remote server management through WinRM**. This policy setting allows you to manage whether the WinRM service automatically starts and listens on the network for HTTP requests on port 5985 (and if enabled, for HTTPS requests on port 5986).

3. Enable the GPO and complete the IPv* filter's textboxes; an example of a relaxed configuration can be see following screenshot:

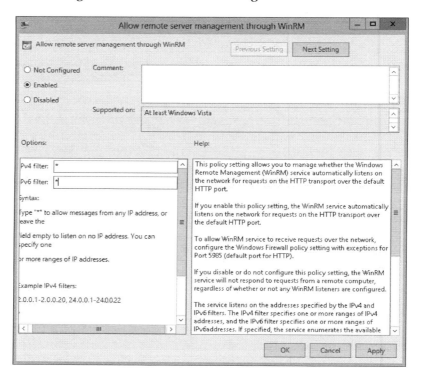

The service listens on the addresses specified by the IPv4 and IPv6 filters. The IPv4 filter specifies one or more ranges of IPv4 addresses, and the IPv6 filter specifies one or more ranges of IPv6 addresses. If specified, the service enumerates the available IP addresses for the computer and uses only the addresses that fall within one of the filter ranges.

You can use the asterisk (*) to indicate that the service listens on all available IP addresses on the computer. When * is used, other ranges in the filter are ignored. If the filter is left blank, the service does not listen on any addresses.

For example, if you want the service to listen only on IPv4 addresses, leave the IPv6 filter empty.

Ranges are specified using the syntax IP1-IP2. Multiple ranges are separated using the comma (,) as the delimiter.

An example of IPv4 filters is `8.8.8.1-8.8.8.20, 8.8.4.1-8.8.4.22`.

Allowing Windows Remote Management through Windows Firewall

1. Locate **Computer Configuration | Policies | Windows Settings | Security Settings | Windows Firewall with Advanced Security | Windows Firewall... | Inbound Rules**, as shown in the following screenshot:

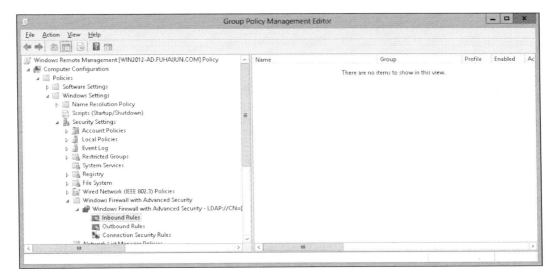

2. Right-click on **Inbound Rules** and click on **New Rule**. Under **Rule Type**, click on **Predefined** and locate **Windows Remote Management**. Be careful here, there's another rule called **Windows Remote Firewall Management**, but that's not what you want. Click on **Next**. This is seen in the following screenshot:

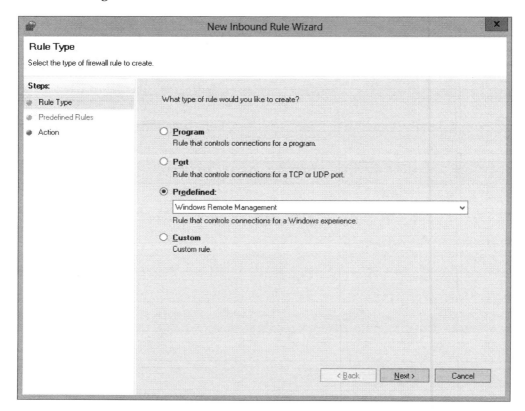

3. Your rules should look something like those shown in the following screenshot. Click on **Next** again:

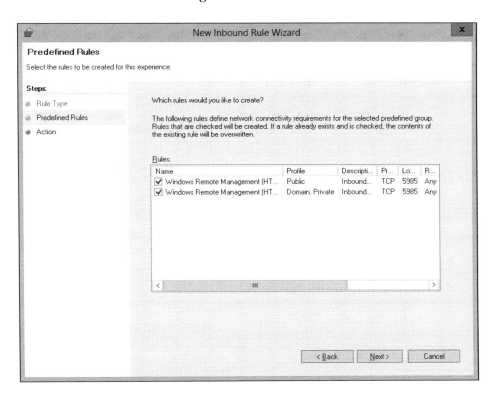

4. Now define what action you want the firewall to take. Click on **Allow the connection**. Then click on **Finish**, as shown in the following screenshot:

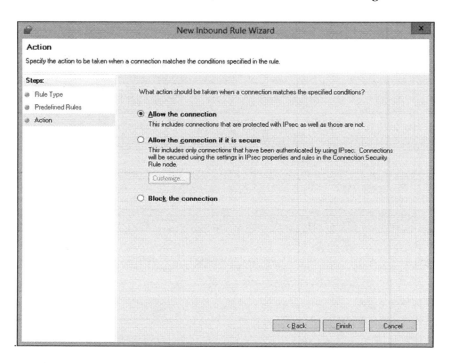

5. When the rules are created, you may choose to make further restrictions, that is, to only allow the IP addresses of your management subnet or perhaps some specific user groups:

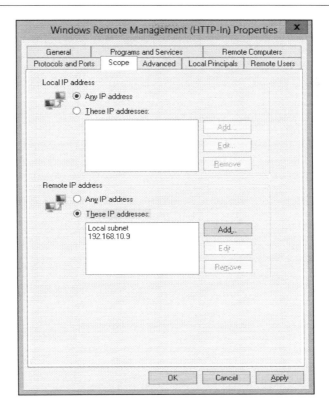

Turning on Service Windows Remote Management (WS-Management)

Now that the firewall is allowing the remoting traffic to go through, we need something to actually listen for it. For that, we need to start Windows' remoting service and make sure it starts automatically.

In addition, the WinRM service is, by default, not started on Windows client operating systems. To configure the WinRM service to start automatically, navigate to **Computer Configuration | Policies | Windows Settings | Security Settings | System Services**. On the right-hand pane, locate **Windows Remote Management** and double-click on it:

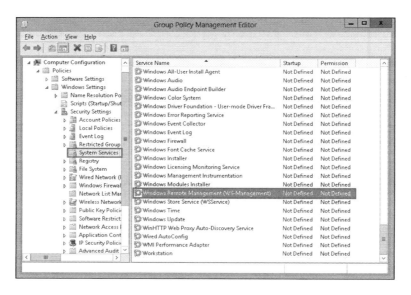

Check the **Define this policy setting** box and set the service startup mode to **Automatic**, as shown in the following screenshot:

We also want to set a service preference here in case the service fails. Navigate to **Computer Configuration | Preferences | Control Panel Settings | Services**. Right-click on **Services**, click on **New | Service**, as shown in the following screenshot:

On the **General** tab, use the following settings:

- **Startup**: Automatic
- **Service Name**: WinRM
- **Service Action**: Start Service

On the **Recovery** tab, set all the failure settings to **Restart the Service**. Click on **OK**:

Doing a Group Policy Update

Assuming the GPO is now enabled and linked to an OU containing the computers targeted for remoting, log on to one of the client machines in the domain and run gpupdate /force or wait for the Group Policy to be deployed to the client machine. Refer to the following screenshot:

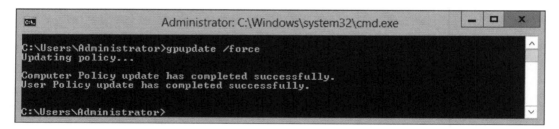

To view the currently applied GPO, use the gpresult command and confirm that the GPO titled **Windows Remote Management** is listed in the **Applied Group Policy Objects** section.

Disabling remoting

You can use Disable-PSRemoting to disable remoting on the local computer. Disable-PSRemoting will only disable the session configuration. All the changes effected by Enable-PSRemoting will not be removed. This includes leaving the WinRM service in the enabled state and leaving all the listeners to enable PS remoting. You will have to manually undo these changes if they are not required by any other component or service on the local computer.

If no other service or components on the local computer need the WinRM service, you can disable it by running the following command:

```
Set-Service winrm -StartupType Manual

Stop-Service winrm
```

To remove all WinRM listeners listening on the default PS remoting port (5985), use the following command:

```
Get-ChildItem WSMan:\localhost\Listener -Recurse | Foreach-Object {
$_.PSPath } | Where-Object { (Get-Item "$_\Port").Value -eq 5985 } |
Remove-Item
```

If the authentication scheme is different from Kerberos or if the client computer is not joined to a domain, HTTPS transport must be used or the destination machine must be added to the TrustedHosts configuration setting. Use winrm.cmd to configure trusted hosts. Note that computers in the trusted hosts list might not be authenticated.

Executing the remoting commands

With remoting, we can execute commands and scripts on a remote computer in a couple of ways. This includes the `Invoke-Command` cmdlet and interactive remoting sessions. Once you have enabled remoting on all your machines, you can use the `Invoke-Command` cmdlet to run commands and scripts on the local computer or remote computers. Here is an example of executing the remoting commands:

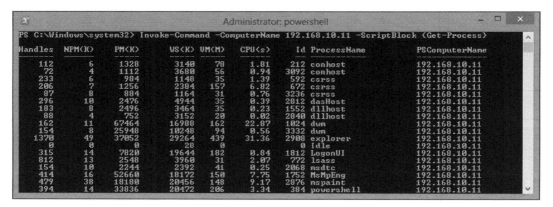

When we appoint an IP address to the `-ComputerName` parameter and set the `-ScriptBlock` parameter as `Get-Process`, the result of execution will be returned to the local computer.

Running ScriptBlock on a remote computer

You can execute a command on a remote computer by using the following method:

```
Invoke-Command -ComputerName Win-8 -ScriptBlock {Get-Service}
```

The `ScriptBlock` parameter can be used to specify a list of commands that you want to run on the remote computer. The `ComputerName` parameter is not required for the running of commands on the local machine. If you want to run the same command on multiple remote computers, you can supply the computer name or IP address as a comma separated list or read a text file's content by using the `Get-Content` cmdlet:

```
Invoke-Command -ComputerName Win-8,Win-8-Client -ScriptBlock {Get-Service}
```

We can also make use of the following command:

```
Invoke-Command -ComputerName (Get-Content c:\servers.txt) -ScriptBlock {Get-Service}
```

This method is called **fan-out** or **1:many** remoting. You can run the same commands on multiple computers just as a single command. All commands and variables in the `ScriptBlock` parameter are evaluated on the remote computer.

If you have a script of commands to run, you can have `Invoke-Command` read it, transmit the content to the remote computers, and have them execute those commands:

```
Invoke-Command -ComputerName Win-8,Win-8-Client –filePath
c:\Scripts\Tasks.ps1
```

The `ComputerName` parameter of the `Invoke-Command` cmdlet accepts multiple computer names, and the `Session` parameter accepts multiple PS sessions. When you run an `Invoke-Command` command, Windows PowerShell runs the commands on all of the specified computers or in all of the specified PS sessions. Windows PowerShell can manage hundreds of concurrent remote connections. However, the number of remote commands that you can send might be limited by the resources of your computer and its capacity to establish and maintain multiple network connections.

If you use something like `-ScriptBlock {Get-Service -Name $serviceName}`, PowerShell exports the remote computer session to have `$serviceName` defined. You can pass variables on the local computer to a remote session with the `-ArgumentList` parameter when using `Invoke-Command`. You can do this using the following command:

```
$serviceName="WinRM"
```

```
Invoke-Command -ComputerName (Get-Content c:\servers.txt) -ScriptBlock
{param($Name) Get-Service -Name $Name} -ArgumentList $serviceName
```

This example shows how to use the `-ArgumentList` parameter to pass the variables to the remote session.

Creating a persistent session with Invoke-Command

Run `Invoke-Command` with the `-ComputerName` parameter, which specifies the name of the remote computer, its NetBIOS name, and its IP address. This parameter can establish a temporary session and execute the remote command every time. Establishing a session every time is a time-consuming operation. It may be fine for a couple of commands but not when you have to execute many more commands and scripts. This is a very efficient method for running a single command or several unrelated commands, even on many remote computers.

To avoid the unnecessary time overhead, we can use a persistent session of the remote computer using the `-Session` parameter. You can create a persistent connection to a remote computer by using the `New-PSSession` cmdlet as shown in the following examples.

When you use the `New-PSSession` cmdlet to create a PS session, Windows PowerShell establishes a persistent connection for the PS session. Then, you can run multiple commands in the PS session, including commands that share data.

```
$session=New-PSSession -ComputerName Win-8
```

Right now, `$session` contains the session details for the persistent connection. We can use `$session` to invoke a command on the remote computer; the syntax for that looks like this:

```
Invoke-Command -Session $session -ScriptBlock {Get-Service}
```

`$session` contains all variables you create/modify when you execute commands on the remote computer. So, subsequent command execution with `$session` as the session will have access to all the variables created/updated on the remote computer. For example:

```
$session=New-PSSession -ComputerName Win-8
Invoke-Command -Session $session -ScriptBlock {$fileCount = (Get-ChildItem C:\ -Recurse).Count}
invoke-command -session $session -ScriptBlock {$fileCount}
```

We could access the `$fileCount` variable only because we used a persistent session to run the command:

Through the use of a persistent session, we will execute commands transfer to a specified host. After the execution is completed, the `Invoke-Command` cmdlet retrieves the execution result. The whole process is completed based on the persistent session. When you use the `New-PSSession` cmdlet to create a PS session, Windows PowerShell establishes a persistent connection for the PS session. Then, you can run multiple commands in the PS session, including commands that share data.

Typically, you create a PS session to run a series of related commands that share data. Otherwise, the temporary connection created by the ComputerName parameter is sufficient for most commands.

Running remote commands as a job

When we transmit a time-consuming operation to the remote host by PowerShell remoting, we have to wait for the commands to complete to return the execution results. In the example shown earlier, this gets the total file count on C drive on the remote machine. It depends on the amount of documentation available on the C drive when operation execution is completed. If the file count is a huge number, waiting for the remote computer operation to be completed is very time consuming. To avoid this, you can use the -asjob parameter to run the command as a background job on the remote computer, as shown in the following command:

```
$session=New-PSSession -ComputerName Win-8

Invoke-Command -Session $session -ScriptBlock { (Get-ChildItem C:\
-Recurse).Count} -asjob
```

Once you execute this, you will see the job details listed as shown in the following screenshot:

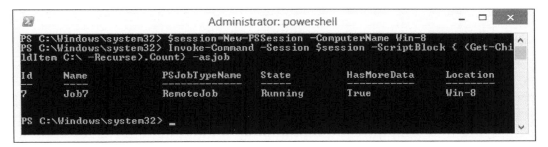

When you use the -asjob parameter with the Invoke-Command cmdlet, the background job gets created locally and runs on the remote computer. Since this job is created locally, we can use *-job cmdlets to manage the job object. The job object will not be destroyed in the current PowerShell process until the process is closed.

For example, you can use the Get-Job cmdlet to monitor the status of the job, and once the job status changes to completed, you can use the Receive-Job cmdlet-to see the output of the script block specified.

```
Get-Job -id 7 |Receive-Job
```

To get the results of the job, use the `Receive-Job` cmdlet. Because the job results are automatically returned to the computer where the job object resides, you can get the results with a local `Receive-Job` command.

Specifying credentials required for remoting

At the start of the chapter, we have mentioned that we can use PowerShell remoting between computers in a workgroup environment. In a domain environment, we can log on as a user only if we have administrator credentials to access any computer in the domain. However, in a workgroup, we have to pass the credentials along with `Invoke-Command`. For example:

```
$cred=Get-Credential

Invoke-Command -ComputerName win-8 -ScriptBlock {Get-Service} -Credential
$cred
```

In this example, `Get-Credential` prompts for the credentials to access a remote computer and uses the same while calling the `Invoke-Command` cmdlet. When you enter the `Get-Credential` cmdlet, a dialog box appears requesting a username and password. When you enter the requested information, the cmdlet creates a `PSCredential` object representing the credentials of the user and saves it in the `$cred` variable.

Entering an interactive remoting session

`Enter-PSSession` and `Exit-PSSession` are the cmdlets used to start/exit an interactive remoting session. To enter an interactive session, we use the following command:

```
Enter-PSSession -ComputerName win-8
```

Once you enter an interactive remoting session, the PowerShell prompt changes to reflect the remote computer name you just connected to. The commands that you type run on the remote computer as though you have typed them directly on the remote computer. This indicates that you are in an interactive remoting session:

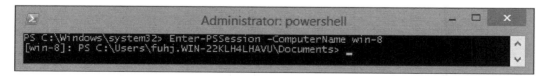

In order to verify that we really have connected to the remote computer through the interactive remoting session, we can implement the `ipconfig` command to check the current thread host information before and after we enter into the interactive remoting session, as shown in the following screenshot:

We can see that the network adapter information of is different before and after entering the interactive remoting session. When we enter the interactive remoting session, we can execute any command just like Telnet. It is not the same as using Telnet, but it provides a similar experience.

Exiting an interactive session

You can use `Exit-PSSession` to come out of an interactive session. You need to pay attention to the specified `-ComputerName` parameter as the `Enter-PSSession` cmdlet starts just a temporary PS session and not a persistent session. Any variables that you create and the command history will be destroyed if you exit this interactive session.

Using a persistent session with interactive remoting

It will be advantageous to use a persistent session so that you can enter and exit the interactive session as many times as you like. All the data, variables, and command history you created in the remote session will persist until you remove the session. You can also do it the same way you used persistent sessions with `Invoke-Command`.

```
$session= New-PSSession -ComputerName win-8
```

```
Enter-PSSession -Session $session
```

Starting interactive remoting with an existing session

It is quite possible that you have created a persistent session to use with `Invoke-Command`. You can use the same persistent session with `Enter-PSSession` to start an interactive remoting session. You can use the `Get-PSSession` cmdlet to see a list of all available/opened PS sessions and then use `Enter-PSSession` to start interactive remoting:

```
PS C:\Windows\system32> Get-PSSession | Format-List *

State                  : Opened
IdleTimeout            : 7200000
OutputBufferingMode    : Block
ComputerName           : win-8
ConfigurationName      : Microsoft.PowerShell
InstanceId             : 2c4ae306-78c4-4a40-a52b-0eeb6c6cd94c
Id                     : 3
Name                   : Session3
Availability           : Available
ApplicationPrivateData : {PSVersionTable}
Runspace               : System.Management.Automation.RemoteRunspace

State                  : Opened
IdleTimeout            : 7200000
OutputBufferingMode    : Block
ComputerName           : win-8
ConfigurationName      : Microsoft.PowerShell
InstanceId             : 613b6a17-62e6-468d-b6a1-e7198966befd
Id                     : 5
Name                   : Session5
Availability           : Available
ApplicationPrivateData : {PSVersionTable}
Runspace               : System.Management.Automation.RemoteRunspace
```

There are several ways to enter an existing PS session for interactive remoting, as shown in the preceding screenshot. You can use any that is convenient to you:

- Using the session ID:

  ```
  Enter-PSSession -Id 3
  ```

- Using the session instance ID:

  ```
  Enter-PSSession -InstanceId 2c4ae306-78c4-4a40-a52b-0eeb6c6cd94c
  ```

- Using the session name:

  ```
  Enter-PSSession -Name Session3
  ```

- Using the -Session parameter:

  ```
  $session=Get-PSSession -Id 3
  Enter-PSSession -Session $session
  ```

In these ways, you can enter an interactive session that contains all data and command history. All of the session scene will be preserved until the current PowerShell process is destroyed.

Disconnecting and reconnecting sessions

In PowerShell v3, you can disconnect and reconnect sessions by using Disconnect-PSSession and Connect-PSSession. These commands will each accept a session object, which you'd usually create with New-PSSession.

A disconnected session leaves a copy of PowerShell up and running on the remote computer. This is a good way to get it to run some long-running task, disconnect, and then reconnect later to check up on it. You can even disconnect a session on one computer, move to another computer, and reconnect to that session.

The following example shows a session being created from a client to a server. The session is then given a task to perform as a background job, and then the session is disconnected. It's important to note that the commands and the background job are on the server, not the client:

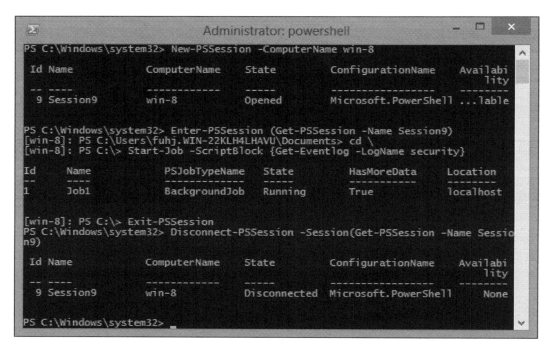

Then, we move to a different machine. We're logged on and running PowerShell as the same user that we were on the previous client computer. We retrieve the session from the remote computer and then reconnect it. We then enter the newly reconnected session, display that background job, and receive some results from it. Finally, we exit the remote session and shut it down via `Remove-PSSession`:

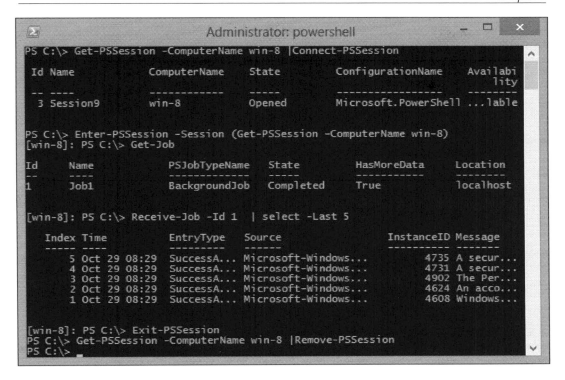

```
PS C:\> Get-PSSession -ComputerName win-8 |Connect-PSSession

 Id Name            ComputerName    State        ConfigurationName       Availabi
                                                                          lity
 -- ----            ------------    -----        -----------------       -------
  3 Session9        win-8           Opened       Microsoft.PowerShell ...lable


PS C:\> Enter-PSSession -Session (Get-PSSession -ComputerName win-8)
[win-8]: PS C:\> Get-Job

Id      Name        PSJobTypeName       State       HasMoreData     Location
--      ----        -------------       -----       -----------     --------
1       Job1        BackgroundJob       Completed   True            localhost


[win-8]: PS C:\> Receive-Job -Id 1  | select -Last 5

   Index Time        EntryType  Source                   InstanceID Message
   ----- ----        ---------  ------                   ---------- -------
       5 Oct 29 08:29 SuccessA... Microsoft-Windows...          4735 A secur...
       4 Oct 29 08:29 SuccessA... Microsoft-Windows...          4731 A secur...
       3 Oct 29 08:29 SuccessA... Microsoft-Windows...          4902 The Per...
       2 Oct 29 08:29 SuccessA... Microsoft-Windows...          4624 An acco...
       1 Oct 29 08:29 SuccessA... Microsoft-Windows...          4608 Windows...


[win-8]: PS C:\> Exit-PSSession
PS C:\> Get-PSSession -ComputerName win-8 |Remove-PSSession
PS C:\>
```

Obviously, disconnected sessions can present management concern because you're leaving a copy of PowerShell up and running on a remote machine, and you're doing so in a way that makes it difficult for someone else to even see that you've done it! That's where session options come into play.

Saving a remote session to a disk

In this section, we look at how we can save a remoting session to a disk so that we don't even have to explicitly create a PS session to execute commands on a remote computer.

Exporting a remote session to a module on a disk

The `Export-PSSession` cmdlet lets us export commands from a remote session and save the same in a PowerShell module on the local disk. This cmdlet can get cmdlets, functions, aliases, and other command types into a PowerShell module.

```
$session = New-PSSession -ComputerName win-8

Invoke-Command -Session $session -ScriptBlock {Import-Module NetTCPIP}

Export-PSSession -Session $session -OutputModule RemoteCommands
-AllowClobber -Module NetTCPIP -Force
```

In the preceding example, we create a persistent session and import a module named NetTCPIP. Then, we use the `Export-PSSession` cmdlet to export all commands, aliases, functions, and so on available in the PS session `$session` to a module on the local hard disk and name it `RemoteCommands`.

If the `Export-PSSession` cmdlet is successful, you will see output similar to what is shown in the following screenshot:

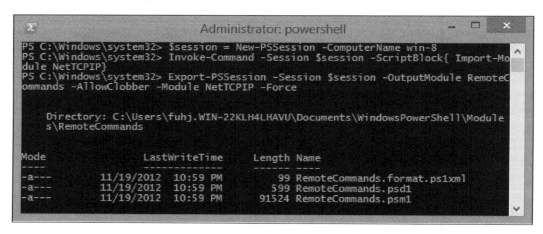

In the preceding output, it is clear that `Export-PSSession` generates `.psm1`, `.psd1`, and `format` data files for the module automatically. Right now, you can load the module to get access to the remote commands.

Importing a module saved on a disk

If you observe the output closely, the path where the module files are stored is the same as that for `$Env:PSModulePath`. So, you don't need to specify the absolute path to the module. The following operation imports all remote commands available in the module to the local session:

```
Import-Module RemoteCommands
```

Then, when we execute a remote command, it establishes the remote session, executes the command in the remote session, and returns the output. All this is done without you really using any remoting-related cmdlet. Of course, if establishing a remote session requires a password, you will be prompted for one.

Limitations of Export-PSSession

Using `Export-PSSession` has the same limitations as implicit remoting. You cannot use `Export-PSSession` to export a PowerShell provider. You cannot start a program with a user interface as it requires access to the interactive desktop. The exported module does not include the session options used to create the session. So, if you need any specific session options to be configured before running remote commands, you need to create a PS session with all the required session options before importing the on-disk module.

Using session configurations

In the earlier section, we saw that, when PowerShell remoting is enabled, the default session configuration gets registered. The `Invoke-Command`, `Enter-PSSession`, and `New-PSSession` cmdlets have a `-ConfigurationName` parameter that can be used to specify a different session configuration rather than the default one.

A session configuration is used to define who can create a PowerShell session on the local computer. When we enable PowerShell remoting using `Enable-PSSession`, we can see a final step performing `Microsoft.PowerShell` session configuration registration. These default session configurations are used when the remote users connecting to a local system do not specify a configuration name. By default, only members of the administrators group have access to these two session configurations.

Based on the preceding description, PowerShell session configurations can be used to:

- Customize the remoting experience for users
- Delegate administration by creating session configuration with varying levels of access to the system

The following cmdlets are available for managing session configurations:

- `Register-PSSessionConfiguration`
- `Unregister-PSSessionConfiguration`
- `Enable-PSSessionConfiguration`
- `Disable-PSSessionConfiguration`
- `Set-PSSessionConfiguration`
- `Get-PSSessionConfiguration`

Creating a new session configuration

The `Register-PSSessionConfiguration` cmdlet can be used to create a new session configuration. You can use a C# assembly or a PowerShell script as a startup script for this new session configuration. This startup script can be used to customize the remoting experience. For example, create a script that imports the `NetTCPIP` module using the `Import-Module` cmdlet:

```
Import-Module NetTCPIP
```

Save this script as `startupscript.ps1` (or with any name of your choice) on the local computer. Now, use the `Register-PSSessionConfiguration` cmdlet to create a new session configuration. This can be done by running the following command:

```
Register-PSSessionConfiguration -Name "NetTCPIP" -StartupScript C:\
StartupScript.ps1
```

The preceding command gives the following output:

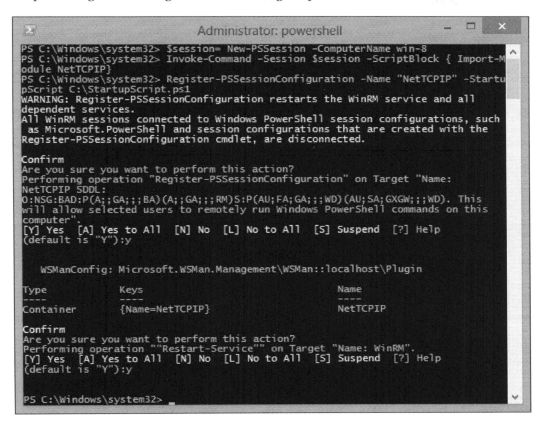

You will be prompted to confirm this action at the end to restart the WinRM service on the local computer. You must enable the script execution on the local computer to be able to use the startup script as a part of session configuration.

Listing available session configurations

The Get-PSSessionConfiguration cmdlet lists all the available session configurations on the local computer. This can be seen in the following screenshot:

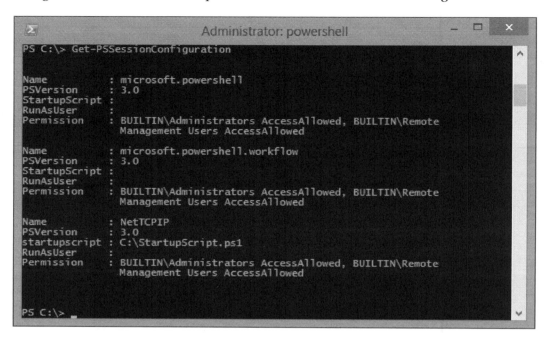

As you see in the preceding output, Get-PSSessionConfiguration lists all available session configurations on the local computer and who has permission to access each configuration. No permissions have been assigned yet to the new active directory configuration.

The `Get-PSSessionConfiguration` cmdlet cannot be used to access a list of PS session configurations from a remote computer. However, we can use the `Get-WSManInstance` cmdlet to achieve this as shown in the following command:

```
Get-WSManInstance winrm/config/plugin -Enumerate -ComputerName win-8 |
Where ` { $_.FileName -like '*pwrshplugin.dll'} | Select Name
```

This will list all the session configuration names as available on the remote computer. You can then use any one of the session configurations to connect to the remote computer using PowerShell remoting.

You must have access to the session configuration on the remote computer to be able to use it within PowerShell remoting.

Custom permissions and PS session configurations

You can use `Set-PSSessionConfiguration` to allow access to invoke the new session configuration. To do this, we can use the following command:

```
Set-PSSessionConfiguration -Name NetTCPIP -ShowSecurityDescriptorUI
```

This opens up the dialog to add permissions to invoke this session configuration. As you can see in the following screenshot, the administrators group has no invoke permission on this session configuration:

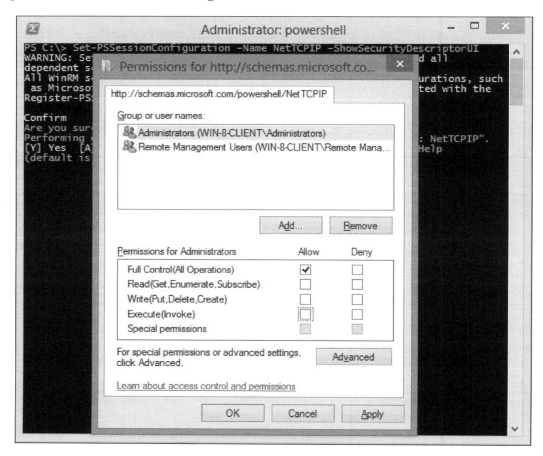

Check the **Allow** checkbox for the **Execute (Invoke)** permission and then click on **OK**. You will be prompted to restart the WinRM service. Now, an administrator or a member of the administrators group will be able to use this session configuration. Similarly, you can add a non-administrator user to the list of users/groups and then assign appropriate permissions. This way, you can have non-administrator users remote into the local computer using PowerShell remoting.

Invoking a custom session configuration

You can use the `New-PSSession`, `Enter-PSSession`, and `Invoke-Command` cmdlets specifying the `-ConfigurationName` parameter to load a session configuration other than the default configuration. The following code snippet shows three different ways to invoke a remote session using a custom session configuration name:

```
$s = New-PSSession -ComputerName win-8 -ConfigurationName NetTCPIP

Enter-PSSession -ComputerName win-8 -ConfigurationName NetTCPIP

Invoke-Command -ComputerName win-8 -ConfigurationName NetTCPIP
-ScriptBlock {Get-Process}
```

We used `Invoke-Command` to load the active directory module within a persistent session and then used that persistent session to import `NetTCPIP` cmdlets into the local session. However, by using a session configuration that imports the Active Directory module as a startup script, we will have all the `NetTCPIP` cmdlets available as soon as we connect to the remote session.

Disabling a session configuration

You can use the `Disable-PSSessionConfiguration` cmdlet to disable an existing session configuration and prevent users from connecting to the local computer by using this session configuration. You can use the `-Name` parameter to specify what session configuration you want to disable. If you do not specify a configuration name, the default `Microsoft.PowerShell` session configuration will be disabled.

The `Disable-PSSessionConfiguration` cmdlet adds a `deny all` setting to the security descriptor of one or more registered session configurations. As a result, you can unregister, view, and change the configurations, but you cannot use them all in one session.

The `Disable-PSRemoting` cmdlet will disable all PS session configurations available on the local computer.

The `Enable-PSSessionConfiguration` cmdlet can be used to enable a disabled configuration. You can use the `-Name` parameter to specify what session configuration you need to enable.

Deleting a session configuration

You can use the `Unregister-PSSessionConfiguration` cmdlet to delete a previously defined session configuration. It is quite possible to delete the default session configuration—`Microsoft.PowerShell`—using this cmdlet. However, this default session configuration gets recreated if you re-run the `Enable-PSRemoting` cmdlet.

Summary

In Windows PowerShell 3.0, you can run remote commands on a single computer or on multiple computers by using a temporary or persistent connection. You can also start an interactive session with a single remote computer. When you work remotely, you type commands in Windows PowerShell on a local computer, but the commands run on a remote computer. The experience of working remotely should be as much like working directly at the remote computer as possible.

In this chapter, we discussed how to enable/disable remoting, execute remote command, and save remote sessions to a disk. We also covered how to use an interactive remoting session and session configuration.

When we submit a remote command, the command will be transmitted to the Windows PowerShell engine of the remote computer through the network and executed on the remote computer. The command results are sent back to the local computer and appear in the Windows PowerShell session on the local computer.

In the next chapter, we will discuss extending PowerShell by writing modules. A module is a set of related Windows PowerShell functionalities that can be dynamic or that can persist on a disk. Modules that persist on disk are referenced, loaded, and persisted as script modules, binary modules, or manifest modules respectively.

4

Extending Windows PowerShell

One of the great features of PowerShell is its extensibility. You are not limited to the commands that Microsoft ships. You can load additional commands and functionalities via a module. Many other Microsoft product teams and third-party vendors deliver PowerShell solutions for their products via modules.

A module is a set of related Windows PowerShell functionalities that can either be dynamic or that can persist on a disk. Modules that persist on a disk are referenced, loaded, and persisted as script modules, binary modules, or manifest modules. Unlike snap-ins, the members of these modules can include cmdlets, providers, functions, variables, aliases, and much more. A module is really nothing more than a PowerShell script with a `.psm1` file extension, although it can include binary code, typically delivered in a DLL file.

In this chapter we will cover:

- Windows PowerShell modules
- PowerShell module types
- The `PSModulePath` environment variable
- Importing, removing, and reloading modules
- Writing a Windows PowerShell module
- Working with multiple versions of PowerShell modules
- Checking PowerShell module dependencies

You can run the `Get-Module` command to see what is loaded in your current session.

Introduction to Windows PowerShell modules

In the previous versions of Windows PowerShell, only developers could create packages using snap-ins that contained .NET Framework classes for cmdlets and providers. Now by using Windows PowerShell modules, you do not have to use a compiled language to create a package for your Windows PowerShell solutions. Modules allow cmdlet developers, script developers, and administrators to package and distribute their solutions.

Windows PowerShell modules allow you to partition, organize, and abstract your Windows PowerShell code into self-contained, reusable units. With these reusable units, administrators, script developers, and cmdlet developers can easily share their modules directly with others. Script developers can also repackage third-party modules to create custom script-based applications. Modules, similar to those in other scripting languages such as Perl and Python, enable production-ready scripting solutions that use reusable, redistributable components, with the added benefit of enabling you to repackage and abstract multiple components to create custom solutions.

PowerShell module types

PowerShell accepts several module types that can be used to package and deploy, just like script modules, binary modules, manifest modules, and dynamic modules.

Script modules

A **script module** is a file (`.psm1`) that contains valid PowerShell code. Script developers and administrators can use this type of module to create modules whose members include functions, variables, and more.

Binary modules

A **binary module** is a .NET Framework assembly (`.dll`) that contains compiled code. Cmdlet developers can use this type of module to create modules that contain cmdlets, providers, and more. (Existing snap-ins can also be used as binary modules.)

Manifest modules

A **manifest module** is a module that includes a manifest (which is described later in this section) to describe its components, but that does not specify a root module in the manifest. A module manifest does not specify a root module when the ModuleToProcess key of the manifest is blank. In most cases, a manifest module also includes one or more nested modules using script modules or binary modules. A manifest module that does not include any nested modules can be used when you want a convenient way to load assemblies, types, or formats.

Dynamic modules

A **dynamic module** is a module that does not persist to disk. This type of module enables a script to create a module on demand that does not need to be loaded or saved to persistent storage. By default, dynamic modules created with the New-Module cmdlet are intended to be short-lived and therefore are not visible using the Get-Module cmdlet.

The PSModulePath environment variable

The PSModulePath environment variable stores the paths to the locations of modules that are installed on the disk. Windows PowerShell uses this variable to locate modules when the user does not specify the full path to a module. The paths in this variable are searched in the order in which they appear.

When Windows PowerShell starts, PSModulePath is created as a system environment variable with the default value $home\Documents\WindowsPowerShell\Modules; $pshome\Modules.

Viewing the PSModulePath variable

If you want to view the PSModulePath variable, you can type the following command:

```
$Env:PSModulePath
```

We can see that PSModulePath is an item of the $Env driver. Of course, we can add other locations to it for specifying custom module library paths. In this way, we can use the Import-Module cmdlet for importing the module to any current path.

Adding locations to the PSModulePath variable

To add paths to the PSModulePath variable, we can use the methods discussed in this section.

If we want to add a temporary value that is available only for the current session, we need to execute the following command at the command line:

```
$Env:PSModulePath=$Env:PSModulePath + ";C:\MyModules"
```

If we want to add a persistent value that is available whenever a session is opened, we need to add the following command to the PowerShell profile:

```
$Env:PSModulePath=$Env:PSModulePath + ";C:\MyModules"
```

After we add the content to the profile, any PowerShell command line will load the variable automatically.

The PSModulePath variable assigns a parameter for the PowerShell engine to search through the multiple paths specified in this variable, to find a directory named by the module name and load the module program when using the Import-Module cmdlet that loads modules into the current session.

Importing PowerShell modules

We can use the Import-Module cmdlet to import modules. When this command is executed, PowerShell searches for the specified module within the directories specified in the PSModulePath variable. When the specified directory named as the module name is found, PowerShell searches for files in the following order:

- Manifest module files (.psd1)
- Script module files (.psm1)
- Binary module files (.dll)

We can list the available modules using the Get-Module cmdlet with the -ListAvailable switch. To import a module, we can use the Import-Module cmdlet. Then we can use the Get-Command cmdlet to get the command list of this module with the -Module switch parameter. Finally, we can execute the cmdlet in the module. The effect of the command is shown in the following screenshot:

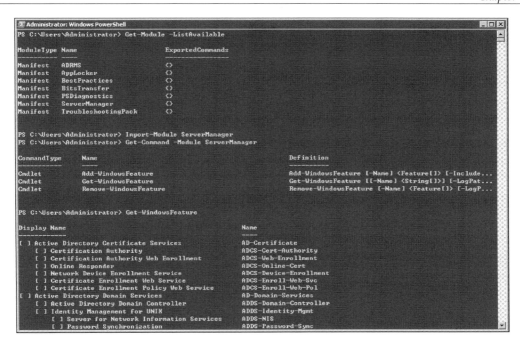

In fact, observant readers may notice that the `Get-WindowsFeature` cmdlet lists all the server roles on this server, which is similar to the **Add Roles Wizard** in Server Manager, as shown in the following screenshot:

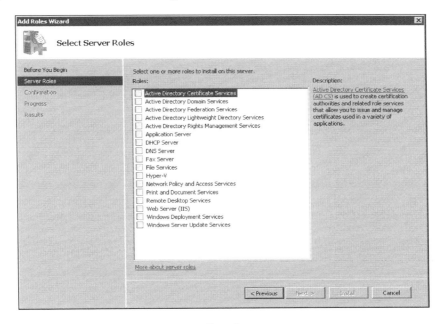

In PowerShell 3.0, modules are imported automatically when any cmdlet or function in the module is used in a command. This feature works on any module in a directory that is included with the value of the PSModulePath variable. The following actions will trigger the automatic import of a module:

- **Using any cmdlet in a module**: For example, executing the Get-Acl cmdlet imports the Microsoft.PowerShell.Security module that contains the Get-Acl cmdlet.

- **Using the Get-Command cmdlet to get the command**: For example, executing Get-Command Get-VpnConnection imports the VpnClient module that contains the Get-VpnConnection cmdlet. A Get-Command command that includes wildcard characters is considered to be a discovery and does not trigger the import of any module.

- **Using the Get-Help cmdlet to get help**: For example, executing the Get-Help Set-PSBreakpoint cmdlet imports the Microsoft.PowerShell. Utility module that contains the Set-PSBreakpoint cmdlet.

By default, the Import-Module cmdlet does not return any object to the pipeline. Sometimes, we may need the cmdlet to return an object that is used for judging whether execution is normal or not. The cmdlet supports a PassThru parameter that can be used to return a PSModuleInfo object for each module that is imported.

When a module is imported using the Import-Module cmdlet, all the module members are imported into the current session by default. If we want to restrict the members that are imported, we use the -function, -cmdlet, -variable, and -alias parameters of the Import-Module cmdlet.

Removing PowerShell modules

The Remove-Module cmdlet removes modules from the current session. If a module contains assemblies (.DLL), the Remove-Module cmdlet will delete the program realization set of all the members but won't uninstall the programs.

```
Remove-Module -Name BitsTransfer
```

We can remove the BitsTransfer module by executing the preceding command.

Reloading PowerShell modules

Sometimes, for the purpose of testing we need to reload the PowerShell modules. For instance, say we write a script module. Now in order to debug the function, we need to reload the modules when the scripts are modified. In this section, we will define a Reload-Module function that is used to reload the specified module. Here is the code for it:

```
Function Reload-Module($ModuleName)
{
if((get-module -list | where{$_.name -eq "$ModuleName"} | measure-
object).count -gt 0)
{
  if((get-module -all | where{$_.Name -eq "$ModuleName"} | measure-
object).count -gt 0)
  {
    Remove-Module $ModuleName
    Write-Host "Module $ModuleName Unloading"
  }
  Import-Module $ModuleName
  Write-Host "Module $ModuleName Loaded"
}
Else
{
  Write-Host "Module $ModuleName Doesn't Exist"
}
}
```

The function checks to make sure the module exists before running any commands, and if it exists, it also checks to make sure it's loaded, before attempting to unload it.

Writing a PowerShell module

In the earlier versions of PowerShell, snap-ins were popular with system administrators who used cmdlets provided by third-party vendors. However, it is easier to achieve the objective of sharing functions and scripts as part of a module. In addition to this, while a snap-in can only contain cmdlets and providers, a module can also contain other common PowerShell items, such as functions, variables, aliases, and PowerShell drives.

Each module should be stored in a subfolder of one of these paths and typically the name of the subfolder is the name of that module; within that folder you should then store the files that make up the module. At the least, we need a *.psm1 file. In this file, a number of functions or variables that make up the module could be placed. In addition to this, it is possible to place PowerShell scripts in *.ps1 files in the module's folder and reference them in the *.psm1 file. As a final touch, a module manifest file can be created, which will give a more professional and rounded feel to your module, but we will discuss manifests later.

Let's look at the process of creating an example module.

Creating script modules

Script modules can contain any valid PowerShell code. We can place a couple of functions in a *.psm1 file to make a module. There is nothing special about a *.psm1 file; it is a normal *.ps1 script file. We can rename any *.ps1 script file that contains our functions to *.psm1 to create a script module.

Firstly, let's create two functions for our module that we will use for sending and receiving TCP messages. The first function will monitor a local TCP port that waits for an external program to connect, accept the messages sent by it, and display the message content in the console. We name it Receive-TCPMessage.ps1. Its code is as follows:

```
Function Receive-TCPMessage
{
  param ( [ValidateNotNullOrEmpty()]
  [int] $Port )
  try
  {
    $EndPoint = New-Object System.Net.IPEndPoint([System.Net.
IPAddress]::Loopback,$Port)
    $Socket = New-Object System.Net.Sockets.TCPListener($EndPoint)
    $Socket.Start()
    $Socket = $Socket.AcceptTCPClient()
    $EncodedText = New-Object System.Text.ASCIIEncoding
    $Stream = $Socket.GetStream()
    $Buffer = New-Object System.Byte[] $Socket.ReceiveBufferSize
    while( $Bytes = $Stream.Read($Buffer,0,$Buffer.Length) )
    {
        $Stream.Write($Buffer,0,$Bytes)
        Write-Output $EncodedText.GetString($Buffer,0,$Bytes)
    }
```

```
      $Socket.Close()
      $Socket.Stop()
   }
   catch{}
}
```

We can see that `Receive-TCPMessage` is an ordinary function with a parameter `$port`. In the code, we use the `New-Object` cmdlet to create two .NET objects called `System.Net.IPEndPoint` and `System.Net.Sockets.TCPListener`. The `System.Net.IPEndPoint` object is used to resolve the loopback address for an IP address. The `System.Net.Sockets.TCPListener` object is used when waiting for a connection and for receiving messages.

The second function is `Send-TCPMessage`; it is saved as `Send-TCPMessage.ps1`. We will use it to connect to a TCP port of the destination host. Its code looks as follows:

```
Function Send-TCPMessage
{
  param ( [ValidateNotNullOrEmpty()]
  [string] $EndPoint,
  [int] $Port,
  [string] $Message )
  $IP = [System.Net.Dns]::GetHostAddresses($EndPoint)
  $Address = [System.Net.IPAddress]::Parse($IP)
  $Socket = New-Object System.Net.Sockets.TCPClient($Address,$Port)
  $Stream = $Socket.GetStream()
  $Writer = New-Object System.IO.StreamWriter($Stream)
  $Writer.AutoFlush = $true
  $Writer.NewLine = $true
  $Writer.Write($Message)
  $Socket.Close()
}
```

We can notice that the preceding code looks like the first function that uses the `System.Net.Sockets.TCPClient` object to establish a connection. The function needs three parameters, namely `$EndPoint`, `$Port`, and `$Message`. The `EndPoint` parameter is used with the `[System.Net.Dns]::GetHostAddresses` method to resolve the domain of an IP address.

Execute these functions. The following screenshot shows how to send and receive TCP messages:

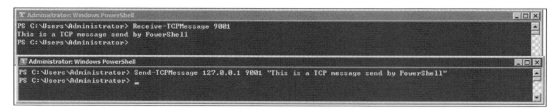

We now save these functions in the `PSNet.psml` file and save them at `C:\Users\Administrator\Documents\WindowsPowerShell\Modules\PSNet\TCPOp`.

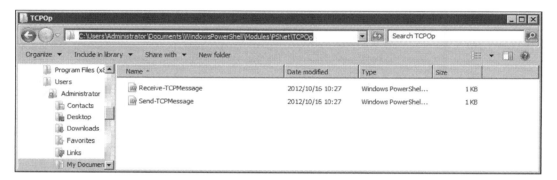

In order to realize code package structure similar to the C# code namespace, we create the subdirectory `PSNet\TCPOp` in the directory specified by the `PSModulePath` variable. Of course, we can create a UDP operation in `PSNet\UDPOp` and add dot-sourcing statements for the script file in the `PSNet.psml` file.

Now, we will talk about how to create the script module file `PSNet.psml`, which is as follows:

```
. $home/Documents/WindowsPowerShell/Module/PSNet/TCPOp/Receive-TCPMessage.ps1
. $home/Documents/WindowsPowerShell/Module/PSNet/TCPOp/Send-TCPMessage.ps1
Write-Host "PSNet Module Added" -BackgroundColor green -ForegroundColor blue
Export-ModuleMember -Function *  # Used for deriving function to members of the module
```

We can see that the first and second statements are used for dot sourcing two script files. The third statement is used for notifying the users that the PSNet module has been added to the current session. The last statement is used for deriving a function for the members of the module.

So far, we have finished the task of writing a script module. If we want to import the module once the PowerShell session has already started, we can add the Import-Module cmdlet into our PowerShell profile.

```
Import-Module PSNet -PassThru
```

Once the PowerShell session has already started, we will get the following results:

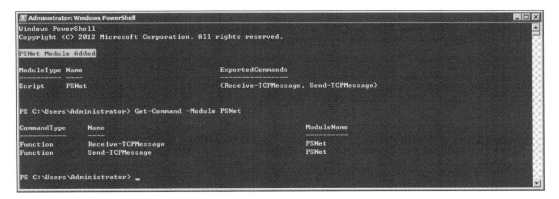

We can see that two functions are members of the module that is available to us in this PowerShell session using the Get-Command cmdlet.

```
Get-Command -Module PSNet
```

We can check whether or not our module PSNet is available using the Get-Module cmdlet with the -ListAvailable switch.

```
Get-Module -ListAvailable
```

We may get the result shown in the following screenshot:

We can see that the PSNet module has a ModuleType of script while other built-in and third-party modules have a ModuleType of manifest or script.

Binary modules

A binary module can be any assembly (.dll) that contains a cmdlet class. By default, all the cmdlets in the assembly are imported when the binary module is imported, unless the CmdletToExport keyword is specified in the manifest file of the binary module to restrict the cmdlet range when using Import-Module to import the module.

In fact, you can load most existing snap-ins as modules instead, which means you don't have to be an administrator to load a new snap-in. There is no need to register them by running InstallUtil.exe. You can simply place them in a folder and tell PowerShell where to find them. In addition to this, any formatting or type files that are referenced by the snap-in cannot be imported as part of a binary module. To import formatting and type files, you must create a module manifest.

The development method of a binary module is completely similar to the method used for developing snap-ins in *Chapter 2, Developing Snap-ins for PowerShell*. Readers can review this chapter for the method to develop snap-ins.

Manifest modules

A manifest module is a Windows PowerShell datafile (.psd1) that describes the contents of a module and determines how a module is processed. A manifest file is a text file that contains a hash table of keys and values. To use the manifest file in a module, place the module manifest file in the root of the module directory.

It is possible to smarten up your modules and give them a more professional look by using module manifests. For instance, you may wish to include some author and versioning information as part of the module, or you may wish to specify minimum versions of PowerShell and/or the .NET Framework that are needed for the components of your module. You should create a module manifest. Microsoft has made creating a basic module manifest easy by giving us the New-ModuleManifest cmdlet. While it is possible to create a module manifest manually (by simply creating a *.psd1 file containing your requirements and placing it in the module folder), using the cmdlet makes it easy to create a basic one. Let's continue with the PSNet module and create a basic module manifest using New-ModuleManifest.

We can specify all of the parameters we wish to include in the manifest and supply them on the command line.

```
New-ModuleManifest -Author "fuhj" `
-CompanyName "Packt Publishing" `
-CopyRight "(c) 2009 fuhj" `
-Description "Sending and receivingTCP message" `
-FileList "PSNet.psm1" `
-FormatsToProcess @() `
-ModuletoProcess "PSNet.psm1" `
-NestedModules @() `
-Path "C:\Users\Administrator\Documents\WindowsPowerShell\Modules\
PSNet\PSNet.psd1" `
-RequiredAssemblies @() `
-TypesToProcess @()
```

You can use Get-Help New-ModuleManifest to examine in more detail other options that you may wish to include in your module manifest. When the command is executed, we get a module manifest file named PSNet.psd1.

```
@{
# Script module or binary module file associated with this manifest.
RootModule = 'PSNet.psm1'
# Version number of this module.
ModuleVersion = '1.0'
# ID used to uniquely identify this module
GUID = '08766c71-a825-4d38-b2a2-477445be6a17'
# Author of this module
```

```
Author = 'fuhj'
# Company or vendor of this module
CompanyName = 'Pocket Publishing'
# Copyright statement for this module
Copyright = '(c) 2009 fuhj'
# Description of the functionality provided by this module
Description = 'Sending and receivingTCP message'
# Functions to export from this module
FunctionsToExport = '*'
# Cmdlets to export from this module
CmdletsToExport = '*'
# Variables to export from this module
VariablesToExport = '*'
# Aliases to export from this module
AliasesToExport = '*'
# List of all files packaged with this module
FileList = 'PSNet.psm1'
}
```

Now that we have created a basic module manifest, we can take that as a template for future modules and customize it as per our needs.

Dynamic modules

Using `Add-Type` and `Import-Module`, you can dynamically compile and load an assembly without any intermediate assembly files to clean up. For instance, to run a cmdlet on a remote machine, you could send over the cmdlet source code and compile, import, and run it all on the fly.

Let's say you have your cmdlet in C# code with the variable $source:

```
PS> $source = @"
public class BasicTest
{
    public static int Add(int a, int b)
    {
        return (a + b);
    }
    public int Multiply(int a, int b)
    {
        return (a * b);
    }
}
```

```
"@
PS> Invoke-Command {(Add-Type -TypeDefinition $args[0] -PassThru).
assembly | Import-Module} -ArgumentList $source
PS> Invoke-Command {(new-object BasicTest).Multiply(5, 2)}
```

All the code will be executed as follows:

The PowerShell session compiles the code with Add-Type and passes the resulting assembly object to Import-Module.

In the preceding example, we can consider a situation where we need to execute a cmdlet in a remote host. But we don't want to upload the compiled assembly file to the remote host, delete files, and clean up environment after the operation is completed. We can read cmdlet source code from local files and then push the code to remote host with a remote session. The source code will be compiled, imported as a module, and run on the remote host. The cmdlet Execute-MyCmdlet is invoked in the remote session and then removed, without the need to remove any intermediate files on the remote system.

```
PS> [string]$source = Get-Content myCmdletcode.cs
PS> $s = New-PSSession remoteHost
PS> Invoke-Command $s {(Add-Type -TypeDefinition $args[0] -PassThru).
assembly | Import-Module} -ArgumentList $source
PS> Invoke-Command $s {Execute-MyCmdlet}
PS> Remove-PSSession $s
```

It's very useful when we need to invoke a cmdlet in an assembly on the remote system without wanting to remove any intermediate files.

Storing modules on a disk

After we have written script, binary, and manifest modules, there are several places where we can store them. They can be stored in the system folder where PowerShell is installed, or in a user's folder. In either case, the module is placed into a module directory, and the entire module is placed in the subdirectories that are named by module name, with the following exceptions:

- Dynamic modules created using the `New-Modules` cmdlet can be named using the `-Name` parameter of the cmdlet
- Modules imported from the assembly object using the `Import-Module` `-Assembly` command are named using the following syntax:

  `"dynamic_code_module_" + assembly.GetName().`

When storing files in the system folder, you have to create the following path:

`C:\Windows\system32\WindowsPowerShell\v1.0\Modules\`

It needs to be emphasized that to modify the directory, administrator privileges are required. When we store files in the user's folder, we have to create the following path:

`C:\Users\Administrator\Documents\WindowsPowerShell\Modules`

Working with multiple versions of modules

Sometimes, we need to develop several versions of modules for different PowerShell versions or Windows versions. We have two or more versions of the module that we need to be able to load in order to support users and do development.

The `PSModulePath` variable contains a semicolon-delimited list of folder paths that PowerShell searches for modules. Some people may think of a PowerShell module as basically a `.dll` (binary module), `.psm1` (script module), or `.psd1` (manifest module) file, but it's never just one file; it's a group of folders and files. In order for PowerShell to find the PSNet module when you type `Import-Module PSNet`, you have to set up a folder in `PSModulePath` named `PSNet` and also a file (`.dll`, `.psm1`, or `.psd1`) named `PSNet`.

As we all know, PowerShell has a `-version` parameter that is used to specify the PowerShell version. We can execute this in the console as follows:

```
powershell.exe -version 3.0
```

We may get a different result when we tell the console to start PowerShell Version 2.0 or Version 3.0, as shown in the following screenshot:

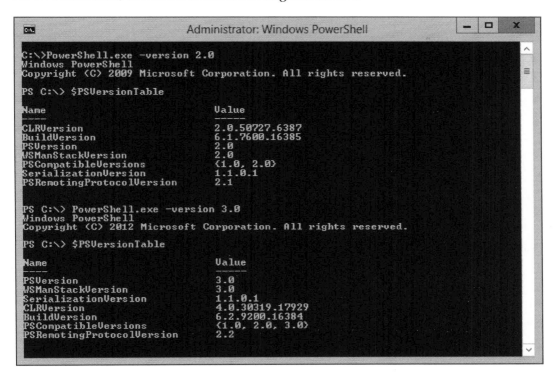

The `Import-Module` cmdlet has a version parameter that is an alias of `MinimumVersion`. We cannot use the version parameter of the `Import-Module` cmdlet to load a specified version of the module. For instance:

```
PS C:\> Import-Module -Name PSWorkflow -MinimumVersion 3.0.0.0
```

This command imports the `PSWorkflow` module. It uses the `MinimumVersion` (alias=`Version`) parameter of `Import-Module` to import only version 3.0.0.0 or greater of the module. You can use the `RequiredVersion` parameter to import a particular version of a module, or use the `Module` and `Version` parameters of the `#requires` keyword to require a particular version of a module in a script.

Although we cannot use the `-version` parameter to specify the module's version, we can rename the module directory and module file to distinguish between different versions of the module. Right now, we are going to copy the PSNet module to PSNet1.3 for our development version, then rename the manifest module file to PSNet1.3.psd1 and rename the script module file to PSNet1.3.psm1. Finally, we must modify the options of the manifest module file in which all the options of the script module file are `ModuleVersion`, `RootModule`, and `FileList`.

We can load the development version to the current session as follows:

```
Import-Module PSNet1.3
```

And then, we can find the development version of PSNet1.3 in the list of available modules:

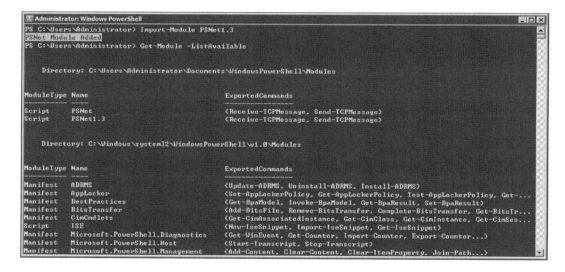

Checking PowerShell module dependencies

One problem with using modules is that sometimes you have a dependency on external code. This means that a script that uses the module must have the module installed, or the script will fail. If you can control the environment, taking an external dependency is not a bad thing. But most times, we write a module used for an external module on the user's computer, and we don't know whether or not this module has been installed on the user's computer; it must be a disaster.

At this time, it is very important that we write some proper error handling code for our module. For example, we need to write some code using **background intelligent transfer service (BITS)** for implementing a specific feature. But we don't know whether the user's computer has the `BitsTransfer` modules. For instance, the user's computer may have installed Windows XP OS, but the `BitsTransfer` modules are a feature of Windows 7 and the later versions of OS. We can use the following code for error handling:

```
if (Get-MyModule -name "BitsTransfer") { call your bits code here }
else { "Bits module is not installed on this system." ; exit}
```

In this case, we use the `Get-MyModule` function to check whether a module has been installed on the user's computer or not. Now, we realize the `Get-MyModule` function. First of all, this function accepts a single string for storing the name of the module that we want to check. Then, the function needs to check whether the specified module is currently loaded or not. If it is not loaded, the `Get-Module` cmdlet is used to see if the module exists on the system. If the module exists but is not loaded, the function loads it and returns `$true`. If the module is loaded, it directly returns `$true`. If the module does not exist, it directly returns `$false`. This section of the script is as follows:

```
Function Get-MyModule
{
Param([string]$name)
if(-not(Get-Module -name $name))
{
if(Get-Module -ListAvailable |
Where-Object { $_.name -eq $name })
{
Import-Module -Name $name
$true
} #end if module available then import
else { $false } #module not available
} # end if not module
else { $true } #module already loaded
} #end function get-MyModule
```

With this function, we can check module dependencies and write more robust code. When we write script code, we also need to know how to deal with a script error if it occurs, in order to avoid it bringing unnecessary trouble to the user.

Signing PowerShell modules

PowerShell supports a concept called **execution policies** in order to help deliver a more secure command-line administration experience. Execution policies define the restrictions under which PowerShell loads files for execution and configuration. The four execution policies are `Restricted`, `AllSigned`, `RemoteSigned`, and `Unrestricted`.

Execution policies

PowerShell is configured to run in its most secure mode by default. This mode is the `Restricted` execution policy, in which PowerShell operates as an interactive shell only. The modes are as follows:

- `Restricted`:
  - Default execution policy
  - Does not run scripts
  - Interactive only

- `AllSigned`:
  - Runs scripts
  - All scripts and configuration files must be signed by a publisher that you trust
  - Opens you to the risk of running signed (but malicious) scripts after confirming that you trust the publisher

- `RemoteSigned`:
  - Runs scripts
  - All scripts and configuration files are downloaded from communication applications, such as Microsoft Outlook, Internet Explorer, Outlook Express, and Windows Messenger; they must be signed by a publisher that you trust
  - Opens you to the risk of running malicious scripts that are not downloaded from these applications, without prompting

- Unrestricted:
  - Runs scripts
  - All scripts and configuration files are downloaded from communication applications, such as Microsoft Outlook, Internet Explorer, Outlook Express, and Windows Messenger; it runs them after confirming that you have understood that the file has originated from the Internet
  - No digital signature is required
  - Opens you to the risk of running unsigned, malicious scripts downloaded from these applications

You can use the `Get-ExecutionPolicy` cmdlet to check the execution policies as follows:

Changing the execution policy

Run the following script from a PowerShell prompt (`AllSigned` is an example):

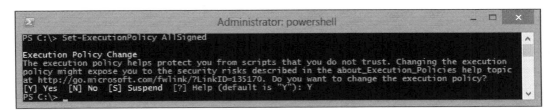

This command requires administrator privileges. Changes to the execution policy are recognized immediately.

If you're executing PowerShell scripts for the first time, PowerShell may just display an error message as you try to run a script:

The default execution policy of PowerShell is Restricted. In this mode, PowerShell operates as an interactive shell only. It does not run scripts, and it loads only configuration files signed by a publisher that you trust. The AllSigned execution policy is best for production since it forces the requirement for digital signatures on all scripts and configuration files.

Script signing background

Adding a digital signature to a script requires that it be signed with a code-signing certificate. Two types are suitable:

- Those created by a certificate authority for a fee (such as VeriSign and Thawte)
- Those created by a user (called a self-signed certificate)

If your scripts are specific to your internal network use, you may be able to self-sign. You can also buy a code-signing certificate from another certificate authority if you like.

For a self-signed certificate, a designated computer is the authority that creates the certificate. The benefits of self-signing include its zero cost as well as creation speed and convenience. The drawback is that the certificate must be installed on every computer that will be running the scripts, since other computers will not trust the computer used to create the certificate. Of course, you can deploy it through a GOP if your computers are in a domain environment.

To create a self-signed certificate, the makecert.exe program is required. This is available as part of the Microsoft .NET Framework SDK or Microsoft Windows Platform SDK. The latest is the .NET Framework 2.0 SDK; after installing, makecert.exe is found in the C:\Program Files\Microsoft Visual Studio 8\SDK\v2.0\Bin\ directory.

You can download it from `http://www.microsoft.com/downloads/details.aspx?familyid=fe6f2099-b7b4-4f47-a244-c96d69c35dec&displaylang=en`.

Setting up a self-signed certificate

You can create a local certificate authority for your computer by running the following command:

You will be prompted for the private key:

Next, you'll be prompted to verify the private key you entered in the preceding screen:

And then, the self-signed certificate will be added into the current user's Certificate Store. Windows will notify users that if you install this root certificate, Windows will automatically trust any certificate issued by this CA. Installing a certificate with an unconfirmed thumbprint is a security risk.

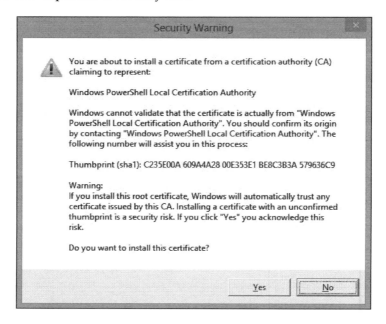

We can run `certmgr.msc` to check the trusted root certification authorities:

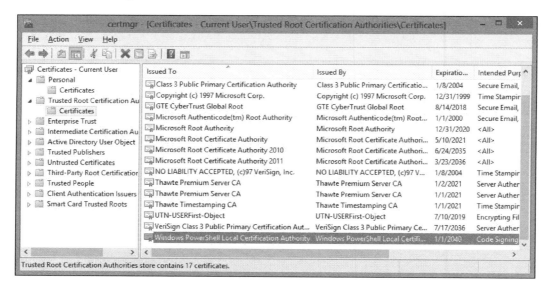

After creating a trusted root certification authority, we will generate a personal certificate from the preceding certification authority:

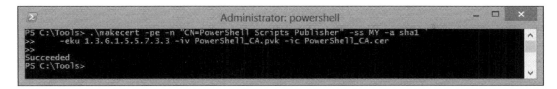

You will be prompted for the private key:

There will now be a certificate present in the personal store:

After performing the preceding steps, verify from PowerShell that the certificate was generated correctly:

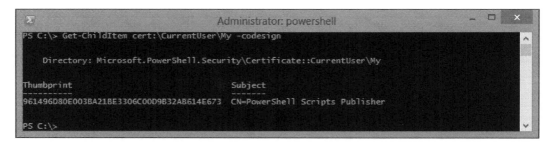

Signing a module

In order to show how to sign a module, we will create a simple module called MyModule in the PowerShell module location C:\Windows\System32\ WindowsPowerShell\v1.0\Modules\MyModule.

We add the following content to the MyModule.psm1 file in the preceding location:

```
MyModule.psm1  X
    1    . C:/Windows/System32/WindowsPowerShell/v1.0/Modules/MyModule/Say-Hello.ps1
    2    Export-ModuleMember  -Function *
```

We can see that the module file is used for dot-sourcing a script file and exporting the module function. And, the content of the script file Say-Hello.ps1 will be as shown in the following screenshot:

```
Say-Hello.ps1  X
    1  ⊟function Say-Hello{
    2  │ Write-Host 'Hello World!'
    3  └}
```

To test the effectiveness of digitally signing a PowerShell module, use the script from the following screenshot:

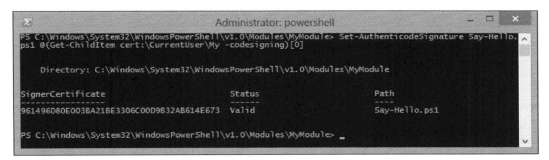

```
PS C:\Windows\system32> Set-ExecutionPolicy AllSigned

Execution Policy Change
The execution policy helps protect you from scripts that you do not trust. Changing the execution
policy might expose you to the security risks described in the about_Execution_Policies help topic
at http://go.microsoft.com/fwlink/?LinkID=135170. Do you want to change the execution policy?
[Y] Yes   [N] No   [S] Suspend  [?] Help (default is "Y"): Y
PS C:\Windows\system32> Import-Module MyModule
  . : File C:\Windows\System32\WindowsPowerShell\v1.0\Modules\MyModule\Say-Hello.ps1 cannot be
loaded. The file C:\Windows\System32\WindowsPowerShell\v1.0\Modules\MyModule\Say-Hello.ps1 is not
digitally signed. The script will not execute on the system. For more information, see
about_Execution_Policies at http://go.microsoft.com/fwlink/?LinkID=135170.
At C:\Windows\system32\WindowsPowerShell\v1.0\Modules\MyModule\MyModule.psm1:1 char:3
+ . C:/Windows/System32/WindowsPowerShell/v1.0/Modules/MyModule/Say-Hello.ps1
+   ~~~~~~~~~~~~~~~~~~~~~~~~~~~~~~~~~~~~~~~~~~~~~~~~~~~~~~~~~~~~~~~~~~~~~~
    + CategoryInfo          : SecurityError: (:) [], PSSecurityException
    + FullyQualifiedErrorId : UnauthorizedAccess
PS C:\Windows\system32>
```

Now sign the script:

```
PS C:\Windows\System32\WindowsPowerShell\v1.0\Modules\MyModule> Set-AuthenticodeSignature Say-Hello.
ps1 @(Get-ChildItem cert:\CurrentUser\My -codesigning)[0]


    Directory: C:\Windows\System32\WindowsPowerShell\v1.0\Modules\MyModule


SignerCertificate                          Status     Path
-----------------                          ------     ----
961496D80E003BA21BE3306C00D9B32AB614E673   Valid      Say-Hello.ps1


PS C:\Windows\System32\WindowsPowerShell\v1.0\Modules\MyModule> _
```

PowerShell appends your digital signature to the end of that file. This signature
verifies that the file came from you and also ensures that nobody can tamper with
the content in the file without detection. After the script is signed, it looks as follows:

```
Say-Hello.ps1  ×

 1  function Say-Hello{
 2    Write-Host 'Hello World!'
 3  }
 4  # SIG # Begin signature block
 5  # MIIEbwYJKoZIhvcNAQcCoIIEYDCCBFwCAQExCzAJBgUrDgMCGgUAMGkGCisGAQQB
 6  # gjcCAQSgWzBZMDQGCisGAQQBgjcCAR4wJgIDAQAABBAfzDtgWUsITrckOsYpfvN
 7  # AgEAAgEAAgEAAgEAAgEAMCEwCQYFKw4DAhoFAAQUwZ2Gxia1deNWAk3Q1Wm42m+z
 8  # 9lCgggJqMIICZjCCAdOgAwIBAgIQZ9xUemK7Pq9PBH6N9yirLzAJBgUrDgMCHQUA
 9  # MDsxOTA3BgNVBAMTMFdpbmRvd3MgUG93ZXJTaGVsbCBMb2NhbCBDZXJ0aWZpY2F
10  # aW9uIEF1dGhvcml0eTAeFw0xMzAyMjUxMzAyMDVaFw0zOTEyMzEyMzU5NTlaMCcx
11  # JTAjBgNVBAMTHFBvd2VyU2hlbGwgU2NyaXB0cyBQdWJsaXNoZXIwgZ8wDQYJKoZ
12  # hvcNAQEBBQADgY0AMIGJAoGBAL3tUPe4+cKWeZHTaeWc/hpru6xXZuVh5qtU4d3S
13  # lLaMhEOFsWAtOgYuLy/iivQ1jNxtngcr1o7OuE3IesU9pzpOk5YDtW7aKJgiSIG
14  # j+wajtlOft3vN+oGDIJLKvUg8Qvy5zUE0394gr6vqX8K5cz01pVDBee/NOeK6ch
15  # ZWxRAgMBAAGjgYYwgYMwEwYDVR01BAwwCgYIKwYBBQUHAwMwbAYDVR0BBGUwY4AQ
16  # /tG NEp/dt +b ab jnC4 caF9MP xQ A3 gNVBAMTMFdpbmRvd3MgUG93ZXJTaGV
```

Import the module again and execute the function:

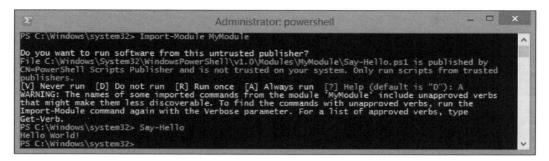

Answer A and the function proceeds to run, and runs without needing prompting thereafter. A new certificate is also created in the **Trusted Publishers** container:

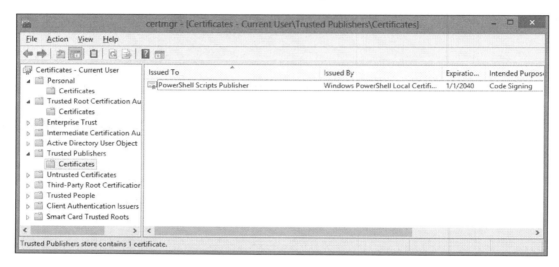

To validate the signature of a script or formatting file, use the
`Get-AuthenticodeSignature` cmdlet:

The `Get-AuthenticodeSignature` cmdlet gets the authenticode signature from a
file. This can be a PowerShell script or formatting file, but the cmdlet also supports
DLLs and other Windows standard executable file types.

Signed modules can be transported by exporting (from the original computer) and
importing (to the new computer) the PowerShell certificates found in the **Trusted
Root Certification Authorities** container. Optionally, the trusted publishers can also
be moved to prevent the first-time prompt. From the **Current User** certificate store,
go to the **Trusted Root Certification Authorities** container and locate the PowerShell
Local Certificate Root certificate. Right-click on it and click on **All Tasks | Export**.

Log in to the target machine as the user under which modules will be running. Open MMC and add the Certificates snap-in for the current user, locating the **Trusted Root Certification Authorities** container. Expand the container to find the **Certificates** store. Right-click on it and select **All Tasks | Import**.

Your signed modules should now run on the new computer. Note that PowerShell will prompt you the first time they are run unless you also import the Trusted Publishers certificate.

Summary

In Windows PowerShell 3.0, modules are a very important feature. You can load most existing snap-ins as a module instead, which means you don't need to have administrator privileges to load a new snap-in. There is no need to register snap-ins by running `InstallUtil.exe`. You can simply place them in any folder you can access and tell PowerShell where to find them.

In this chapter, we discussed how to extend PowerShell by writing modules. The content covered how to import, remove, and reload PowerShell modules, create a module, and sign a module. This is a great encouragement to DBAs and systems administrators to create PowerShell cmdlets to automate a number of processes, and make them accessible via modules. It has also enabled Microsoft to provide modules to accompany added roles or features of the OS that ease the administrative workload. Getting access to these modules is a simple process of installing the correct role or feature and then importing the module. As IT organizations strive towards greater automation, it is well worth checking out the automation possibilities that these modules bring.

In the next chapter, we will have a look at the Windows Server 2012 Server Core installation option, which allows you to use Windows Server capabilities in a shell-like interface without any graphical interface. Also, we will cover how to use PowerShell to manage and configure Server Core instead of the normal command-line interface `cmd`.

5

Managing Core Infrastructure with PowerShell

A few years ago, Microsoft added a new feature called Server Core to the Windows Server operating system. Server Core is an option for installing the operating system with a minimal **Graphical User Interface (GUI)**, which means less services footprint, less hardware requirements, and a more secure surface. Because Server Core is a minimal installation of GUI, each and every single administration task is done via the command line. In Windows Server 2012, a lot of new PowerShell modules have been developed in order to make the management of Server Core much easier.

In this chapter we will discuss the following points:

- What is Server Core?
- How to make PowerShell the default shell
- Preparing your operating system using PowerShell
- Managing and configuring core infrastructure roles

The default shell for the Server Core is `cmd.exe`, so before we start building our core infrastructure, let's do a nice trick and change the default shell from the traditional **command-line interface (cmd)** to Windows PowerShell.

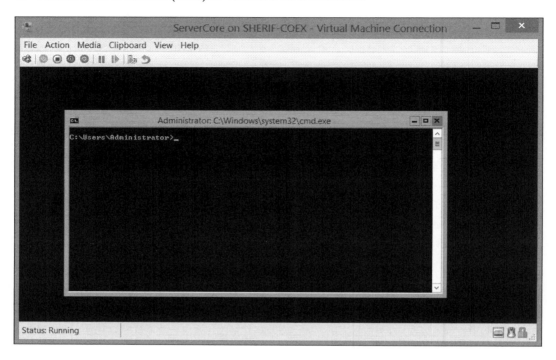

In order to accomplish this task, change the value of the `Shell` registry key under `HKLM:\Software\Microsoft\Windows NT\CurrentVersion\winlogon` from `cmd.exe` to `PowerShell.exe`. We can do this by either using the registry editor `RegEdit` or Windows PowerShell.

To do that using PowerShell, we need to start Windows PowerShell by executing PowerShell in the cmd window, and then using the `Set-ItemProperty` cmdlet to change the registry key value.

```
C:\Users\Administrator> PowerShell.exe
PS > Set-ItemProperty "HKLM:\Software\Microsoft\Windows NT\
CurrentVersion\winlogon" Shell PowerShell.exe
```

After changing the registry key value, log out and log in again to apply the new changes.

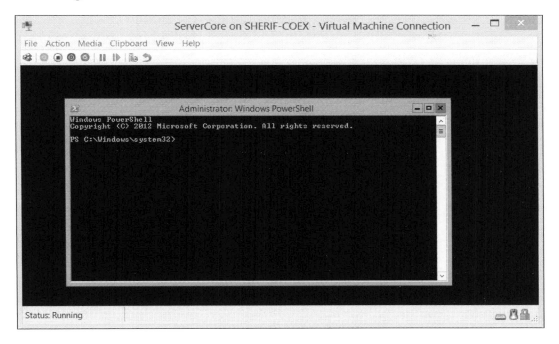

Preparing the operating system for first time use

Now, after changing the default shell to PowerShell, it is time to do some basic preparation for the server before starting to build the infrastructure roles and services. Usually, after installing the operating system or running the Sysprep generalization utility, you need to rename the computer to a specific naming convention to meet organization standards, assign a static IP address to your server, change the time zone, and so on. Although these kinds of tasks look very easy in the normal Windows Server GUI, the situation is different in Server Core where the GUI is no longer available. So, PowerShell will help us achieve our purpose.

Task 1 – changing the computer name

In this task, we will change the computer name that was generated during the installation of the operating system to a more meaningful name. In this example, we will use HQ-DC-01 to refer to the Domain Controller server in the headquarters. For this purpose, we will use the Rename-Computer cmdlet to rename the computer and then use the Restart-Computer cmdlet to restart the computer to apply the changes.

```
PS > Rename-Computer –NewName HQ-DC-01
PS > Restart-Computer
```

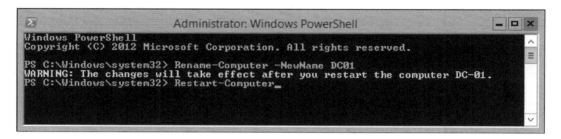

Task 2 – changing the time zone settings

In this task, we will change the default time zone to Greenwich Standard Time. For this purpose, we will use the time zone utility to change the time zone.

```
#Display the Current Time Zone
PS > TZutil /g

#Display the list of available Time Zones
PS > TZutil /l

#Set the new Time Zone
PS > TZutil /s "Greenwich Standard Time"
```

 Use TZutil with the Invoke-Command cmdlet to change the time zone settings on remote computers.

Task 3 – setting the Network Interface Card (NIC) configuration

In this task, we will change the configuration for the **Network Interface Card (NIC)**; this task will be accomplished in two steps. The first step is to use the New-NetIPAddress cmdlet, which is a part of the NetTCPIP module, to set the IP address and default gateway configuration. The second step is to use the Set-DNSClientServerAddress cmdlet, which is part of the DnsClient module, to set the DNS configuration for the client computer.

```
#Setting static IP Address Configuration
PS > New-NetIPAddress -IPAddress 192.168.0.2 -InterfaceAlias Ethernet
-DefaultGateway 192.168.0.1 -AddressFamily IPv4 -PrefixLength 24

#Setting Client DNS Settings
PS > Set-DnsClientServerAddress -InterfaceAlias Ethernet
-ServerAddresses 192.168.0.1,192.168.0.2
```

If you want to revert the TCP/IP settings and use the DHCP assignment method for automatic IP addresses assignment, you have to perform the following steps:

1. Remove the IP address and subnet mask settings.
2. Remove the network route (default gateway) setting.
3. Reset the DNS client configuration.
4. Enable the DHCP assignment on the interface.

You can use the following code:

```
#Remove static IP Address Setting
PS > Remove-NetIPAddress -InterfaceAlias Ethernet

#Remove network route
PS > Remove-NetRoute -InterfaceAlias Ethernet

#Reset Client DNS Settings
PS > Set-DnsClientServerAddress -ResetServerAddresses

#Enable the DHCP option on the interface
PS > Set-NetIPInterface -InterfaceAlias Ethernet -Dhcp Enabled
```

Task 4 – managing Windows Server roles and features

Managing server roles and features is one of the most important, basic, and repetitive tasks when dealing with a server operating system such as Windows Server. In this task, we will learn how to use the `ServerManager` module to display, add, and remove Windows roles and features.

Example 1

In this example, we will use the `Get-WindowsFeature` cmdlet to list all the installed roles and features on the local server.

```
#Get list of all installed Roles and Features
PS > Get-WindowsFeature | where Installed -eq $true
```

Refer to the following screenshot:

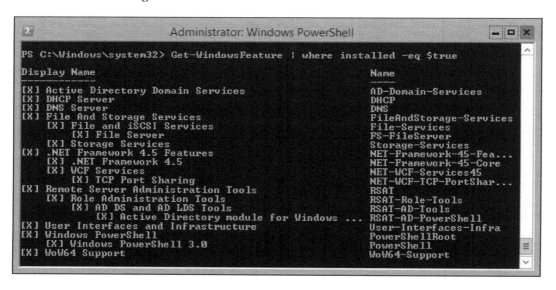

Installing Windows features using PowerShell is very useful even if you have a full graphical user interface, especially when you want to install a set of prerequisites for a product such as Exchange Server or SharePoint Server on multiple servers.

For this purpose, we will use the `Install-WindowsFeature` cmdlet that comes with a couple of very interesting switches, `-IncludeAllSubFeature` and `-IncludeManagementTools`, which make the installation easier.

- `IncludeAllSubFeature`: This is useful if you want to install a role or feature that has subfeatures and you want to install all of them in one step; it's a good candidate for roles such as Web Server and File Server.

- `IncludeManagementTools`: When you install a role or feature using PowerShell, it will install the role itself only without the management console. For example, if you install **Internet Information Services (IIS)** using PowerShell, it will not install the IIS Management Tool until you add the `IncludeManagementTools` switch.

Example 2

In this example, we will install the Web Server role with all subfeatures and management tools.

```
#Install-WindowsFeature
PS > Install-WindowsFeature Web-Server -IncludeAllSubFeature
-IncludeManagementTools
```

Deploying the Active Directory Domain Services (ADDS) role

The Directory Service is one of the core services that must be implemented when we consider building an integrated, secure, and centralized infrastructure. It is required for any organization looking for an integrated, central administration process for network resources, managing identities, and access control. There are three deployment scenarios related to the Active Directory deployment:

- Creating a new Active Directory forest
- Creating a new Active Directory Domain in an existing forest
- Creating a new Active Directory Domain Controller in an existing domain

These deployment options are available as part of **Active Directory Domain Services Configuration Wizard**.

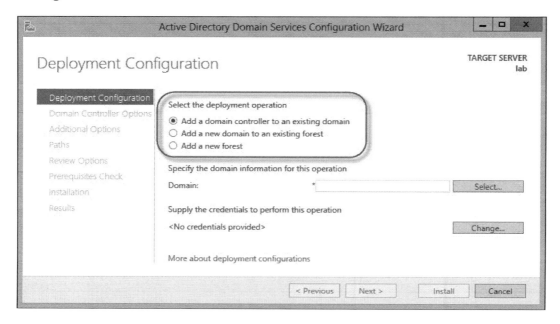

Before you start deploying the Active Directory, you need to add the Active Directory Domain Services Windows role first. Installing this role will install the required binary files to set up the Active Directory Domain Services and will also install the ADDSDeployment module that is required to deploy Active Directory using Windows PowerShell.

For this purpose, we will use the Add-WindowsFeature cmdlet:

```
#Install "Active Directory Domain Services" windows feature
PS > Add-WindowsFeature AD-Domain-Services
```

Scenario 1 – installing a new Active Directory Forest

In this scenario, we will install a new Active Directory Forest and an Active Directory Domain called contoso.local, and the functional level Windows Server 2012 for both the forest and domain in addition to installing and configuring the DNS server role. The following example explains how to accomplish this task by using the Install-ADDSforest cmdlet with the following group of parameters:

- DomainName: Defines the root's domain name

- `DomainNetbiosName`: Defines the NetBIOS name for the domain
- `ForestMode`: Specifies the forest functional level
- `DomainMode`: Specifies the domain functional level
- `SafeModeAdministratorPassword`: Defines the administrator password required for starting up a domain controller in an active directory restore mode
- `InstallDNS`: Installs and configures the DNS server role; the default value is `true` if the parameter is not used

For the functional level for both the forest and domain, use the level name or the following equivalent values:

Functional level	Name	Value
Windows Server 2003	Win2003	2
Windows Server 2008	Win2008	3
Windows Server 2008 R2	Win2008R2	4
Windows Server 2012	Win2012	5

You can use the following code:

```
PS > Install-ADDSForest -DomainName contoso.local
-SafeModeAdministratorPassword (ConvertTo-SecureString P@ssw0rd
-AsPlainText -Force) -DomainMode Win2012 -DomainNetbiosname Contoso
-ForestMode Win2012 -InstallDNS
```

Scenario 2 – installing a new domain in an existing forest

In this scenario, we will install a new Active Directory child domain called `corp` in the existing Active Directory Forest called `contoso.local` and with a domain functional level, that is, Windows Server 2012 in addition to installing and configuring the DNS server role. The following example explains how to accomplish this task by using the `Install-ADDSdomain` cmdlet with the following group of parameters:

- `NewDomainName`: Defines the new domain name
- `ParentDomainName`: Defines the parent domain name for the new domain
- `DomainMode`: Specifies the domain functional level

- SafeModeAdministratorPassword: Defines the administrator password required for starting up a domain controller in the safe mode and the active directory restore mode

- InstallDNS: Installs and configures the DNS server role; the default value is true if the parameter is not used

- DomainType: Defines the domain type, which can be either Child or Tree

- CreateDnsDelegation: Creates a DNS delegation for the new DNS server.

You can use the following code:

```
PS > Install-ADDSDomain -NewDomainName corp -ParentDomainName contoso.
local -SafeModeAdministratorPassword (ConvertTo-SecureString P@ssw0rd
-AsPlainText -Force) -CreateDnsDelegation -Credential (Get-Credential
Contoso\Administrator) -DomainMode Win2012 -DomainType ChildDomain
```

Scenario 3 – installing a new domain controller in an existing domain

In this scenario, we will install a new Active Directory Domain Controller in the existing Active Directory Domain in addition to installing and configuring the DNS server role. The following example explains how to accomplish this task by using the Install-ADDSdomaincontroller cmdlet with the following group of parameters:

- DomainName: Defines the name of the domain that the Domain Controller will be a part of

- NoGlobalCatalog: Defines if the domain controller will hold a Global Catalog replica or not

- Site: Defines which Active Directory site the domain controller will be a part of

- ReplicationSourceDC: Defines the source domain controller for replication

- SafeModeAdministratorPassword: Defines the administrator password required for starting up a domain controller in the safe mode and the active directory restore mode

- InstallDNS: Installs and configures the DNS server role

- CreateDnsDelegation: Creates a DNS delegation for the new DNS server

- ReadOnlyReplica: Use this option if you want to install a read-only domain controller

You can use the following code:

```
PS > Install-ADDSDomainController -NoGlobalCatalog:$false
-CreateDnsDelegation:$false -Credential (Get-Credential)
-DomainName "contoso.local" -InstallDns:$true -ReplicationSourceDC
"DC01.contoso.local" -SiteName "Default-First-Site-Name"
-SafeModeAdministratorPassword (ConvertTo-SecureString P@ssw0rd
-AsPlainText -Force)
```

Managing and configuring the Domain Name System (DNS) role

The **Domain Name System** (**DNS**) is one of the most popular infrastructure roles not only for IT specialists but also for normal Internet users. DNS is an application-layer protocol responsible for the hierarchical naming structure for the different IT components either connected locally to the intranet or exposed to the Internet.

In this section, we will learn about the new Windows PowerShell modules for DNS that have been introduced in Windows Server 2012 and how you can use them to perform different DNS configuration tasks.

By default if you are using Windows 8 or Windows Server 2012, you will have the DnsClient PowerShell module installed to allow you to manage and troubleshoot the DNS client component. However, the DnsServer PowerShell module will be available on Windows Server once you install the DNS role.

Task 1 – configuring DNS server resource records

In this task, we will learn how to create a different type of DNS resources records. In this example, we will create records of types A, CName, and MX. For the purpose of this task, we will use the Add-DnsServerResourceRecord* cmdlets where * represents the type of the record.

 You can use the Add-DnsServerResourceRecord cmdlet and define the type of the resource record as a parameter such as –MX or -CName.

```
#Add DNS Server 'A' Resource Record
PS > Add-DnsServerResourceRecordA -Name FileServer -Ipv4Address
192.168.1.20 -ZoneName Contoso.local
```

```
#Add DNS Server 'CName' Resource Record
PS > Add-DnsServerResourceRecordCName -Name OWA -HostNameAlias
EXCH-MBXCAS-02.Contoso.local -ZoneName Contoso.local

#Add DNS Server 'MX' Resource Record
PS > Add-DnsServerResourceRecordMX -Name Mail -MailExchange
EXCH-HUB-01.Contoso.local -ZoneName Contoso.local -Preference 10
```

Task 2 – creating primary forward and reverse lookup zones

In this task, we will learn how to create different DNS zones. For the purpose of this task, we will use the `Add-DnsServerPrimaryZone` cmdlet to create primary forward and reverse lookup zones.

```
#Add DNS Forward Zone
PS > Add-DnsServerPrimaryZone -Name 'Labs' -ReplicationScope Domain
-DynamicUpdate Secure

#Add DNS Server Reverse Lookup zone
PS > Add-DnsServerPrimaryZone -NetworkId '192.168.1.0/24'
-ReplicationScope Forest -DynamicUpdate NonsecureAndSecure
```

Task 3 – adding a DNS server forwarder

In this task, we will learn how to add a forwarder to the forwarders list in the DNS server. For the purpose of this task, we will use the `Add-DnsServerForwarder` cmdlet.

```
#Add DNS Server Forwarder
PS > Add-DnsServerForwarder –IPAddress '4.2.2.3','8.8.8.8'
```

Task 4 – exporting DNS server zones

In this task, we will learn how to back up the DNS server. For the purpose of this task, we will use the `Export-DnsServerZone` cmdlet to export the DNS zone to a file that contains all records from this zone.

 The DNS backup file will be stored by default under the DNS physical directory `C:\Windows\System32\Dns`.

```
#Export DNS Zones
PS > ForEach($Zone in (Get-DnsServerZone | Where IsAutoCreated -eq
$false))
```

```
{
Export-DnsServerZone -Name $Zone.ZoneName -FileName $Zone.ZoneName
}
```

Deploying and configuring the Dynamic Host Configuration Protocol (DHCP) role

The main purpose of using **Dynamic Host Configuration Protocol (DHCP)** is to automatically assign the IP addresses and the other TCP/IP configuration to the network devices. This part explains how to use Windows PowerShell to install and configure the DHCP role. In order to complete the DHCP deployment process, you should accomplish the following tasks.

Task 1 – installing the DHCP server role

The first step in deploying the service is installing the DHCP server role. For this purpose, we will use `Add-WindowsFeature` to install the server role and also to install the `DHCPServer` module that contains the DHCP-related cmdlets and functions.

```
#Install DHCP Server Role
PS > Add-WindowsFeature DHCP
```

Task 2 – setting up the DHCP server scope

In this task, we will set up the DHCP server scope that defines the network subnet configuration. In this example, we will create a DHCP scope called Contoso for the `192.168.0.0` subnet with a subnet mask `255.255.255.0` and then activate it.

```
#Adding DHCP server IPv4 scope
PS > Add-DhcpServerv4Scope -Name "Contoso" -StartRange 192.168.0.1
-EndRange 192.168.0.254 -SubnetMask 255.255.255.0 -State Active
```

Task 3 – configuring DHCP scope options

In this task, we will set up the DHCP scope options that define settings such as DNS Domain Name, DNS Server Address, WIN Server, and Default Gateway. In this example, we will configure the DHCP scope options for the DHCP scope created in the previous example.

```
#Configuring DHCP Scope options (e.g. DNS Server and Router)
PS > Set-DhcpServerv4OptionValue -DnsDomain contoso.local -DnsServer
192.168.0.2 -Router 192.168.0.1
```

Task 4 – configuring DHCP scope exclusion

In this task, we will configure range exclusion for the DHCP scope. Usually, range exclusion is used when you want to exclude a range of specific IP addresses from your scope so that you can use it for static assignment for network devices. In this example, we will configure exclusion for 30 IP addresses in the DHCP scope created in the first example.

```
#Configuring DHCP scope exclusion
PS > Add-DhcpServerv4ExclusionRange -ScopeId 192.168.0.0 -StartRange
192.168.0.100 -EndRange 192.168.0.130
```

Task 5 – configuring DHCP scope reservations

In this task, we will configure IP address reservations in the DHCP scope. DHCP reservation is used to reserve a specific IP address for a specific device (for example, network printer) in order to make sure that your device is always assigned the same IP address. It is similar to the idea of range exclusion, but the difference is DHCP assigns the same IP address to the same device every time automatically instead of defining range exclusion and then assigning it manually to each and every device.

In this example, we will reserve the IP address 192.168.0.10 for the network printer with the MAC address F4-DA-F1-78-00-6D.

```
#Add DHCP IP Address Reservation
PS > Add-DhcpServerv4Reservation -ScopeId 192.168.0.0 -IPAddress
192.168.0.10 -ClientId F4-DA-F1-78-00-6D -Description "Multi-Function
Network Printer in 3rd floor"
```

Task 6 – authorizing the DHCP server in Active Directory

In this task, we will authorize the DHCP server in Active Directory in order to start leasing the IP addresses to the clients. In this example, we will use the Add-DhcpServerInDC cmdlet to add the DHCP server created in the previous steps to the list of the authorized DHCP servers in the Active Directory.

```
#Authorize DHCP Server in Domain Controller
PS > Add-DhcpServerInDC -DnsName "DhcpServer.contoso.local"
```

Managing Windows Firewall

Windows Firewall is a built-in component in Windows operating systems that allows you to control the incoming and outgoing network traffic and communications.

Task 1 – enabling or disabling Windows Firewall profiles

In this task, we will use the `Set-NetFirewallProfile` cmdlet to disable all Windows Firewall profiles, and then enable the firewall public profile.

```
#Disable all Firewall Profiles
PS > Set-NetFirewallProfile –All –Enabled False

#Enable Windows Firewall Public Profile
PS > Set-NetFirewallProfile –Name Public –Enabled True
```

Task 2 – creating Windows Firewall rules

In this task, we will use the `New-NetFirewallRule` cmdlet to create a new Windows Firewall rule.

Example 1

This example explains how to create a firewall rule that blocks all outbound traffic to any FTP protocol.

```
PS > New-NetFirewallRule -Name "Block FTP" -DisplayName "Block FTP"
-Direction Outbound -Action Block -Protocol TCP -LocalPort FTP
```

Example 2

This example explains how to create a firewall rule that allows inbound traffic coming from an application (for example, Skype).

```
PS > New-NetFirewallRule -Name "Skype" -DisplayName "Skype" -Direction
Inbound -Action Allow -Program "C:\Program Files (x86)\Skype\Phone\
Skype.exe"
```

Using the Best Practice Analyzer (BPA)

Best Practice Analyzer is a Windows management tool that assesses and evaluates the server configuration against Microsoft's best practices and compliances, then reports the healthy and violated best practices, and then provides ways to fix it.

Task 1 – displaying the list of best practice models

In this task, we will use the Get-BpaModel cmdlet to display the list of available models and then filter them to get the models that have not run on the server before.

```
#Get list of all BPA models
PS > Get-BpaModel

#Get list of all BPA filtered by LastScanTime propert
PS > Get-BpaModel | where LastScanTime -eq Never
```

The list in the following screenshot shows the available BPA models and their properties:

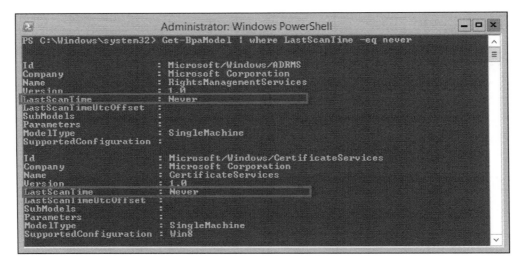

Task 2 – invoking a best practice model

In this task, we will use the Invoke-BpaModel cmdlet to start scanning the server for the best practices and compliances violations and problems for File Services.

```
#Invoke File Services BPA Model
PS > Invoke-BpaModel -ModelId Microsoft/Windows/FileServices
```

The following screenshot shows the output of invoking a single BPA model:

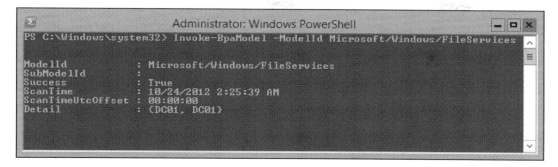

Task 3 – showing the best practice model result

In this task, we will use the `Get-BpaResult` cmdlet to display the result of the File Services best practice scan that has been invoked in the previous example.

```
#Get File Services BPA Model scan results
PS > Get-BpaResult -ModelId Microsoft/Windows/FileServices
```

The following screenshot shows the results of the BPA model execution:

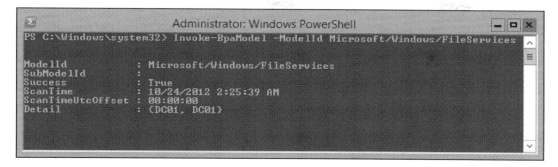

Summary

Windows Server Core is a great addition to the Windows Server operating system. It provides a new non-traditional concept of Windows, but the main challenge is to perform the normal administration tasks with no **Graphical User Interface (GUI)**, especially for the administrator with no shell background.

In this chapter, we have seen how Windows PowerShell can make life easier in terms of deploying, managing, and configuring the different server roles and features even without a GUI.

In the next chapter, we will discuss on how to manage organizational units, user accounts, user passwords and groups by using the Active Directory module. The Active Directory module for Windows PowerShell consolidates a group of cmdlets. You can use these cmdlets to manage your Active Directory domains.

6

Managing Active Directory with PowerShell

Active Directory (AD) is a directory service created by Microsoft for Windows domain networks. It is included in most Windows Server operating systems. Active Directory provides a central location for network administration and security. Server computers that run Active Directory are called domain controllers. An AD domain controller authenticates and authorizes all users and computers in a Windows domain-type network along with assigning and enforcing security policies for all computers and installing or updating software. For example, when a user logs in to a computer that is part of a Windows domain, Active Directory checks the submitted password and determines whether the user is a system administrator or a normal user.

In Windows Server 2000, Windows Server 2003, and Windows Server 2008, administrators used a variety of command-line tools and **Microsoft Management Console (MMC)** snap-ins to connect to their Active Directory domains and AD **Lightweight Directory Services (LDS)** configuration sets for the purpose of monitoring and managing them. The Active Directory module for Windows PowerShell now provides a centralized experience for administering your directory service.

The Active Directory module for Windows PowerShell consolidates a group of cmdlets. You can use these cmdlets to manage your Active Directory domains, AD LDS configuration sets, and Active Directory Database Mounting Tool instances in a single, self-contained package.

In this chapter we will cover:

- Creating, listing, renaming, modifying, and deleting an organizational unit
- Creating a user account
- Getting and listing the properties of a user account
- Preventing the password change of a user
- Creating a security or distribution group

First of all, we should introduce some concepts of Active Directory services.

Active Directory-related concepts

Active Directory is a complicated technology. The following introduction to it will involve some proper nouns. In order to facilitate the reader's understanding, we first explain some concepts.

Introduction to Active Directory

Active Directory provides information about the storage network object and makes the information available to users and network administrators that use the Active Directory services. Active Directory can store all kinds of information about the object, and also make the information easily accessible to administrators and users who may need to find and use it. It uses information of the structured data storage directory as the logical structure of its foundation; at the same time it will be integrated safely in the Active Directory. Through the network login, the system administrator can manage the entire network of directory data and units, and empowered network users can also access the network on any local resource.

Active Directory includes two aspects: a directory object and a directory service.

A directory object stores information about all kinds of objects of a physical nature, which helps to understand the active directory from the static point of view. We have to consider the "catalogue" or "folder" as only an object or an entity, with no major difference.

A directory service enables the directory containing all the information and resources to play the role of a service. Active Directory is a distributed directory service. Although information can be spread in many sets of different computers, users can quickly access it. Since many machines have the same information, Active Directory has a strong fault-tolerance ability. Because of this, no matter where the user access and information are, Active Directory provides a unified view to all users.

Namespace

Essentially, Active Directory is a namespace. We can add the namespace for any given name at the analytic boundary. The boundary referred to the name can provide or associate the range for mapping the entire information. Name resolution provides a name that is translated into a name that represents object or information processing.

Object

Objects are the Active Directory information entities; we usually see them as properties, but they are sets of attributes, which often represent physical entities, such as user accounts and filenames. Objects, with the help of the attribute description of their basic characteristics such as a user account attribute, may include customer name, telephone number, e-mail address, and home address.

Container

A container is Active Directory's name part of the space and directory object. It also has attributes, but the directory object is different. It does not represent a tangible entity, but represents a store object space; since it represents only a store object space, it is a small namespace.

Trees

In any namespace, a directory tree points to the object container and a hierarchical structure. The leaves and the nodes of the tree are often objects, and a tree without any leaves or nodes is a **container**. A directory tree expresses the mode of connection of objects; it also shows the path from one object to another object.

In the Active Directory, the directory tree is the basic structure. With every container as a starting point, using the layer-upon-layer method, it can constitute a subtree. A simple directory can constitute a tree, and a computer network or a domain can form a tree. In fact, a directory tree describes a kind of path relationship.

Domain

A **domain** is the fundamental, logical building block for the partitioning of Active Directory. Partitioning is a very important concept of directory services because it allows the use of multiple directory partitions rather than one massive store. Consequently, each domain's directory needs to store only the information about the objects located in that domain, and as a result of this, Active Directory as a whole becomes very scalable.

Installing an Active Directory Domain Service (ADDS)

In the default installation of Windows 2012, Active Directory is not installed by default. We can install AD DS by using Server Manager or by using PowerShell in Windows Server 2012. When installing AD DS by using Server Manager, Active Directory Domain Server Configuration Wizard (dcpromo.exe) is deprecated from the beginning in Windows Server 2012.

New AD server roles in Windows 2012

You can use **Active Directory Domain Services** (**AD DS**) in Windows Server 2012 to deploy domain controllers more rapidly and easily, increase flexibility when auditing and authorizing access to files, and more easily perform administrative tasks through consistent graphical and scripted management experiences.

Active Directory Certificate Services

Active Directory Certificate Services (**AD CS**) in Windows Server 2012 is the server role that allows you to build a **public key infrastructure** (**PKI**) and provides public key cryptography, digital certificates, and digital signature capabilities for your organization.

Active Directory Domain Services

By using the **Active Directory Domain Services** (**AD DS**) server role, you can create a scalable, secure, and manageable infrastructure for management of users and resources, and provide support for directory-enabled applications such as Microsoft Exchange Server.

Active Directory Lightweight Directory Services

Active Directory Lightweight Directory Services (**AD LDS**) is a **Lightweight Directory Access Protocol** (**LDAP**) directory service that provides flexible support for directory-enabled applications without the dependencies and domain-related restrictions of AD DS.

Active Directory Rights Management Services

Active Directory Rights Management Services (AD RMS) in Windows Server 2012 is the server role that provides you with management and development tools that work with the security technologies in the industry. This includes encryption, certificates, and authentication, which are used to help organizations create reliable information protection solutions.

Managing Active Directory with PowerShell

The Active Directory module for PowerShell consolidates a group of cmdlets. You can use these cmdlets to manage your Active Directory domains, AD LDS configuration sets, and Active Directory Database Mounting Tool instances in a single, self-contained package. In the following sections, we will show examples to demonstrate how to operate Active Directory using PowerShell. In our examples, we add the computer `Win8Client` as a client to a domain `fuhaijun.com` with a domain controller named `win2012-ad`.

Account management

We can use the Active Directory module in PowerShell to manage your user and computer accounts in **Active Directory Domain Services (AD DS)**. And now we will show how to use the Active Directory module to accomplish many of the common tasks that are associated with managing users.

User management

You can use the Active Directory module for Windows PowerShell to manage users in AD DS in Windows Server 2012. This section contains topics that explain how to use the Active Directory module to accomplish many of the common tasks that are associated with managing users.

Creating an AD User

The following example shows how to use the Active Directory module for Windows PowerShell to create a new user in AD DS.

We create a new user (TestUser) with a password (p@ssword) in an organizational unit (Test) in the fuhaijun.com domain:

```
New-ADUser -SamAccountName TestUser -Name "A Test User" -AccountPassword
(ConvertTo-SecureString -AsPlainText "p@ssw0rd" -Force) -Enabled $true
-Path 'OU=Test,DC=FUHAIJUN,DC=COM'
```

Here, using the -Force parameter, we try to convert a plain text string to a security string used as a password. And the -Path parameter is used for specifying a domain path that the user creates.

Setting a user account to Expire

Sometimes, we need to create an account for a temporary user with a limited time available. Within the specified time range, this account can be used, but after that period the account will be disabled.

```
Set-ADUser TestUser -AccountExpirationDate 11/27/2014
```

We can see that it is very simple. The Set-ADUser cmdlet is used for setting the user (TestUser) to expire on 11/27/2014.

Forcing a user to change the password at the next login

In order to ensure that the newly created user account's password remains confidential, you can force the user to change his/her password at the next login.

```
Set-ADUser -Identity TestUser -ChangePasswordAtNextLogon $true
```

We force the user (TestUser) to change the password by allocating the -ChangePasswordAtNextLogon switch parameter.

Preventing users from changing the password

When some user account is a special user account, such as a user account shared by multiple users, we need to prevent users from modifying the password.

```
Set-ADAccountControl -Identity TestUser -CannotChangePassword $true
```

The -CannotChangePassword parameter is used for preventing the user (TestUser) from modifying the password.

Computer management

If a computer needs to be operated in a domain, it must be connected to the domain. The following examples explain how to use the Active Directory module in PowerShell to perform many of the tasks associated with computer management.

Joining a computer to a domain

You must run the following command on a local computer if you want to add the local computer to the fuhaijun.com domain by using the current logged-in user's credentials.

```
Add-Computer -DomainOrWorkgroupName fuhaijun
```

When we need to add the computer Win8Client to the fuhaijun.com domain and specify a domain controller with the -server parameter using the current credentials, we can run the following command on the local computer:

```
Add-Computer Win8Client -DN fuhaijun -Server Win2012-ad
```

Of course, we can also add a local computer to the OU in the directory specified by the -OUPath parameter using the current logged-in user:

```
Add-Computer -DomainOrWorkgroupName fuhaijun -OUPath
OU=testOU,DC=fuhaijun,DC=com
```

Renaming a computer

Sometimes we need to rename a computer. We can rename the local domain-joined computer by executing the following command:

```
Rename-Computer -NewName win8client2 -DomainCredential fuhaijun\
administrator -Restart
```

The preceding example demonstrates how to change a domain-joined computer's name to Win8Client2 with the parameter -DomainCredential for specifying the privilege of a domain controller administrator. In order for changes to take effect after modifying the hostname, the -Restart parameter is used to restart the computer after execution is finished. This command is run on the local computer.

Group management

A group is the concept for organization of objects with the same characteristics. Based on the operation of the group, the management tasks for the group members can be accomplished.

Viewing group permissions

If you want to manage a group, first of all you need to know the permissions of the current group. You can run the following command from the AD:\> drive; the drive must be connected to the domain where the group exists.

```
Get-ACL (Get-ADGroup UserGroup) | fl * -f
```

Executing the preceding command, we can get the following result:

```
PS C:\> cd ad:
PS AD:\> Get-ACL (Get-ADGroup UserGroup) | fl * -f

PSPath                   : Microsoft.ActiveDirectory.Management\ActiveDirectory:
                           ://RootDSE/CN=UserGroup,DC=fuhaijun,DC=com
PSParentPath             : Microsoft.ActiveDirectory.Management\ActiveDirectory:
                           ://RootDSE/DC=fuhaijun,DC=com
PSChildName              : CN=UserGroup
PSDrive                  : AD
PSProvider               : Microsoft.ActiveDirectory.Management\ActiveDirectory
CentralAccessPolicyId    :
CentralAccessPolicyName  :
AccessToString           : NT AUTHORITY\SELF Allow
                           NT AUTHORITY\Authenticated Users Allow
                           NT AUTHORITY\SYSTEM Allow
                           BUILTIN\Account Operators Allow
                           FUHAIJUN\Domain Admins Allow
                           NT AUTHORITY\Authenticated Users Allow
                           BUILTIN\Windows Authorization Access Group Allow
                           BUILTIN\Pre-Windows 2000 Compatible Access Allow
                           BUILTIN\Pre-Windows 2000 Compatible Access Allow
                           BUILTIN\Pre-Windows 2000 Compatible Access Allow
                           BUILTIN\Pre-Windows 2000 Compatible Access Allow
                           BUILTIN\Pre-Windows 2000 Compatible Access Allow
```

We use the Get-ADGroup cmdlet to obtain the existing group, UserGroup, then pass it to the Get-ACL cmdlet, and finally transmit it to the Format-List cmdlet for formatting the output to the list.

Creating a group

Once we have viewed the group permissions, we need to create a group for managing a series of AD objects. The following example demonstrates how to create a group named ProductAdmins in the fuhaijun.com domain:

```
New-ADGroup -Name "Product Admins" -SamAccountName ProductAdmins
-GroupCategory Security -GroupScope Global -DisplayName "Product
Administrators" -Path "CN=Users,DC=fuhaijun,DC=Com"
```

When this command executes, we can find a new group named `ProductAdmins` by using ADSI Edit, as shown in the following screenshot:

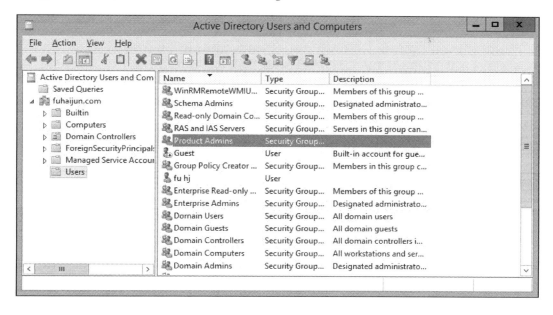

Adding and removing members of a group

The most common maintenance operation is to add and remove group members. We can use the `Add-ADGroupMember` cmdlet for adding a user `fuhj` to the group `ProductAdmins`.

```
Add-ADGroupMember -Identity ProductAdmins -Member fuhj
```

The parameter `-Identity` is used for specifying the group to to which to add the new member, and the parameter `-Member` is used for specifying the operating group's new member. After the command is executed, we can find the `ProductAdmins` group in the `fuhj` user's properties on the **Member Of** tab.

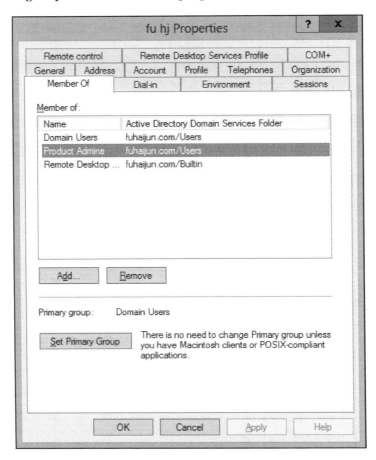

When we need to remove a group, we can use the `Remove-ADGroup` cmdlet for removing an Active Directory group object. You can use this cmdlet to remove security and distribution groups.

```
Get-ADGroup -filter 'Name -like "Product*"' | Remove-ADGroup
```

The preceding example shows how to get all the groups whose names start with `Product` and then remove them.

The -Identity parameter specifies the Active Directory group to be removed. You can identify a group by its **distinguished name (DN)**, GUID, **security identifier (SID)**, **Security Accounts Manager (SAM)** account name, or canonical name. You can also set the -Identity parameter to an object variable such as $<localADGroupObject>, or you can pass an object through the pipeline to the -Identity parameter. For example, you can use the Get-ADGroup cmdlet to retrieve a group object and then pass the object through the pipeline to the Remove-ADGroup cmdlet. If ADGroup is being identified by its DN, the -Partition parameter will be automatically determined.

For AD LDS environments, the -Partition parameter must be specified except in the following two conditions:

- The cmdlet is run from an Active Directory provider drive
- A default naming context or partition is defined for the AD LDS environment

To specify a default naming context for an AD LDS environment, set the msDS-defaultNamingContext property of the Active Directory **directory service agent (DSA)** object (nTDSDSA) for the AD LDS instance.

Organizational unit management

The OU is a particularly useful type of directory object in domains. OUs are Active Directory containers into which you can place users, groups, computers, and other OUs. An OU cannot contain objects from other domains. OUs can contain other OUs. An OU is the smallest scope or unit to which you can assign Group Policy settings or delegate administrative authority. By using OUs, you can create containers within a domain that represent the hierarchical and logical structures in your organization.

Creating a new organizational unit

We can create a new organizational unit named UserAccounts, which is located in the domain fuhaijun.com, as shown in the following example:

```
New-ADOrganizationalUnit -Name UserAccounts -Path "DC=FUHAIJUN,DC=COM"
```

We can also use the -instance parameter to specify a template from a completely set OU object, as follows:

```
$ouTemplate = Get-ADOrganizationalUnit "OU=UserAccounts,DC=FUHAIJUN,DC=com" -properties seeAlso,managedBy;

New-ADOrganizationalUnit -name UserReports -instance $ouTemplate
```

In the preceding example, we can see that we create an OU named `UserReports` from the template `$ouTemplate`.

Listing organizational units

We can use the `Get-ADOrganizationalUnit` cmdlet to get one or more Active Directory organizational units. This cmdlet gets an organizational unit object or performs a search to retrieve multiple organizational units.

```
Get-ADOrganizationalUnit -Filter 'Name -like "*"' | ft -AutoSize
```

When we execute this command, we get the result as shown in the following screenshot:

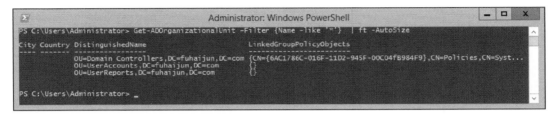

We can see that all organizational units created in the preceding examples have been listed out. The `Format-Tables` cmdlet is used for formatting the output display.

Renaming an organizational unit

We can use the `rename-ADObject` cmdlet for changing the name of an organizational unit.

```
Rename-ADObject "OU=TestOU, DC=Fuhaijun,DC=Com" -NewName Groups
```

Rename the object having the distinguished name `OU=TestOU,DC=Fuhaijun,DC=Com` to `Groups`. After executing the command, the name of the OU `TestOU` will be changed to `Groups`.

Of course, we can also use the `-Identity` parameter with the object GUID in order to locate the organizational unit object to be renamed.

```
Rename-ADObject -Identity "d465ddc9-a5e6-4998-91aa-09e33fe22369" -NewName
Groups
```

Note that the `-Partition` parameter is not specified because the object is in the default naming context of the domain.

Modifying an organizational unit

We can modify the description of the organizational unit with the distinguished name `OU=TestOU,DC=Fuhaijun,DC=COM` by using the `Set-ADOrganizationalUnit` cmdlet.

```
C:\PS>Set-ADOrganizationalUnit -Identity "OU=TestOU,DC=Fuhaijun,DC=COM"
-Description "This Organizational Unit is a test OU of Fuhaijun.COM"
```

Of course, we can also modify several properties at once. The `Get-ADOrganizationalUnit` cmdlet can help us obtain the destination organizational unit, and then assign it to a variable `$AsianSalesOU`. Then we can set the properties of the variable and use the `Set-ADOrganizationalUnit` cmdlet with the `-Instance` parameter to save the modification to the object. The command would be as follows:

```
$AsianSalesOU = Get-ADOrganizationalUnit "OU=Asia,OU=Sales,OU=UserAccount
s,DC=Fuhaijun,DC=COM"

$AsianSalesOU.StreetAddress = "No. 20 Chang An Avenue"

$AsianSalesOU.City = "Beijing"

$AsianSalesOU.PostalCode = "100000"

$AsianSalesOU.Country = "China"

Set-ADOrganizationalUnit -Instance $AsianSalesOU
```

Moving an organizational unit

When we need to adjust the organization structure, we need to move an OU to another location; to do so we must use the `Move-ADObject` cmdlet.

```
Move-ADObject "OU=ManagedGroups,DC=Fuhaijun,DC=Com" -TargetPath
"OU=Managed,DC=Fuhaijun,DC=Com"
```

As we can see, we use the `-TargetPath` parameter to specify the destination path. Meanwhile, we can also use this cmdlet to move other AD objects.

Deleting an organizational unit

As one of the daily tasks is to maintain the Active Directory, removing an Active Directory organizational unit is also very important. The following example will show how to delete an organizational unit:

```
C:\PS>Remove-ADOrganizationalUnit -Identity
"OU=TestOU,DC=FUHAIJUN,DC=COM" -Recursive

Are you sure you want to remove the item and all its children?

Performing recursive remove on Target: 'OU=Accounting,DC=Fuhaijun,DC=com
'.

[Y] Yes  [A] Yes to All  [N] No  [L] No to All  [S] Suspend  [?] Help
(default is "Y"):y
```

The preceding example shows how to remove an organizational unit and all of its children. If the organizational unit is protected from deletion, the organizational unit and its children will not be deleted. If the organizational unit is not protected even if any of the children are, both the organizational unit and the children will be deleted.

It is also possible to remove an organizational unit using its object GUID as the identity while suppressing the confirmation prompt.

```
Remove-ADOrganizationalUnit -Identity "d465ddc9-a5e6-4998-91aa-
09e33fe22369" -confirm:$false –ProtectedFromDeletion $false
```

We used the `-Identity` parameter to specify the object GUID for an organizational unit and the `-confirm:$false` parameter to suppress the confirmation prompt. If the flag for `-ProtectedFromDeletion` is set to `True`, this cmdlet does not delete the OU and it returns an error.

Domain controller management

You can use the Active Directory module for Windows PowerShell to manage your domain controllers and the operation's master roles in AD DS.

Finding a domain controller

The following example demonstrates how to find a domain controller for the `Fuhaijun.com` domain:

```
Get-ADDomainController -Discover -DomainName fuhaijun.com
```

The execution result is as follows:

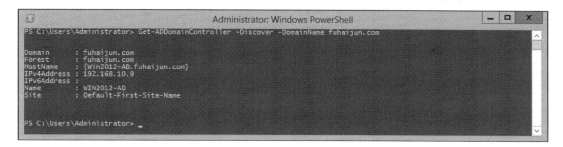

We can find all the information about the domain controller, including the hostname, IP address, and so on. If you want to find all the domain controllers for the domain and you are currently logged in, just use the following command line:

```
Get-ADDomainController -filter *
```

When this command is executed, you get all the details as shown in the following screenshot:

Finding a domain controller's site

After we find the domain controller, we can also find the domain controller's site using the Get-ADDomainController cmdlet with the -Identity parameter, as follows:

```
Get-ADDomainController -Identity Win2012-AD | FT Name,Site
```

Finding the global catalog servers in a forest

The Get-ADForest cmdlet gets the Active Directory forest specified by the parameters. You can specify the forest by setting the -Identity or -Current parameters. The -Identity parameter specifies the Active Directory forest that is required. You can identify a forest by its **fully qualified domain name (FQDN)**, DNS hostname, or NetBIOS name. You can also set the parameter to a forest object variable, such as $<localForestObject>, or you can pass a forest object through the pipeline to the -Identity parameter.

```
Get-ADForest Fuhaijun.com | FL GlobalCatalogs
```

Summary

The Active Directory module for Windows PowerShell provides command-line scripting for administrative, configuration, and diagnostic tasks, with a consistent vocabulary and syntax. The Active Directory module enables end-to-end manageability with Exchange Server, Group Policy, and other services.

In this chapter, we discussed how to manage organizational units, user accounts, user passwords, and groups by using the Active Directory module. The Active Directory module for Windows PowerShell can help users to manage the AD effectively through the PowerShell. If you are an administrator managing domains, computers, users, groups, mailboxes, organizational units, and so on, using the Active Directory module for PowerShell, you may no longer find it difficult to manage time for efficiently managing all the AD objects and preparing AD reports for all the computers present in your organization. It will ease the task of managing AD objects and will also save a substantial lot of time of the administrator or of the help-desk person who is managing them.

In the next chapter, we will discuss how to manage a server with PowerShell. We will also look at adding roles and features, managing networks, group policy, managing IIS, and the DNS server.

7
Managing the Server with PowerShell

Having PowerShell built into Windows Server 2012 gives you flexibility while managing your server. Several PowerShell cmdlets let you perform many of the key administrative jobs that you may need to do on a daily basis, including installing features for your Windows Server, backing up your server, analyzing the server, managing IIS, and many others. PowerShell lets you perform many of these tasks consistently on a batch basis.

Managing your web servers and web farms is an ideal scenario for PowerShell. With PowerShell, you can configure IIS as well as manage applications, sites, application pools, and many other aspects of IIS. Managing the core server configuration of IIS is one key aspect of working with IIS. Another scenario is working with the websites themselves, including the sites, directories, and web applications on the server. From working with your server configuration to deploying your applications, PowerShell can help you accomplish this in a scalable, automated, and consistent fashion.

In this chapter we will cover:

- Working with Server Manager cmdlets
- Managing Group Policy
- Managing IIS with PowerShell
- Managing DNS Server
- Managing Hyper-V with PowerShell
- Managing AppLocker with PowerShell

All demos in this book are based on Windows Server 2012 and PowerShell 3.0.

Working with Server Manager cmdlets

Windows Server 2012 eases the task of managing and securing multiple server roles in an enterprise with the Server Manager console. Server Manager in Windows Server 2012 provides a single source for managing a server's identity and system information, displaying server status, identifying problems with server role configuration, and managing all roles installed on the server.

Server Manager makes server administration more efficient by allowing administrators to do the following using a single tool:

- View and make changes to server roles and features installed on the server
- Perform management tasks associated with the operational lifecycle of the server, such as starting or stopping services, and managing local user accounts
- Perform management tasks associated with the operational lifecycle of roles installed on the server, including scanning certain roles for compliance with best practices
- Determine server status, identify critical events, and analyze and troubleshoot configuration issues or failures

Adding roles or features by using PowerShell

PowerShell cmdlets can be used for server management. In Windows Server 2012, we can use the Get-WindowsFeature cmdlet to retrieve roles and features that are available on a computer. We can see the features that have been installed; those features will be marked with checkboxes ([X]) in its display name. The Install-WindowsFeature and Uninstall-WindowsFeature cmdlets are used for installing and uninstalling a role or feature:

1. Open a PowerShell session with elevated user rights. To do this, navigate to **Start | All Programs | Accessories | Windows PowerShell** and right-click on the Windows PowerShell shortcut. Then click on **Run as administrator**.

2. Load the Server Manager module into the PowerShell session before working with Server Manager cmdlets. Type the following and press *Enter*:

```
Import-Module Servermanager
```

3. If you do not know the command name of the role, role service, or feature that you want to install, type the following and then press *Enter* to return a list of all command names in the **Name** column. The command name is required for the next step.

```
Get-WindowsFeature web-*
```

When the command is executed, we get all the Windows features that have their names starting with 'web-'. It looks like the following screenshot:

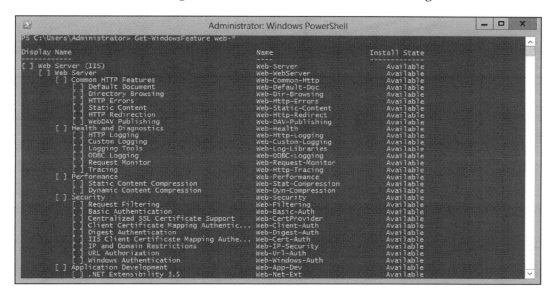

4. Type the following command, in which the name represents the command name of the role, role service, or feature that was obtained in the previous step, and then press *Enter* to install the role or feature. The `-restart` parameter restarts the computer automatically after installation is complete, if a restart of the computer is required by the role or feature.

```
Install-WindowsFeature Telnet-Client
```

Since the process of feature installation runs for a long duration, in order to let the user know the current progress of the installation, the installation will show a progress bar with the percentage of the installation completed, as shown in the following screenshot:

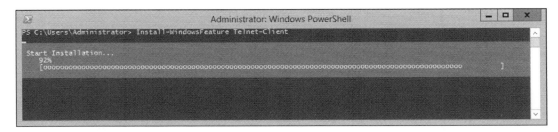

If you want to install several features at a same time, you can use the Get-WindowsFeature cmdlet to obtain some feature objects, and then pass them to the Install-WindowsFeature cmdlet. Say we want to install all features for IIS7.5; in this case, we type the following and press *Enter*:

```
Get-WindowsFeature web-*  |Install-WindowsFeature
```

After these features have been installed, we can check the installation status, as shown in the following screenshot:

```
Administrator: Windows PowerShell                                      _  □  x
PS C:\Users\Administrator> Get-WindowsFeature web-*

Display Name                                    Name               Install State
------------                                    ----               -------------
[X] Web Server (IIS)                            Web-Server             Installed
    [X] Web Server                              Web-WebServer          Installed
        [X] Common HTTP Features                Web-Common-Http        Installed
            [X] Default Document                Web-Default-Doc        Installed
            [X] Directory Browsing              Web-Dir-Browsing       Installed
            [X] HTTP Errors                     Web-Http-Errors        Installed
            [X] Static Content                  Web-Static-Content     Installed
            [X] HTTP Redirection                Web-Http-Redirect      Installed
            [X] WebDAV Publishing               Web-DAV-Publishing     Installed
        [X] Health and Diagnostics              Web-Health             Installed
            [X] HTTP Logging                    Web-Http-Logging       Installed
            [X] Custom Logging                  Web-Custom-Logging     Installed
            [X] Logging Tools                   Web-Log-Libraries      Installed
            [X] ODBC Logging                    Web-ODBC-Logging       Installed
            [X] Request Monitor                 Web-Request-Monitor    Installed
            [X] Tracing                         Web-Http-Tracing       Installed
        [X] Performance                         Web-Performance        Installed
            [X] Static Content Compression      Web-Stat-Compression   Installed
            [X] Dynamic Content Compression     Web-Dyn-Compression    Installed
        [X] Security                            Web-Security           Installed
            [X] Request Filtering               Web-Filtering          Installed
            [X] Basic Authentication            Web-Basic-Auth         Installed
            [X] Centralized SSL Certificate Support  Web-CertProvider  Installed
            [X] Client Certificate Mapping Authentic... Web-Client-Auth Installed
            [X] Digest Authentication           Web-Digest-Auth        Installed
            [X] IIS Client Certificate Mapping Authe... Web-Cert-Auth   Installed
            [X] IP and Domain Restrictions      Web-IP-Security        Installed
            [X] URL Authorization               Web-Url-Auth           Installed
            [X] Windows Authentication          Web-Windows-Auth       Installed
        [X] Application Development             Web-App-Dev            Installed
            [X] .NET Extensibility 3.5          Web-Net-Ext            Installed
```

You can install multiple roles, role services, and features by using commas to separate the command names, as shown in the following example:

```
Install-WindowsFeature Telnet-Server,Hyper-V
```

In this example, we install the Telnet Server and Hyper-V roles.

Advantages of PowerShell cmdlets for Server Manager

PowerShell cmdlets for Server Manager offer some significant advantages over the ServerManagerCmd.exe command. After Windows PowerShell and the Server Manager cmdlet sets are installed by using the **Deployment Image Servicing and Management (DISM)** tool, Windows PowerShell cmdlets can be run on a computer that is running the Server Core installation option of Windows Server 2012. Instructions for installing Windows PowerShell and the Server Manager cmdlet sets on the Server Core installation option of Windows Server 2012 are available in Remote Management with Server Manager.

Managing networking using PowerShell

Managing network settings and services is a core task for administrators of Windows Server-based networks. Examples of network configuration tasks include configuring interfaces, IP addresses, default gateways, and similar tasks.

In previous versions of Windows Server, such tasks usually had to be performed using a combination of GUI tools and various command-line utilities. But with the significantly increased Windows PowerShell capabilities built into Windows Server 2012, you can now perform most network administration tasks from the Windows PowerShell command line or by running Windows PowerShell scripts.

Running the Get-NetIPAddress cmdlet displays a list of all interfaces on the server:

From the preceding command output, you can see that the interface you are looking for is identified by the alias `Ethernet 2`. To view the existing TCP/IP configuration of this interface, you can use `-InterfaceAlias` with the `Get-NetIPAddress` cmdlet as follows:

The preceding command output shows that the Ethernet interface currently has `192.168.10.9/24` as its IPv4 address.

You can add a second IP address to the interface by executing the following command:

```
New-NetIPAddress -InterfaceAlias "Ethernet 2" -IPAddress  192.168.10.20 `
-AddressFamily IPv4 -PrefixLength 24
```

The resulting command output looks like this:

By using `-InterfaceAlias` with the `Get-NetIPAddress` cmdlet again, you can verify that the command accomplishes the desired result.

```
Get-NetIPAddress -InterfaceAlias Ethernet
```

When the command is executed, all the information of `Ethernet 2` will be listed out. It looks like the following:

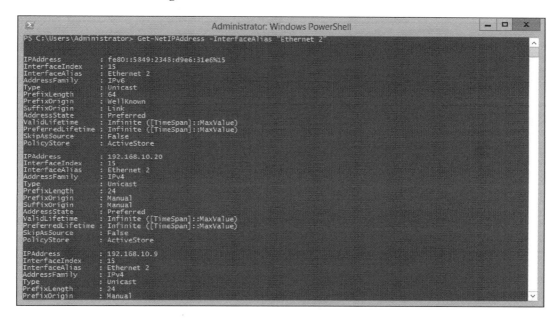

Viewing the **Advanced TCP/IP Settings** window for the interface from the **Network Connections** folder confirms the result. We can see two IP addresses have been added to the interface. It is shown in the following screenshot:

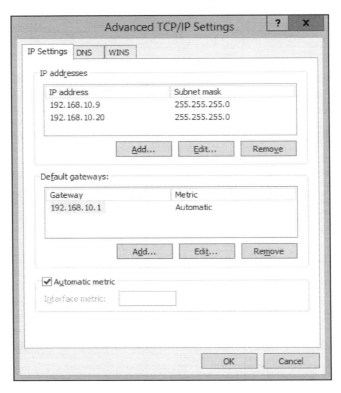

You can enable and disable bindings on a network adapter by using Windows PowerShell. For example, start by using the Get-NetAdapterBinding cmdlet to display the bindings for the specified interface:

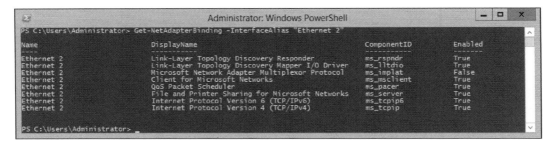

To disable a specific binding such as QoS Packet Scheduler, you can use the `Disable-NetAdapterBinding` cmdlet as follows:

```
Disable-NetAdapterBinding -Name "Ethernet 2" -ComponentID ms_lltdio
```

You can use the `Enable-NetAdapterBinding` cmdlet to re-enable the binding.

You can disable a specific network adapter or even all network adapters using Windows PowerShell. For example, the following command disables the adapter named `Ethernet 2`.

```
Disable-NetAdapter -Name "Ethernet 2" -Confirm:$false
```

To disable all network adapters on the server, you can use the following command:

```
Disable-NetAdapter -Name *
```

Note that all remote connectivity with the server will be lost if you do this. To enable any network adapters that are disabled, you can use the `Enable-NetAdapter` cmdlet.

Managing Group Policy with PowerShell

While most administrative tasks for Group Policy can be most easily performed by using GUI tools such as the GPMC and the Group Policy Management Editor, some tasks can also be performed using Windows PowerShell. You can use the Windows PowerShell Group Policy cmdlets to automate many of the same tasks for domain-based **Group Policy objects** (GPOs) that you perform in the user interface by using the **Group Policy Management Console (GPMC)**.

The Group Policy cmdlets can only be run on a computer that has the Group Policy Management Console installed. You can use Windows PowerShell to configure and manage Group Policy in an Active Directory environment based on Windows Server 2012.

Importing a GroupPolicy module

You can import the cmdlets manually by running the following commands from Windows PowerShell:

```
Import-Module ServerManager
Add-WindowsFeature GPMC
Get-Command -Module GroupPolicy
```

The following screenshot shows that we have imported a `GroupPolicy` module and checked all the commands of the module:

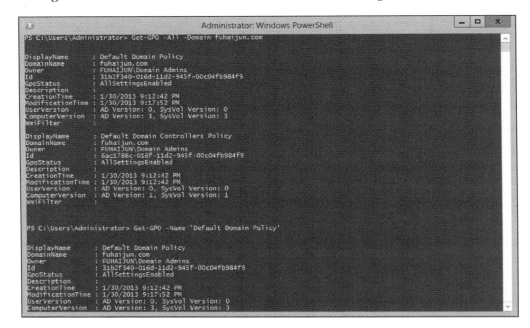

We can use the `Get-GPO` cmdlet to get one GPO or all the GPOs in a domain. The usage of the `Get-GPO` cmdlet is as shown in the following screenshot:

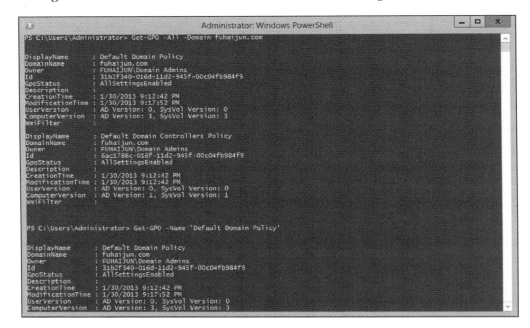

Creating GPOs with PowerShell

Only domain administrators, enterprise administrators, and members of the Group Policy Creator Owners group can create GPOs. These users must run Windows PowerShell in an elevated state. You can use the `Domain` parameter to explicitly specify the domain for this cmdlet. If you do not specify the domain explicitly, the cmdlet uses the default domain. The **default domain** is the domain that is used to access network resources by the security context under which the current session is running. This domain is typically the domain of the user that is running the session. For example, the domain of the user who has started the session by opening Windows PowerShell from the **Program Files** menu, or the domain of a user that is specified in a `runas` command. However, computer startup and shutdown scripts run under the context of the `LocalSystem` account. The `LocalSystem` account is a built-in local account, and it accesses network resources under the context of the computer account. Therefore, when this cmdlet is run from a startup or shutdown script, the default domain is the domain to which the computer is connected.

Next, you can use the `New-GPO` cmdlet to create a new GPO as follows:

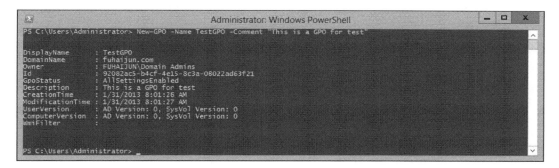

This command creates a GPO in the domain of the user. The GPO is created with the specified comment.

Managing IIS with PowerShell

The web server management module (`WebAdministration`) for Windows PowerShell, which includes IIS cmdlets, can let you manage the configuration and operation of IIS. It implements a namespace model that includes application pools, websites, web applications, and virtual directories.

In Windows Server 2012, the Windows PowerShell icon is pinned to the task bar by default. However, you must start Windows PowerShell only once to make the **Import all modules** task appear. You can manually add the IIS module to the instance of Windows PowerShell that you have opened by using the following command at the PowerShell prompt:

```
Import-Module WebAdministration
```

If we want to operate the IIS objects, we must import the WebAdministration module. The following screenshot shows how to import this module and shows all the websites in this computer:

In the preceding example, we import the WebAdministration module and list the websites on the current computer. The IIS module implements a virtual drive named IIS. The root virtual folders are AppPools, websites, and SslBindings. In the AppPools folder, runtime data such as the current operation of the worker processes, application domains, and requests can be found. The sites folder contains website folders, as well as application procedures and virtual directories.

To use the Windows PowerShell cmdlets for IIS, you must be a member of the IIS Administrators group or you must have been delegated the appropriate authority.

Creating a new website

We can create a new IIS website by using the New-Website cmdlet with the settings specified in the parameter values.

```
New-Website -Name testsite -Port 80 -HostHeader testsite -PhysicalPath
c:\temp
```

The following screenshot shows that we create a website named testsite and specify the physical path as c:\temp.

Meanwhile, we can find the websites in the IIS Manager as shown in the following screenshot:

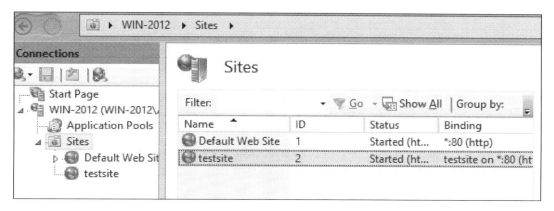

Modifying IIS binding

Sometimes, after we create a website, in order to adapt to a change of environment, we need to modify a property of an existing IIS site binding. We can execute the Set-WebBinding cmdlet to modify IIS binding as follows:

```
Set-WebBinding -Name 'Default Web Site' -BindingInformation "*:80:"
-PropertyName Port -Value 1234
```

In the preceding example, we change the setting for the Port property for the default website from 80 to 1234.

Creating an FTP site

We can create a new FTP site using the New-WebFtpSite cmdlet. FTP 7 or later must be installed for this cmdlet to function successfully.

```
New-WebFtpSite -Name testFtpSite -Port 21 -PhysicalPath c:\test
-HostHeader mySite -IPAddress 127.0.0.1
```

When this command is executed, an FTP site named `testFtpSite` will be created. The FTP site will listen on port 21 and the physical path is `c:\test`. This is shown in the following screenshot:

Creating a virtual directory

A virtual directory simply designates a folder that appears in a path but is not actually a subfolder of the preceding folder in the path in IIS. Virtual directories present a unified virtual view of user information from multiple systems so that it appears to reside in a single system. In PowerShell, we can use the `New-WebVirtualDirectory` cmdlet to create a virtual directory. The example is as follows:

```
New-WebVirtualDirectory -Site "Default Web Site" -Name TestVDir
-PhysicalPath c:\inetpub\virtualdir
```

The example creates a new virtual directory named `TestVDir` on the default website.

Creating a WebAppPool

Application pools are used to separate sets of IIS worker processes that share the same configuration and application boundaries. Application pools are used to isolate our web applications for better security, reliability, availability, and performance and keep them running without impacting each other. The worker process serves as the process boundary that separates each application pool so that when one worker process or application is having an issue or recycles, other applications or worker processes are not affected. We can use the `New-WebAppPool` cmdlet for creating a new application pool as shown in the following example:

```
New-WebAppPool MyAppPool
```

This example creates a new IIS application pool named `MyAppPool`.

Backing up and restoring WebConfiguration

In order to mitigate mistake we make when we modify the IIS configuration, we can back up the configuration of IIS into a configuration file. If any errors occurred, we can restore the backup configuration.

The following example demonstrates how to create a backup of your IIS configuration in a folder named `MyIISConfigBackup`.

```
Backup-WebConfiguration -Name MyIISConfigBackup
```

We can also use the `Get-WebConfigurationBackup` cmdlet to get a list of available IIS configuration backups.

```
Get-WebConfigurationBackup
```

Restoring the IIS configuration backup is very simple. We can use the `Restore-WebConfiguration` cmdlet with the `-Name` parameter to restore a configuration file named `MyIISConfigBackup`, as shown in the following example:

```
Restore-WebConfiguration -Name MyIISConfigBackup
```

When the IIS configuration backup file is no longer needed, we can use the `Remove-WebConfiguration` cmdlet with the `-Name` parameter to remove it.

```
Remove-WebConfiguration -Name MyIISConfigBackup
```

All the examples of this section are shown in the following screenshot:

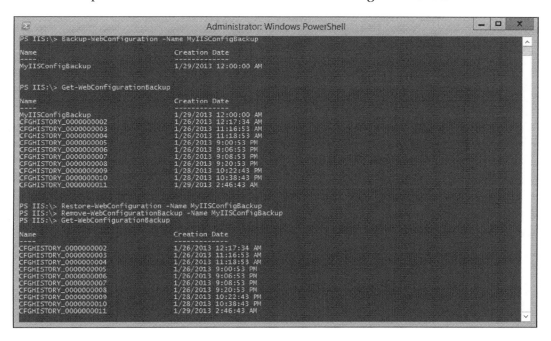

In the preceding screenshot, we have demonstrated the maintenance process of an IIS configuration backup file.

Managing a DNS server using PowerShell

You can manage Windows Server 2012 DNS servers using Windows PowerShell. Common DNS server management tasks are adding resource records to zones, configuring forwarders, configuring root hints, and so on.

For example, let's view a list of zones on a DNS server that is also a domain controller for the `fuhaijun.com` domain:

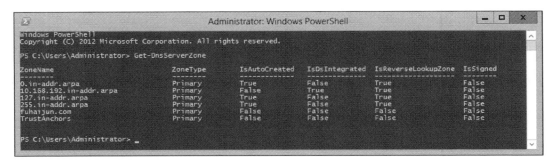

To view a list of resource records of type A (address) in the `fuhaijun.com` zone, we can pipe the output of the `Get-DnsServerResourceRecord` cmdlet into the `Where-Object` cmdlet as follows:

To add a new A resource record for a test server, you can use the `Add-DnsServerResourceRecordA` cmdlet as follows:

```
Add-DnsServerResourceRecordA -IPv4Address 192.168.10.1 -Name gateway
-ZoneName fuhaijun.com
```

You can also add other types of resource records such as PTR, CN, or MX records using the `Add-DnsServerResourceRecordA` cmdlet, by replacing A with the record type, for example, `Add-DnsServerResourceRecordPTR`, `Add-DnsServerResourceRecordCN`, and `Add-DnsServerResourceRecordMX`. And you can use the `Remove-DnsServerResourceRecord` cmdlet to remove resource records from a zone.

When we set up a DNS server, we can use the `Test-DNSServer` cmdlet to verify whether it was configured correctly or not. As we all know, DNS Server 8.8.8.8 is a server for the Google Public DNS service. Whereas, `192.168.10.9` is a DNS Server I installed in my private network. And `192.168.10.10` is just a common workstation, not a DNS server. We can use the `Test-DNSServer` cmdlet to check the three preceding IP addressed separately, as follows:

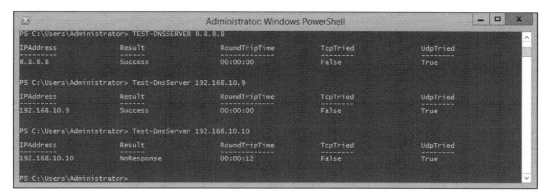

We can see the result of these commands; DNS servers return `Success` and the non-DNS Server returns `NoRespnse`. The `Test-DNSServer` cmdlet can check whether a server is a valid DNS server.

Managing Hyper-V with PowerShell

Microsoft Hyper-V, known as Windows Server Virtualization, is a native hypervisor that enables platform virtualization on an x86-64 system. Microsoft Hyper-V and VMware ESX Server are based on the hardware support Bare-Metal virtualization products. Their biggest difference is that Microsoft Hyper-V adopts a microkernel structure, and the ESX Server is a product of a single kernel.

The main characteristic of a single kernel is that the hardware driver present in the Hypervisor layer is shared by all virtual machines on the Hypervisor. When a virtual machine OS needs to access the hardware, it uses the Hypervisor driver model. This kind of single-kernel Hypervisor can provide very good performance, but it has defects in safety and compatibility. Due to the drivers and some third-party code running in a very sensitive area, the model has a large attack surface. Another problem is stability. The model relies on shared drivers, so any bug will affect all of the virtual machines. In addition, you also require the Hypervisor to support all of the drivers, and this causes this layer to be relatively large in size.

The Hyper-V adopts a microkernel structure; it is a thin Hypervisor. Because it does not need third-party drivers, Hyper-V has the advantage on volume. In addition, since the microkernel volume is low, the running efficiency is very high. A driver runs in each partition within the virtual machine OS to be able to access the hardware directly by using the Hypervisor. It makes each partition independent of the others, so it has better security and stability.

The Hyper-V technology provides an environment that you can use to create and manage virtual machines and their resources. Each virtual machine is an isolated, virtualized computer system that is capable of running its own operating system. This allows you to run multiple operating systems at the same time on the same physical computer. In the following sections, we will introduce how to manage Hyper-V with PowerShell.

Installing Hyper-V on Windows Server 2012

We can use the Server Manager from the control panel to add the Hyper-V role. On the desktop, right-click on **PowerShell** in the task bar, and then click on **Run as Administrator**. In Windows PowerShell 3.0, there is no need to import the Server Manager cmdlet module into the PowerShell session before running cmdlets that are part of the module. A module is automatically imported the first time you run a cmdlet that is part of the module. We can run the Get-WindowsFeature cmdlet to verify installation, as shown in the following screenshot:

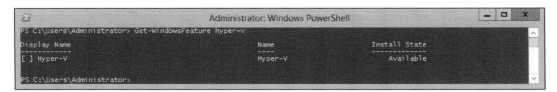

We can see Hyper-V has not been installed. We can then use the Install-WindowsFeature Hyper-V cmdlet to install Hyper-V, as shown in the following screenshot:

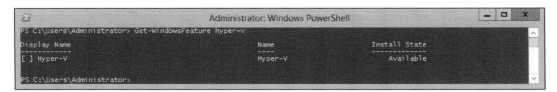

After you add Hyper-V to your computer, a restart is required to complete the process. This restart is necessary to start the Windows Hypervisor and the Virtual Machine Management service. After that occurs, you can create and run virtual machines on this computer.

Creating a virtual machine

If you want to create a virtual machine that can be accessed by networking, you must create a virtual hard disk first, and then create a virtual machine. Finally, connect the virtual network adapter to a virtual switch. The Hyper-V module supplies the needed cmdlet for our operations.

We can create a virtual hard disk by using the New-VHD cmdlet with the following parameters:

- -Path: Specifies the path of the virtual hard disk
- -ParentPath: Specifies the path to the parent of the differencing disk to be created
- -SizeBytes: The maximum size, in bytes, of the virtual hard disk to be created

For example, we can create a VHDX-format differencing virtual hard disk with a parent path of D:\vhd\webserver.vhdx, as shown in the following screenshot:

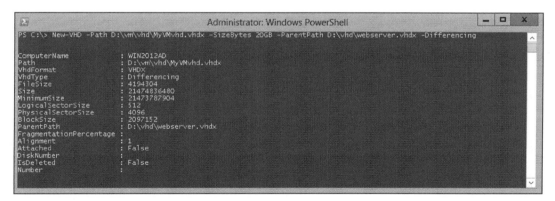

We can create a virtual machine by using the New-VM cmdlet with the following parameters:

- -Name: Specifies the name of the new virtual machine
- -Path: Specifies the path of the virtual machine

- -VHDPath: Specifies the path to the parent of the differencing disk to be created

- -MemoryStartupBytes: Specifies the amount of memory, in megabytes, to assign to the virtual machine

For example, we can create a virtual machine named MyVM with 2 GB of memory and an existing virtual hard disk that uses the VHDX format connected to it, as shown in the following screenshot:

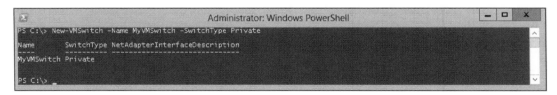

Starting and stopping a virtual machine

We can start or stop the virtual machine MyVM by using the Start-VM or Stop-VM cmdlet. The parameter -Name is the name of the virtual machine.

```
Start-VM -Name MyVM
```

```
Stop-VM -Name MyVM
```

Modifying a virtual machine

Sometimes, we need to add a virtual switch on a Hyper-V host. The New-VMSwitch cmdlet is used to add a virtual switch. The parameter SwitchType specifies the type of switch to be created. The allowed values are Internet and Private, just as shown in the following screenshot:

```
Administrator: Windows PowerShell                          _ □ x
PS C:\> New-VMSwitch -Name MyVMSwitch -SwitchType Private

Name        SwitchType NetAdapterInterfaceDescription
----        ---------- ------------------------------
MyVMSwitch  Private

PS C:\> _
```

Meanwhile, we can create a VMNetworkAdapter and add it to a specified virtual machine connecting to the virtual switch by using the Add-VMNetworkAdapter cmdlet.

```
Add-VMNetworkAdapter -VMName MyVM -SwitchName MyVMSwitch
```

If we want to add a new hard drive for a virtual machine, we can use the `Add-VMHardDiskDrive` cmdlet with the `-VMName` parameter for specifying the VM's name and the `-Path` parameter for the hard drive to be saved.

```
Add-VMHardDiskDrive -VMName MyVM -Path D:\vm\vhd\disk1.vhdx
```

We can add a DVD drive to a virtual machine when we need to install a new guest OS for it by using the `Add-VMDvdDrive` cmdlet. The `-VMName` parameter specifies the virtual machine. The `-Path` parameter specifies the location of the ISO image that will be mounted to the virtual machine.

```
Add-VMDvdDrive -VMName MyVM -Path D:\CentOS6.3_KS1-x86_64.iso
```

Operating a virtual machine snapshot

A virtual machine snapshot captures the state, data, and hardware configuration of a virtual machine. Snapshots provide a fast and easy way to revert a virtual machine to a previous state.

We can create a snapshot of a virtual machine by using the `Checkpoint-VM` cmdlet.

```
Checkpoint-VM -Name MyVM -SnapshotName BeforeInstall
```

We can retrieve a list of the snapshots of a virtual machine by using the `Get-VMSnapshot` cmdlet, as shown in the following screenshot:

We can restore a virtual machine snapshot by using the `Restore-VMSnapshot` cmdlet, as shown in the following screenshot:

We can delete a snapshot or snapshot tree by using the `Remove-VMSnapshot` cmdlet.

```
Remove-VMSnapshot -Name BeforeInstall -VMName MyVM
```

Managing AppLocker with PowerShell

AppLocker is a new feature used for Software Restriction Policies. AppLocker contains new capabilities and extensions that allow users to create rules to allow or deny applications' permission to run based on the unique identities of files, and to specify which users or groups can run those applications. Of course, you can create and manage AppLocker rules by using Windows PowerShell cmdlets.

Microsoft supplies an AppLocker module, which contains five cmdlets that are used to help create, test, maintain, and troubleshoot an AppLocker policy. To edit or update a GPO by using the AppLocker cmdlet, you must have the Edit Setting permission. By default, members of the Domain Admins group, the Enterprise Admins group, and the Group Policy Creator Owners group have this permission. To perform tasks by using the Local Security policy snap-in, you must be a member of the Local Administrators group on the computer.

Importing the AppLocker PowerShell module

To use the AppLocker cmdlet, you must first import the AppLocker module by using the following command at the PowerShell prompt:

```
Import-Module AppLocker
```

Retrieving application information

Now, after importing the AppLocker module, you need to retrieve application information for preparing to deny others access. For this purpose, we use the `Get-AppLockerFileInformation` cmdlet with the following parameters:

- `-Path`: List of paths to the files from which the file information is retrieved.
- `-Directory`: Defines the directory containing the files from which the file information is retrieved. To search all subfolders and files in the directory, include the `Recurse` parameter.
- `-FileType`: Defines the generic file type to find. The file type options are `exe`, `secript`, `WindowsInstaller`, or `dll`.

For example, we can get the file information for the `mspaint.exe` file at `C:\Windows\System32\`.

We can get the file information for all of the executable files in the
`C:\Windows\System32` directory, as shown in the following screenshot:

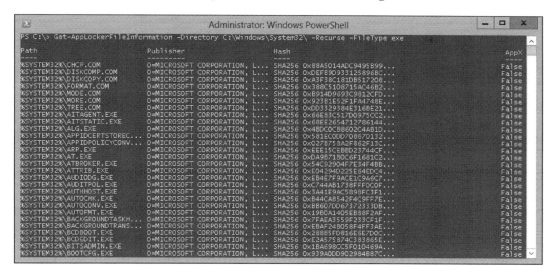

Retrieving an AppLocker policy

Before we modify the AppLocker policy, we should first get the AppLocker policy
from the local GPO. We can use the `Get-AppLockerPolicy` cmdlet with the
following parameters:

- `-Local`: Gets the AppLocker policy from the local GPO.

- `-Domain`: Gets the AppLocker policy from the GPO that is specified by the
  path in the LDAP parameter.

- `-LDAP`: This is the LDAP path of the Group Policy object. It must specify a
  unique GPO.

- `-XML`: Specifies that the AppLocker policy be output as an XML-formatted
  string.

For example, we can get the local AppLocker policy as an `AppLockerPolicy` object,
as shown in the following screenshot:

We can also get the AppLocker policy of the unique GPO specified by the LDAP path as an `AppLockerPolicy` object.

Setting an AppLocker policy

We can set the AppLocker policy for the specified GPO. If no **Lightweight Directory Access Protocol (LDAP)** is specified, the local GPO is the default. The `Set-AppLockerPolicy` cmdlet has the following parameters:

- `-XMLPolicy`: Specifies the path where the AppLocker policy XML file is saved.
- `-PolicyObject`: Specifies the AppLocker object that contains the AppLocker policy.
- `-LDAP`: The LDAP path of the Group Policy object. If this parameter is not specified, the local AppLocker policy is set.
- `-Merge`: If the `-Merge` parameter is used, rules in the specified AppLocker policy will be merged with the AppLocker rules in the target GPO specified in the LDAP path. The merged policies will remove rules with duplicate rule IDs. If the `-Merge` parameter is not specified, the new policy will overwrite the existing policy.

For example, we can set the local AppLocker policy to the policy specified in `D:\Policy.xml`.

```
Get-AppLockerPolicy -Local -Xml -XMLPolicy C:\Policy.xml
```

We can also set the GPO specified in the LDAP path to contain the AppLocker policy that is specified in `C:\Policy.xml`.

```
Set-AppLockerPolicy -XMLPolicy C:\Policy.xml -LDAP "LDAP://Win2012AD.
fuhaijun.com/CN={31B2F340-016D-11D2-945F-00C04FB984F9},CN=Policies,CN=Sys
tem,DC=fuhaijun,DC=com"
```

Generating rules for a given user or group

We can use a list of file information to automatically generate rules for a given user or group. It can generate rules based on publisher, hash, or path information. We can use the `Get-AppLockerFileInformation` cmdlet to create the list of file information, and then pass the information to the `New-AppLockerPolicy` cmdlet. The `New-AppLockerPolicy` cmdlet with the following parameters creates a new AppLocker policy from a list of file information:

- `-FileInformation`: A file can contain publisher, path, and hash information. Some information may be missing, such as publisher information for an unsigned file.

- `-RuleType`: Specifies the type of rules to create from the file information.

- `-RuleNamePrefix`: Specifies a name to add as a prefix to each rule that is created.

- `-User`: Defines the user or group that rules are applied to. You can provide the value in one of the following formats:
    - DNS user name (`domain\username`)
    - User Principal Name (`username@domain.com`)
    - SAM user name (`username`)

- `-Optimize`: Instructs that similar rules should be grouped together.

For example, we can create an AppLocker policy that allows rules for all of the executable files in `C:\Windows\System32`. The policy contains publisher rules for those files with publisher information and hash rules for those that do not.

Testing the AppLocker policy against a fileset

After you create AppLockerPolicy rules, you can use the `Test-AppLockerPolicy` cmdlet to test whether a specified list of files is allowed to run or not on the local computer for a specified user. The `Test-AppLockerPolicy` cmdlet has following parameters:

- `-PolicyObject`: Specifies the policy object that contains the AppLocker policy

- -Path: Specifies the list of file paths to test
- -User: Defines the user or group to be used for testing the rules in the specified AppLocker policy
- -Filter: Filters the output by the policy decision for each input file

We can use the AppLocker policy in C:\Policy.xml to test whether or not mspaint.exe and taskmgr.exe are allowed to run for users who are members of the Everyone group, as shown in the following screenshot:

Summary

Using Windows PowerShell commands in Windows Server 2012 for basic administration and networking tasks can save a lot of time. This is true not only because you can script the tasks for application on multiple computers, but you can also save time by not having to navigate through frequently complex **user interface (UI)** dialog boxes when you use PowerShell to configure individual computers.

In this chapter, we discussed how to add roles or features and manage Group Policy. We also discussed the module extension manager, IIS, DNS Server, Hyper-V, and AppLocker.

DevOps is a modern term and there is some disagreement about what it demands, but at the heart it is all about making changes safely through automation and bridging the gap between operators and developers. There is a lot to do in this area, but Windows Server 2012 and PowerShell 3.0 have made excellent progress towards accomplishing those goals. PowerShell won't be the only tool in your automatic DevOps toolbox, but it should be in every efficient developer's toolbox.

In the next chapter, we will take a look at the usage of Windows PowerShell in managing and configuring unified communication (UC) components, especially Microsoft Exchange Server, Lync Server, and Office 365.

8
Managing Unified Communication Environments with PowerShell

Unified communication (UC) has become one of the most important components of any organization, regardless of the size of the business, not only because of the integration between different components but also because of the added value for end users that can stay connected to the business, and be reachable and in control. The term unified communication from a technological perspective always refers to e-mails, **Instant Messaging (IM)**, voice message, **Voice over IP (VoIP)**, and a lot of other amazing technologies that everyone uses on a daily basis.

Today, a lot of vendors in the market are providing comprehensive unified communication solutions for different types of business sectors. However, in this chapter the focus will be on Microsoft unified communication on-premise and cloud-hosted solutions, and how Windows PowerShell can be used to configure and manage them easily.

This chapter will discuss how to start using Windows PowerShell to perform the basic and advanced administration tasks for Exchange Server, Lync Server, and Office 365.

In this chapter we will cover:

- What Exchange Management Shell is
- How to use PowerShell to do Exchange Management tasks
- What Lync Management Shell is
- How to use PowerShell to do Lync Management tasks
- Windows PowerShell with Office 365 and Exchange Online Service

What Exchange Management Shell is

Exchange Management Shell (EMS) is a normal Windows PowerShell console that runs a set of Exchange-related Windows PowerShell snap-ins and cmdlets that are loaded when Exchange Management Shell is started up. It also shows a basic and quick guidance for using it and some effective daily Exchange Management Shell tips each time you open it.

EMS is the Windows PowerShell interface that allows you to easily perform Exchange Server administrative tasks, such as creating mailboxes, configuring mail flow policies, and managing security permissions in addition to being able to execute normal Windows PowerShell cmdlets and functions.

On having a deeper look at EMS shortcut properties, you will obviously notice that Exchange Management Shell is nothing more than running a `powershell.exe` file with an Exchange script.

The Exchange script loaded by Exchange Management Shell is located at **%SystemDrive%** | **Program Files** | **Microsoft** | **Exchange Server** | **V15** | **Bin** | **RemoteExchange.ps1**.

Exchange Management Shell tips

- Use the `Get-ExCommand` cmdlet to list the Exchange Server cmdlets and functions only
- Use the `Get-Tip` cmdlet to get a new Exchange tip
- Use the `Get-ExBlog` cmdlet to open the Exchange Server team blog

How to make Windows PowerShell understand Exchange Server cmdlets

Launching EMS is a quick and nice way to jump into the Exchange PowerShell environment and start doing things. However, sometimes you may want to write a long, complex script with a lot of debugging, comments, and breakpoints so that you can move from the traditional Windows PowerShell blue console to Windows PowerShell **Integrated Scripting Environment** (**ISE**) for a better scripting experience. Moreover, you may want to bring the Exchange environment to the ISE so a couple of options are available in order to achieve this goal.

Option 1 – do it like EMS

In this method, we will load into Windows PowerShell ISE the cmdlets and functions related to Exchange Server, by running the RemoteExchange.ps1 script inside the PowerShell ISE and then executing the Connect-ExchangeServer –Auto cmdlet to connect to the Exchange Server in your organization.

Option 2 – loading Exchange Server snap-ins

In this method, you will load the snap-ins related to Exchange Server directly into Windows PowerShell ISE without using the `RemoteExchange.ps1` script. During Exchange Server installation, the Exchange DLLs and snap-ins are installed and registered in the system.

You can get a list of the Windows PowerShell snap-ins available in the current PowerShell session using the `Get-PSSnapin` cmdlet, with the `-Registered` parameter used to display the list of registered snap-ins even if they are not added or available in the current Windows PowerShell session. In order to get the list of PowerShell snap-ins registered by Exchange Server, just filter the cmdlet results by the word `Exchange`. And the wildcard symbol * is used to idetifiy all snap-ins that contain the word `Exchange`.

```
#Get list of Exchange available PowerShell Snap-ins
PS> Get-PSSnapin -Registered *Exchange*
```

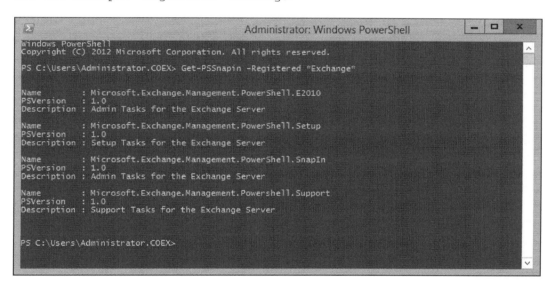

Now after getting the list of available Exchange PowerShell snap-ins, we need to load it into the current PowerShell session using the `Add-PSSnapin` cmdlet.

Since the Exchange had registered four snap-ins, to quickly load them into Windows PowerShell, use the pipeline trick to get the list of Exchange PowerShell snap-ins and add them directly.

```
#Add Exchange Server PowerShell Snap-ins
PS> Get-PSSnapin –Registered *Exchange* | Add-PSSnapin
```

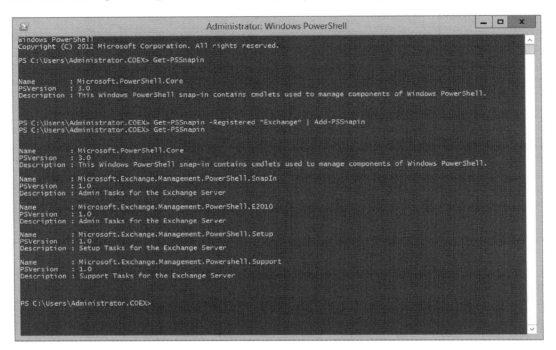

Managing Exchange using PowerShell Remoting

In *Chapter 3, Using PowerShell Remoting*, we had a long discussion about Windows PowerShell Remoting and how PowerShell uses different ways to allow you to connect to a remote computer using a remote shell. For Exchange Server, we use implicit remoting to connect to the **Client Access Server (CAS)** using a virtual directory called PowerShell in order to get the Exchange cmdlets and load them on the local computer.

To connect to Exchange using implicit remoting, perform the following steps:

1. Create a new PowerShell Remoting session using the `New-PSSession` cmdlet.

2. Import the created session to the local computer using the `Import-PSSession` cmdlet.

   Use the following script:

   ```
   #Create new implicit remoting session
   ```

   ```
   $Session = New-PSSession -ConfigurationName Microsoft.Exchange
   -ConnectionUri "http://Exch.Contoso.local/PowerShell" -Credential
   (Get-Credential) -Authentication Kerberos
   ```

   ```
   #Import the PowerShell remoting Session
   ```

   ```
   Import-PSSession -Session $Session
   ```

In order to disconnect the Exchange remoting session, use the `Remove-PSSession` cmdlet:

```
#Remove Exchange Remoting Session
```

```
PS > Remove-PSSession -Session $Session
```

Getting started with Exchange scripting

In this section, we will help you get started with Exchange Server scripting and automation using a set of Windows PowerShell scenarios and examples.

Scenario 1 – creating multiple mailboxes from CSV file

In this scenario, you are a messaging administrator who want to create multiple exchange mailboxes using a CSV file that contains new employees' information sent by the HR department.

1. Import the CSV file using the `Import-CSV` cmdlet, and then store the imported data in a defined variable.

2. Define a variable called `OU` to store the **organizational unit (OU)** location information, and then prompt the user to enter the OU name.

3. Define a variable called `Domain` to store the domain suffix information, and then prompt the user to enter the domain suffix.

4. Use the `ForEach` loop to iterate over the list of users imported from the CSV file.

5. Use the `New-Mailbox` cmdlet within the `ForEach` loop defined in the previous step to create a new user account in the active directory, and then create a mailbox for this user account.

Use the following script:

```
#Import a file named "UsersList.CSV" and save it in variable called
"$UsersList"
$UsersList = Import-Csv C:\UsersList.csv

#Prompt the user to enter the name of the OU that will store the new
user accounts (e.g. IT)
$OU = Read-Host -Prompt "Enter the name of the OU..."

#Prompt the user to enter the Domain Suffix (e.g. Contoso.local)
$Domain = Read-Host -Prompt "Enter the domain suffix..."

#Iterating over the $UsersList to create an account for each user
ForEach($User in $UsersList)
{
    New-Mailbox -FirstName $User.Firstname `
    -LastName $User.Lastname `
    -DisplayName ($User.Firstname + " " + $User.Lastname) `
    -Name ($User.Firstname + " " + $User.Lastname) `
    -Alias $User.Alias `
    -SamAccountName $User.Alias `
    -UserPrincipalName "$User.Alias@$Domain" `
    -Password (ConvertTo-SecureString -String "P@ssw0rd" `-AsPlainText
-Force) `
    -OrganizationalUnit $OU `
    -ResetPasswordOnNextLogon $true
}
```

Scenario 2 – creating a shared mailbox

In this scenario, you are messaging administrator who receive a request from the sales team asking for a shared mailbox for the department so that any member of the sales team can have the ability to read, and also reply to customer inquiries received on this alias.

1. Create a shared mailbox using the `New-Mailbox` cmdlet with the `-Shared` switch.

2. Create a new distribution group for the sales team using the New-DistributionGroup cmdlet, and grant it access on the shared mailbox created in the previous step so that any member of the team can get access to the shared mailbox without having to having to manually assign, send, and receive rights for each user. The distribution group type should be Security to be able to assign security permissions on it.

3. Assign a FullAccess permission to the group created in the previous step on the shared mailbox using the Add-MailboxPermission cmdlet to grant the group members the ability to access the mailbox.

4. Assign a SendAs permission using the Add-RecipientPermission cmdlet to allow group members to send e-mails (reply) from the shared mailbox alias.

Use the following script:

```
#Enter the alias of Shared Mailbox to be created
$MBalias = Read-Host -Prompt "Enter Shared Mailbox name..."

#Enter the alias of Distribution Group to be access to Shared mailbox
$DGalias = Read-Host -Prompt "Enter Distribution Group name..."

#Create a new shared mailbox
New-Mailbox -Name $MBalias -Shared

#Create a new security distribution group
New-DistributionGroup -Type Security -Name $DGalias -SamAccountName
$DGalias

#Assign FullAccess rights on the shared mailbox to the distribution group
Add-MailboxPermission -Identity $MBalias -User $DGalias -AccessRights
FullAccess -InheritanceType All

#Assign SendAs rights to disribution groupn on the shared mailbox
Add-RecipientPermission $MBalias -Trustee $DGalias -AccessRights
"SendAs"
```

Scenario 3 – creating a resource (room/equipment) mailbox

In this scenario, you are messaging administrators who receive a request from the corporate facilities team asking for help in automating the process of making meeting room and equipment reservations.

1. Create a resource mailbox using the `New-Mailbox` cmdlet with the `-Room` or `-Equipment` parameter to define the type of resource mailbox you want to create, that is, either `Room` or `Equipment`.

2. Automate a resource calendar reservation using the `Set-CalendarProcessing` cmdlet with the following group of parameters:

   ○ `-AutomateProcessing`: To allow auto acceptance of a resource reservation

   ○ `-MaximumDurationInMinutes`: To define the maximum duration for a single resource reservation

   ○ `-AddOrganizerToSubject`: To show the organizer's name in the reservation subject

   ○ `-EnableResponseDetails`: To send a detailed response for resource reservation acceptance or rejection

   ○ `-ProcessExtenralMeetingMessages`: To define whether the resource can be reserved by external users or not

Use the following script:

```
#Enter the name of the resource mailbox
$Mailbox = Read-Host -Prompt "Enter the name of the resource
mailbox..."

#Enter the type of required resource
Do {$type = Read-Host -Prompt "Enter the type of the resource (1 for
Room, 2 for Equipment)"}
While (($type -ne 1) -and ($type -ne 2))

#Create resource mailbox with a selected type
If ($type -eq 1)
{New-Mailbox -Name $Mailbox -Room}
elseif($type -eq 2)
{New-Mailbox -Name $Mailbox -Equipment}

#Define resource reservation
Set-CalendarProcessing -Identity $Mailbox -AutomateProcessing
AutoAccept -MaximumDurationInMinutes 120 -AddOrganizerToSubject $true
-EnableResponseDetails $true -ProcessExternalMeetingMessages $false
```

Scenario 4 – creating a distribution group

In this scenario, you are messaging administrators who want to create a distribution group for corporate departments, to make the communication between team members and corporate departments faster and easier.

1. Import the CSV file using the `Import-CSV` cmdlet, select the column containing the department information using the `Select-Object` cmdlet, and then group the department rows in department column using the `Group-Object` cmdlet in order to unify the duplicate values.

2. Select the column that contains the results of departments' column filtering and grouping using the `Select-Object` cmdlet, then store the imported data in a defined variable.

3. Use the `ForEach` loop to iterate over the list of departments extracted from the CSV file.

4. Use the `New-DistributionGroup` cmdlet within the `ForEach` loop defined in the previous step to create a new distribution group for each department.

5. Use the `ForEach` loop to iterate over the list of users extracted from the CSV file.

6. Use the `Update-DistributionGroupMember` cmdlet to add each user to the related department's distribution group.

Use the following script:

```
#Import a file named "UsersList.CSV", select and group the department,
save it in variable called "$DepartmentsList"
$UsersInfo = Import-Csv C:\UsersList.csv
$DepartmentsList = $UsersInfo | Select Department | Group Department |
Select Name

#Iterating over the $DepartmentsList to create a distribbution group
for each department.
ForEach($Department in $DepartmentsList)
{
    New-DistributionGroup -Type Distribution -Name $Department.Name
-SamAccountName $Department.Name.Trim() -DisplayName $Department.Name
-MemberJoinRestriction Open -OrganizationalUnit "DGs"
}

#Iterating over the $UsersInfo to add each user to the related a
distribbution group according to department.
ForEach($User in $UsersInfo)
{
    Update-DistributionGroupMember -Identity $User.Department -Members
$User.Alias -Confirm:$false
}
```

Scenario 5 – defining a MailTip for a distribution group

In this scenario, you are messaging administrators who want to add a MailTip for the technical support department's distribution group that is asking the users to check the IT support portal before opening an incident request.

1. Use the `Set-DistributionGroup` cmdlet to add a MailTip to the required distribution group.

2. Use the `-MailTip` parameter to define the MailTip text.

Use the following script:

```
#Enter the Distribution Group Name/Alias
$Alias = Read-Host -Prompt "Enter the Distribution Group Name/
Alias..."

#Enter the MailTip Text
$TipText = Read-Host -Prompt "Enter the MailTip Test..."

#Update the DG with the MailTip
Set-DistributionGroup -Identity $Alias -MailTip $TipText
```

Scenario 6 – creating a dynamic distribution group

Unlike a normal distribution group, a dynamic distribution group does not have criteria for members but has one for membership. In other words, you do not have to add each member to the group, but you need to define filtering criteria so that each time you send an e-mail to this group, the Exchange server will query active directory using the mentioned criteria and send the message to the list retrieved from this query.

In this scenario, you are messaging administrators who want to create a dynamic distribution group for a Technology department that contains subdepartments, such as Software, Networking, Infrastructure, and Security.

1. Create a dynamic distribution group using the `New-DynamicDistributionGroup` cmdlet.

2. Use the `-IncludedRecipients` parameter to define the recipients to be included in this group.

3. Use the -RecipientContainer parameter to define the scope of the recipients based on their location in active directory.

4. Use the -ConditionalDepartment parameter to define which departments should be included in the group based on the department property of the user object in the active directory.

Use the following script:

```
New-DynamicDistributionGroup -Name "Information Technology Team"
-IncludedRecipients MailboxUsers -RecipientContainer "Contoso.local/
HQ/IT" -Alias "ITteam" -ConditionalDepartment "Software","Security","N
etworking","Infrastructure" -OrganizationalUnit "DDGs"
```

Scenario 7 – creating multiple mailbox databases from a CSV file

In this scenario, you are messaging administrators who want to minimize the administration efforts of Exchange mailbox databases. So, we create multiple Exchange mailbox databases for each department in our organization using a CSV file that contains new employee information sent by the HR department.

1. Import the CSV file using the Import-CSV cmdlet, select the column that contains department information using the Select-Object cmdlet, and then group the department column using the Group-Object cmdlet in order to unify the duplicate values.

2. Select the column that contains the results of the group of department columns using the Select-Object cmdlet, and then store the imported data in a variable.

3. Use the ForEach loop to iterate over the list of departments extracted from the CSV file.

4. Use the New-MailboxDatabase cmdlet within the ForEach loop defined in the previous step to create new mailbox databases.

5. Use the Mount-Database cmdlet within the ForEach loop to mount the database created in the previous step.

Use the following script:

```
#Import a file named "UsersList.CSV", select and group the department,
save it in variable called "$DepartmentsList"
$DepartmentsList = Import-Csv C:\UsersList.csv | Select Department |
Group Department | Select Name
```

```
#Iterating over the $DepartmentsList to create a database for each
department, and then mount it.
ForEach($Department in $DepartmentsList)

{
New-MailboxDatabase -Name $Department.Name -Server "EXCH-MB-01"
-EdbFilePath ("c:\Mailbox\" + "$Department.Name" + "\" + $Department.
Name + ".edb") | Mount-Database
}
```

Scenario 8 – exporting mailboxes to PST files

In this scenario, you are messaging administrators who want to back up the current Exchange Server environment using an alternative way that allows an easier and faster way to restore a single mailbox. So we will use Windows PowerShell to export every Exchange mailbox to PST files. For the purpose of achieving this task, we will use the New-MailboxExportRequest cmdlet.

1. In order to get the New-MailboxExportRequest cmdlet, we have to load the Microsoft.Exchange.Management.PowerShell.E2010 PowerShell snap-in.

2. Use the Get-MailboxDatabase cmdlet to retrieve a list of all the available Exchange mailbox databases.

3. Use the ForEach loop to iterate over the list of mailbox databases retrieved in the previous step.

4. Use the Test-Path and New-Item cmdlets to validate the existence of a folder for each database, and create it if it does not exist.

5. Use the Get-Mailbox cmdlet with the –Database parameter to retrieve a list of all the available Exchange mailboxes per database.

6. Use the ForEach loop to iterate over the list of mailboxes retrieved in the previous step.

7. Use the New-MailboxExportRequest cmdlet within the ForEach loop defined in the previous step to export each mailbox to the PST file.

8. Use the –IsArchive parameter with the New-MailboxExportRequest cmdlet to export the archived mailbox to the PST file.

Use the following script:

```
#Load Exchange PowerShell Snap-in
Add-PSSnapin Microsoft.Exchange.Management.PowerShell.E2010

#Iterating over the mailboxes database
ForEach ($DB in Get-MailboxDatabase)
{
    #check the existence of database backup folder
    if( !(Test-Path "\\EXCH\Backup\$DB") )
    {
#Create backup folder for database if not exist
New-Item -ItemType Directory -Name $DB.Name -Path "\\EXCH\Backup\"
}
    #Iterating over the mailboxes for in each database
      ForEach ($Mailbox in (Get-Mailbox -Database $DB.Name) )
      {
          #Export each mailbox into releated database folder
          New-MailboxExportRequest -Mailbox $Mailbox.Alias -FilePath
("\\EXCH\Backup\" + $DB.Name + "\" + $Mailbox.Alias + ".pst")
      }
}
```

Scenario 9 – importing a mailbox from PST files

In this scenario, you are messaging administrators who are trying to restore an Exchange database from a backup but facing a problem due to a corrupted backup file. So, we need to restore the mailboxes by importing the PST file for each mailbox. For the purpose of achieving this task, we will use the New-MailboxImportRequest cmdlet.

1. In order to get the New-MailboxImportRequest cmdlet, we have to load the Microsoft.Exchange.Management.PowerShell.E2010 PowerShell snap-in.

2. Use the Get-GetChilditem cmdlet to retrieve the list of all the available PST files.

3. Use the ForEach loop to iterate over the list of files retrieved in the previous step.

4. Use the New-MailboxImportRequest cmdlet within the ForEach loop defined in the previous step to import each mailbox to the PST file.

5. Use the –IsArchive parameter with the New-MailboxImportRequest cmdlet to import the PST file to the archived mailbox.

Use the following script:

```
#Load Exchange PowerShell Snap-in
Add-PSSnapin Microsoft.Exchange.Management.PowerShell.E2010

#Iterating over the backup file to get the list of *.pst files
ForEach ($file in (Get-ChildItem "\\EXCH\Backup\" -Recurse -Include
*.pst))
{
    #parse file name and remove the extension to get the user alias
    $Alias = $file.Name.Replace(".pst","")

    #Import the PST file to the user inbox
    New-MailboxImportRequest -Mailbox $Alias -FilePath $file.Name
}
```

Scenario 10 – hiding mailbox users from Global Address List (GAL)

In this scenario, you are messaging administrators and your manager has asked you to hide the users under the Directors OU from the corporate GAL.

1. Get the list of Exchange mailboxes using the Get-Mailbox cmdlet with the –OrganizationUnit parameter in order to filter by OU name.

2. Use the Set-Mailbox cmdlet with the -HiddenFromAddressListsEnabled parameter to hide the retrieved mailboxes from the GAL.

Use the following script:

```
PS > Get-Mailbox -OrganizationalUnit "Directors" | Set-Mailbox
-HiddenFromAddressListsEnabled $true
```

Scenario 11 – getting mailbox users who never accessed their mailboxes

In this scenario, you are messaging administrators and you have got a request from the HR asking for a list of users who never access their mailboxes.

1. Get the list of Exchange mailboxes using the Get-Mailbox cmdlet.

2. Use the Get-MailboxStatistics cmdlet to get more insight on the mailboxes retrieved in the previous step.

3. Use the Where-Object cmdlet to filter the list and show only the mailboxes with no available LastLogonTime information.

Use the following script:

```
PS > Get-Mailbox | Get-MailboxStatistics | Where LastLogonTime -eq
$null
```

Scenario 12 – generating an organization mailbox statistics report

In this scenario, you are messaging administrators and you want to generate a mailbox statistics report for all the Exchange mailboxes in the organization.

1. Get the list of Exchange mailboxes using the `Get-Mailbox` cmdlet.
2. Use the `Get-MailboxStatistics` cmdlet to get more insight on the mailboxes retrieved in the previous step.
3. Use the `Where-Object` cmdlet to filter the list and show only the mailboxes with the available `LastLogonTime` information.
4. Use the `Select-Object` cmdlet to select the items to be included in the report.
5. Use the `Export-CSV` cmdlet to export the results to a CSV file.

Use the following script:

```
#Generating CSV report for Exchange Mailboxes Statistics
Get-Mailbox | Get-MailboxStatistics | Where LastLogonTime –ne $null |
Select DisplayName, ItemCount, LastLogonTime, MailboxType
, TotalItemSize, Database, ServerName, IsArchiveMailbox | Export-Csv
C:\Reports\MailboxStatisticsReport.csv
```

Scenario 13 – generating a mailbox size report

In this scenario, you are messaging administrators and want to generate a mailbox size report for all the Exchange mailboxes in the organization that exceed a specific size.

1. Prompt the user to enter the size that he/she wants to search for.
2. Get the list of Exchange mailboxes using the `Get-Mailbox` cmdlet.
3. Use the `Get-MailboxStatistics` cmdlet to get more insight on the mailboxes retrieved in the previous step.
4. Use the `Where-Object` cmdlet to filter the list and show only the mailboxes with `TotalItemSize` that exceed the specified size.

5. Use the `Select-Object` cmdlet to select the items to be included in the report.

6. Use the `Export-CSV` cmdlet to export the results to a CSV file.

Use the following script:

```
#Get the maximum size of mailbox
$MailboxSize = Read-Host -Propmt "Enter maximum mailbox size (e.g.
320MB)"

#Generating CSV report for Exchange Mailboxes Size
Get-Mailbox | Get-MailboxStatistics | Where TotalItemSize -gt
$MailboxSize | Select DisplayName, ItemCount, LastLogonTime,
MailboxType, TotalItemSize, Database, ServerName, IsArchiveMailbox |
Export-Csv C:\Reports\MailboxStatisticsReport.csv
```

What Lync Server Management Shell is

Like EMS, Lync Server provides a Windows PowerShell interface that allows you to perform Lync Server administrative tasks available in Lync Control Panel using Windows PowerShell. An interesting fact about Lync Server is that most of its configurations and settings cannot be done using the GUI but can be done using only Windows PowerShell.

Lync Server Management Shell is a normal Windows PowerShell console running a set of Lync-related cmdlets and functions loaded on Windows PowerShell startup. EMS uses a set of Windows PowerShell snap-ins to load Exchange cmdlets, however Lync Server Management Shell uses PowerShell modules to load Lync cmdlets.

On having a deeper look at Lync Server Management Shell's shortcut properties, you will obviously notice that Lync Server Management Shell runs a `powershell.exe` file that loads the Lync Server PowerShell module.

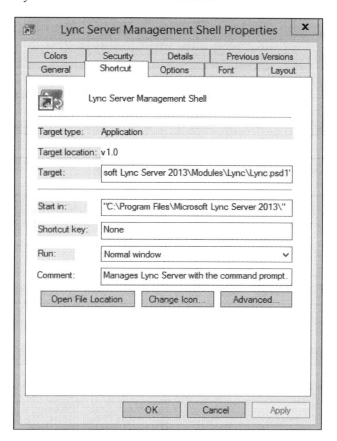

 The Lync Server module loaded by Lync Server Management Shell is located at **%SystemDrive%** | **Program Files** | **Microsoft** | **Common Files** | **Microsoft Lync Server 2013** | **Modules** | **Lync** | **Lync.psd1**.

How to make PowerShell understand Lync Server cmdlets

As we do with Exchange Server, if we want to launch Lync Server Management Shell, we have to either execute Lync Server Management Shell to load Lync Server cmdlets within the normal blue shell window or load related Lync PowerShell modules within the PowerShell ISE for a better experience when writing scripts that deal with Lync management.

Loading a Lync Server module

In this method, we will load Lync Server PowerShell modules directly on Windows PowerShell ISE. During the Lync Server installation preparation, a couple of Windows PowerShell modules are getting installed and registered in the system.

To get the list of PowerShell modules imported in the current PowerShell session, we will use the Get-Module cmdlet with the -ListAvailable parameter to display the list of available modules in our system even if they were not imported in the current PowerShell session. In order to get the list of PowerShell modules installed by Lync Server, use the Get-Module cmdlet with the -ListAvailable parameter and then filter by the word Lync.

```
#Get list of LYNC available PowerShell modules
PS> Get-Module –ListAvailable *Lync*
```

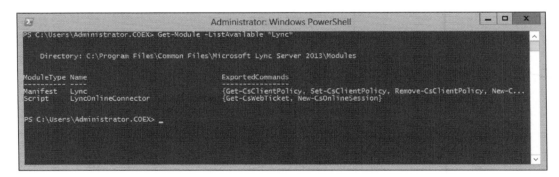

Now after getting the list of available Lync PowerShell modules, we have to load them into the current Windows PowerShell session using the `Import-Module` cmdlet. Since the Lync had registered two modules, you can import them directly in one step by using the pipeline method to get the list of Lync modules and import them directly.

```
#Import Lync Server PowerShell Modules
PS > Get-Module –ListAvailable *Lync* | Import-Module
```

Managing Lync using PowerShell Remoting

Like Exchange Server, Lync Server uses implicit remoting to connect to a frontend server using a virtual directory called `OcsPowerShell`, in order to load the Lync cmdlets on the local computer.

To connect to Lync using implicit remoting, perform the following steps:

1. Create a new PowerShell Remoting session using the `New-PSSession` cmdlet.
2. Import the created session to the local computer using the `Import-PSSession` cmdlet.

Use the following script:

```
#Create new implicit remoting session
$Session = New-PSSession -ConnectionUri "https://Lync.Contoso.local/
OcsPowerShell" -Credential (Get-Credential)

#Import the PowerShell remoting Session
Import-PSSession –Session $Session
```

In order to disconnect the Lync remoting session, use the `Remove-PSSession` cmdlet:

```
#Remove Lync Remoting Session
Remove-PSSession –Session $Session
```

Getting started with Lync scripting

In this section, we will help you getting started with Lync Server scripting and automation using a set of Windows PowerShell scenarios and examples.

Scenario 1 – enabling Lync to user accounts

In this scenario, you are voice administrators who have recently installed Lync Server in the corporate network and want to enable the users for Lync in order to be able to use the Lync client on their machines.

1. Get the list of available users using the Get-CsAdUser cmdlet, and then filter the results to make sure that retrieved users have e-mail addresses and are not enabled for Lync use.

2. Define a variable called Users to store the list of filtered users.

3. Use the ForEach loop to iterate over the list of users.

4. Define a variable called SIP to store the parsed string of the user's SIP address.

5. Use the Enable-CsUser cmdlet within the ForEach loop defined in the previous step to enable each user for Lync capabilities. Use the Get-CSPool cmdlet to get the Lync pool.

Use the following script:

```
#Get list of users who are not enabled for lync
$Users = Get-CsAdUser -Filter {(Enabled -ne $true) -and
(WindowsEmailAddress -ne $null)}

#Iterating over the list of users to enable each one of them
Foreach($User in $Users)
{
    $sip = "sip:" + $User.WindowsEmailAddress

    #Enable users for LYNC
    Enable-CsUser -Identity $User.SamAccountName -RegistrarPool (Get-
CSPool).Identity -SipAddressType EmailAddress -SipAddress $sip
}
```

Scenario 2 – configuring IM file transfer filtering configuration

In this scenario, you are messaging administrators who want to add an extra layer of security to the Instant Messaging communication between the users. So, you enable file transfer filtering to block specific file extensions from being sent over Lync. By default, Lync Server creates a file transfer filter configuration with a global scope across the Lync environment. So, let's create another configuration with SiteScope.

Create a new file transfer filtering configuration using the `New-CsFileTransferFilt erConfiguration` cmdlet with the following group parameters:

- `-Identity site: <Site_Name>`: Defines the scope of the policy that is to be applied

- `-Action`: This parameter defines whether to block all the file extensions or to just block specific ones; by default, a list of extensions is added when you select to block any extensions

- `-Extension`: Modifies the list of extensions by adding, removing, or replacing extensions from the current list

- `-WarningAction`: Defines how to warn the sender about the file transfer rejection

- `-InMemory`: Temporarily keeps the policy in memory instead of committing it on the server

Use the following script:

```
#Create a new file transfer filtering configuration
New-CsFileTransferFilterConfiguration -Identity site:CoEx -Action
Block -Extensions @{Add=".ps1"} -WarningAction Stop
```

Scenario 3 – configuring IM URL filtering

In this scenario, you are messaging administrators who want to add an extra layer of security to the IM communication between the users. So, we will enable URL filtering to block hyperlinks from being sent over Lync.

Create a new file transfer filtering configuration using the `New-CsImFilterConfiguration` cmdlet with the following parameters:

- `-Identity site:<Site_Name>`: Defines the scope of the policy that is to be applied
- `-Action`: Defines the default action, either `Allow`, `Block`, or `Warn`, of the policy
- `-BlockFileExtension`: Blocks hyperlinks containing the file extension
- `-WarnMessage`: Sets the message to appear with hyperlinks if you choose the `Warn` action
- `-IgnoreLocal`: Bypasses this policy for local intranet URLs; the default value is `true`

Use the following script:

```
#Create a new url filtering configuration
New-CsImFilterConfiguration -Identity site:CoEx -Enabled $true
-BlockFileExtension $true -Action Warn -WarnMessage "This is might
contain a harmful content" -IgnoreLocal $false
```

Scenario 4 – bulk assignments of client PIN

In this scenario, you are voice administrators who want to assign a **Personal Identification Number (PIN)** to the newly created and enabled Lync users.

1. Get the list of available users using the `Get-CsAdUser` cmdlet, and then filter the results to make sure that the retrieved users are enabled for Lync.
2. Get the client PIN information for each user retrieved in the previous step using the `Get-CsClientPinInfo` cmdlet, and then filter the results to get only the users with no PIN.
3. Assign a random client PIN using the `Set-CsClientPin` cmdlet, or add the `-PIN` switch to define the PIN value.

Use the following script:

```
#Set Client PIN
Get-CsAdUser -Filter {(Enabled -eq $true)} | Get-CsClientPinInfo |
Where IsPinSet -eq $false | Set-CsClientPin
```

Or you can also use the following script:

```
#Get list of users with no PIN
$Users = Get-CsAdUser -Filter {(Enabled -eq $true)} | Get-
CsClientPinInfo | Where IsPinSet -eq $false

#define the initial start for PIN value
$PINinit = 50000

#iterating of users list
Foreach($User in $Users)
{
    #setting the user PIN info
    Set-CsClientPin -Identity $User.Identity -Pin $PINinit
    #increase the PIN by 1 each
    $PINinit++
}
```

Scenario 5 – getting number of users using OCS/Lync

In this scenario, you are voice administrators who want to generate a simple report showing which users are using **Office Communication Server (OCS)** and which are using Lync Server.

1. Get the list of available users using the `Get-CsUser` cmdlet.

   ° `-OnOfficeCommunnicationServer`: Gets the list of users on Office Communication Server

   ° `-OnLyncServer`: Gets the list of users on Lync Server

2. Use `(Get-CsUser).Count` to count the number of records returned in the result.

Use the following script:

```
#Write the number of users on OCS
Write-Host "Office Communication Server Users:" (Get-csUser
-OnOfficeCommunicationServer).Count -ForegroundColor Green
#Showing the list of OCS Users
Get-csUser -OnOfficeCommunicationServer | Select DisplayName,
SamAccountName, sipAddress, LineURI, EnterpriseVoiceEnabled | ft

#Write the number of users on LYNC
Write-Host "Lync Server Users:" (Get-csUser -OnLyncServer).Count
-ForegroundColor Green
#Showing the list of Lync Users
Get-csUser -OnLyncServer | Select DisplayName, SamAccountName,
sipAddress, LineURI, EnterpriseVoiceEnabled | ft
```

Scenario 6 – setting the conference disclaimer

In this scenario, you are voice administrators who want to set a disclaimer for a conference so that each user can see it before joining the conference. For example, you want to inform the users that the meeting will be recorded.

Set the conference disclaimer using the `Set-CsConferenceDisclaimer` cmdlet.

Use the following script:

```
#Setting conference dislaimer
Set-CsConferenceDisclaimer -Header "Welcome to Contoso Conferencing
Center" -Body "Kindly, note that according to corporate policy this
meeting will be recorded"
```

Microsoft Office 365

Office 365 is the Microsoft cloud implementation for Exchange Server, Lync Server, SharePoint Server, and Office Web Apps. Office 365 is a Software-as-a-Service solution that provides you with the same experience as traditional on-premise technologies with an equivalent for each product.

On-premise product	Equivalent cloud product
Microsoft Exchange Server	Microsoft Exchange Online
Microsoft Lync Server	Microsoft Lync Online
Microsoft SharePoint Server	Microsoft SharePoint Online
Microsoft Office Professional	Microsoft Office Web Apps

Office 365 allows you to use the internal directory service to authenticate online services and also implement a hybrid environment that operates both on-premise and cloud-hosted solutions.

Office 365 and Windows PowerShell

In Office 365, Windows PowerShell is a critical component for performing almost every single administration task, and most tasks are not available on the management portal. So in order to start using Windows PowerShell for Office 365, you have to download and install the following components:

- Microsoft Online Service Sign-In Assistant
- Microsoft Online Service Module for Windows PowerShell

 Download links for Microsoft Online Service components are available at `http://onlinehelp.microsoft.com/en-us/office365-enterprises/hh124998.aspx`.

After installing the Microsoft Online Service Module for Windows PowerShell, the following modules should be available in your system:

- `MSOnline`
- `MSOnlineExtended`

Managing Office 365 using PowerShell

Now to start using the preceding modules, you have to either use Microsoft Online Service Module for the Windows PowerShell shortcut or import the modules using the `Import-Module` cmdlet to load the Microsoft Online Service cmdlets and functions. Then, use the `Connect-MsolService` cmdlet to connect to your Office 365 account.

```
#Import MSOnline Modules
Get-Module -ListAvailable *MSOnline* | Import-Module

#Connect to Office 365 account
Connect-MsolService -Credential (Get-Credential username@domain.
onmicrosoft.com)
```

The following screenshot shows the Microsoft Online Services Module for Windows PowerShell:

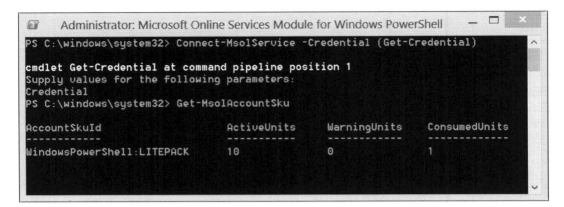

Managing Microsoft Exchange Online using PowerShell

In order to manage Exchange Online using Windows PowerShell, we use the same method that we use for Microsoft Exchange Server implicit remoting, but with minor changes in the session configuration.

The differences between the session configuration for Microsoft Exchange Server and Exchange Online is as follows:

- The use of basic authentication for Exchange Online instead of Kerberos authentication for Exchange Server because we are connecting to a website hosted on the IIS server and not on a member of the local active directory domain.

- `-ConnectionUri` is `https://ps.Outlook.com/PowerShell` instead of `https://Exchange-Server-FQDN/PowerShell`

- The `-AllowRedirection` parameter allows a connection to Microsoft Exchange Online using a unified address, then redirects the connection to an alternate URL based on the instruction that is returned by the remote destination.

Use the following script:

```
#Create new implicit remoting session
$Session = New-PSSession -ConfigurationName Microsoft.Exchange
-ConnectionUri "https://ps.Outlook.com/PowerShell" -Credential (Get-
Credential) -Authentication Basic -AllowRedirection

#Import the PowerShell remoting Session
Import-PSSession -Session $Session
```

The following screenshot shows the connection to Exchange Online and a warning that the connection will be redirected to another URI.

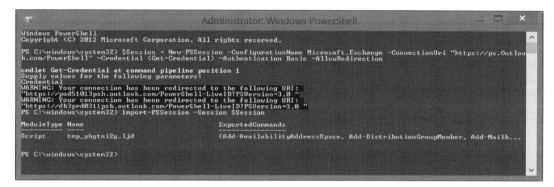

After connecting to Microsoft Exchange Online, you can start using the normal Microsoft Exchange Server cmdlets and functions.

For more information on available PowerShell cmdlets for Microsoft Exchange Online, please visit http://help.outlook.com/en-us/140/dd575549.aspx.

Summary

In this chapter, we talked about unified communication as a concept and how it becomes an important component, especially where complex business requirements exist. Also, we saw how Windows PowerShell can help in managing such solutions in a much faster and convenient way, especially for the cloud-hosted scenario as in Office 365.

In the next chapter, we will go on to discover Windows PowerShell in a different area and for different technologies. Our focus will be on the collaboration and data platforms represented in Microsoft SharePoint Server, SharePoint Online, and Microsoft SQL Server. Definitely, no one can deny how complex it is to deal with these technologies, especially for people who do not have any previous experience. So, the target of the next chapter will be to show how PowerShell can make an administrator's life easier and happier.

9

Managing Collaboration and Data Platforms with PowerShell

Many years ago, if you were working on a project where you wanted to share files, archive documents, or set a project time plan, the most proper way at that time was using a very simple network-sharing mechanism for creating a shared folder for each project and a spreadsheet under each project containing the names of the persons or departments contributing on that project. Do not be surprised by such a solution. At that time, this was one of the easiest ways to achieve your goal.

A few years later, the collaboration software such as Microsoft SharePoint Server was introduced to the market to provide a better way of communication and collaboration between people to achieve their tasks and goals in a more convenient way. Later on, the collaboration software was reinvented to be a platform where people would not only use it but also customize and integrate it with other components to meet the organization's requirements and obtain the best value.

Well, it is a must to mention that collaboration platforms do not work alone. You must have a data platform at the backend serving it. In our chapter, we will focus on the Microsoft SharePoint Server and pursue this chance to spot Microsoft SQL Server, which is the data platform behind it.

In this chapter we will cover:

- What is SharePoint Management Shell
- How to use PowerShell to do SharePoint Management tasks
- How to manage SharePoint online using PowerShell?
- What is SQL Server PowerShell?
- How to use PowerShell to do SQL Server Management Tasks?

What is SharePoint Management Shell

After a long discussion about management shells in the previous chapter, I believe that now you can easily guess what SharePoint Management Shell is. Yes, you are right, SharePoint Management Shell is the Windows PowerShell interface for SharePoint **Application Programming Interface (API)** that allows you to interact directly with SharePoint Server via Windows PowerShell cmdlets and functions. Refer to the following screenshot:

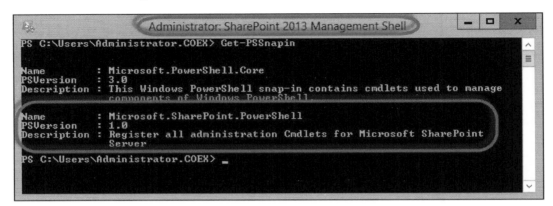

As usual, SharePoint Management Shell has a shortcut to launch it directly like Lync Management Shell and Exchange Management Shell. This shortcut is always nothing more than running a `powershell.exe` file with a Windows PowerShell script that loads the products' snap-ins, modules, binaries, and assemblies. The following screenshot shows how we launch this shortcut:

The SharePoint script loaded by SharePoint Management Shell is located under `%SystemDrive%/Program Files/Common Files/Microsoft Shared/Web Server Extensions/15/Config/PowerShell/Registration/SharePoint.ps1`.

Looking at the `SharePoint.ps1` script you will notice that the script is simply doing the following three things:

- Setting the PowerShell runspace thread option to `ReuseThread` to make sure that every cmdlet is running within the same thread

- Adding the `Microsoft.SharePoint.PowerShell` snap-in

- Setting the console's location to the users' home folder

The following screenshot shows the content of the `SharePoint.ps1` script:

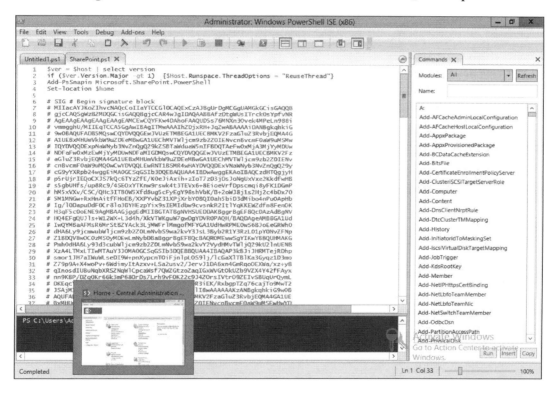

How to make Windows PowerShell understand the SharePoint server cmdlets

In order to use the SharePoint Server cmdlets in Windows PowerShell, you can either directly launch SharePoint Management Shell to quickly jump into the SharePoint PowerShell environment, or execute the `SharePoint.ps1` script in your runspace environment, or use the `Add-PSSnapin` cmdlet to add the `Microsoft.SharePoint.PowerShell` snap-in into your Windows PowerShell session using the following instructions:

```
#Add SharePoint Server PowerShell Snap-ins
PS> Add-PSSnapin Microsoft.SharePoint.PowerShell
```

Getting started with SharePoint scripting

In this part we will help you get started with SharePoint Server scripting and automation using a set of Windows PowerShell scenarios and examples.

Scenario 1 – creating a new site collection

In this scenario, you are a SharePoint administrator who wants to create a SharePoint site collection for your corporate intranet usage. For this purpose you will use the `New-SPSite` cmdlet with the following group of parameters:

- `-Url`: This parameter defines the URL of the site collection.
- `-Name`: This parameter defines the title of the site.
- `-Description`: This parameter writes a short description for the site collection.
- `-Template`: This parameter defines which template will be used to create the site. Use the `Get-SPWebTemplate` cmdlet to get the list of available templates.
- `-OwnerAlias`: This parameter defines the alias of the site collection's owner `<Domain\User>`.
- `-Language`: This parameter defines the **Local ID (LCID)** of the language.

For more information about the list of LCIDs, check the following link:

`http://msdn.microsoft.com/en-us/goglobal/bb964664.aspx`

The script will be as follows:

```
#Creating new SharePoint Site Collection
New-SPSite -Url http://SharePoint.Contoso.local/sites/Contoso -
Name "Contoso Team Site" -Description "Team collaboration
intranet site for Contoso Team" -Template STS#0 -Language
1033 -OwnerAlias "Contoso\SherifT"
```

Scenario 2 – creating a new website

In this scenario, you are a SharePoint administrator who wants to create a set of SharePoint sites (subsites) for different corporate teams and departments under an existing SharePoint site collection. For this purpose, you will use the `New-SPWeb` cmdlet with the following group of parameters:

- `-Url`: This parameter defines the URL of the site collection.
- `-Name`: This parameter defines the title of the site.
- `-Description`: This parameter writes a short description for the site collection.
- `-Template`: This parameter defines which template will be used to create the site. Use the `Get-SPWebTemplate` cmdlet to get the list of available templates.
- `-AddToTopNav`: This parameter adds the site to the top-level navigation bar.
- `-UseParentTopNav`: This parameter uses the parent's navigation bar as the top-level navigation bar.
- `-AddToQuickLaunch`: This parameter adds the subsite to the quick launch.

The script will be as follows:

```
#Creating new SharePoint web site
New-SPWeb -Url http://SharePoint.Contoso.Local/Sites/Contoso/
Blog -Name "Contoso Blog" -Template BLOG#0 -AddToTopNav -
UseParentTopNav –AddToQuickLaunch
```

Scenario 3 – creating a new quota template

In this scenario, you are a SharePoint administrator who wants to create a new quota template for the SharePoint site using Windows PowerShell. Unfortunately, there is no native cmdlet for creating a new quota template; however, you can call SharePoint assemblies using Windows PowerShell to create a new quota template.

This scenario shows a step-by-step procedure for creating a new quota template:

1. Create an object `$template` of the SharePoint quota template using the `New-Object` cmdlet.
2. Define the properties of the SharePoint quota template, such as name, storage maximum level, and storage warning level.
3. Create an object `$service` of the SharePoint content service.
4. Add the template to the content service's object using the `$service.QuotaTemplates.Add($template)` method.
5. Update the content service using the `$service.Update()` method.

The script is as follows:

```
#Create Object of SharePoint Quota Template
$Template = New-Object Microsoft.SharePoint.Administration.
SPQuotaTemplate

#Define template name
$Template.Name = "Blogs Quota Template"

#Assign Storage Maximum Level
$Template.StorageMaximumLevel = 100MB

#Assign Storage Warning Level
$Template.StorageWarningLevel = 80MB

#Creating object of SharePoint Content Service
$Service = [Microsoft.SharePoint.Administration.
SPWebService]::ContentService

#Add the template to the content service
$Service.QuotaTemplates.Add($Template)

#Update Content Service to create the template
$Service.Update()
```

Scenario 4 – backing up your SharePoint environment

In this scenario, you are a SharePoint administrator who wants to perform a complete backup of the SharePoint environment components. By default, there is not a single cmdlet that can back up the whole SharePoint environment; however, you can use a combination of cmdlets to back it up.

These following steps show the SharePoint cmdlets that you need to use in order to perform a complete SharePoint environment backup.

1. Back up the SharePoint configuration database using the `Backup-SPConfigurationDatabase` cmdlet.

2. Back up the SharePoint farm using the `Backup-SPFarm` cmdlet.

3. Back up the SharePoint sites using the `Backup-SPSite` cmdlet.

The script is as follows:

```
#Define the Back-up folder
$BackupFolder = "C:\SharePointBackup"


#Backup SharePoint Configuration Database
Backup-SPConfigurationDatabase -Directory $BackupFolder


#Backup SharePoint Farm
Backup-SPFarm -Directory $BackupFolder -BackupMethod Full


#Backup SharePoint Sites
ForEach($Site in Get-SPSite)
{
    Backup-SPSite -Identity $Site.Url -Path (Join-Path $BackupFolder
($Site.Url.Remove(0,$Site.Url.LastIndexOf("/")+1) + ".bak"))
}
```

Managing SharePoint Online using PowerShell

One of the services provided by Microsoft Office 365 is SharePoint Online, where you have Microsoft SharePoint Server hosted on the cloud like the Lync Online and Exchange Online mentioned in the previous chapter.

Microsoft SharePoint Online provides SharePoint Online Management Shell similar to SharePoint Management Shell for the on-premise SharePoint. SharePoint Online Management Shell is a Windows PowerShell module that allows you to easily manage and control your hosted SharePoint via Windows PowerShell.

 Download the SharePoint Online Management Shell from `http://www. microsoft.com/en-eg/download/details.aspx?id=35588`.

After installing the SharePoint Online Management Shell binaries, you will get a new shortcut called "SharePoint Online Management Shell". This shortcut refers to the Windows PowerShell module called `Microsoft.Online.SharePoint.PowerShell`, which is similar to `Microsoft.SharePoint.PowerShell` with "Online" referring to SharePoint Online.

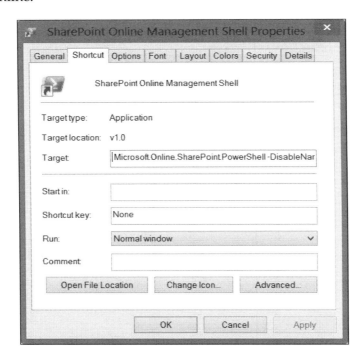

How to load SharePoint Online Management Shell

In order to use the SharePoint Online cmdlets and functions, use the `Import-Module` cmdlet with the `-DisableNameChecking` switch to import the `Microsoft.Online.SharePoint.PowerShell` module. The `-DisableNameChecking` switch is used because the SharePoint Online module has a set of cmdlets that start with unapproved `-standard-` verbs, so it used to avoid any warning message regarding those unapproved verbs.

For a list of Windows PowerShell verbs, you can refer to the following:

- http://social.technet.microsoft.com/wiki/contents/articles/4537.powershell-approved-verbs-en-us.aspx
- http://msdn.microsoft.com/en-us/library/windows/desktop/ms714428(v=vs.85).aspx
- http://blogs.msdn.com/b/powershell/archive/2009/07/15/final-approved-verb-list-for-windows-powershell-2-0.aspx

The script will be as follows:

```
#Import SharePoint Online Module
PS > Import-Module Microsoft.Online.SharePoint.
PowerShell -DisableNameChecking
```

How to connect to SharePoint Online

Now, after importing the SharePoint Online module, you definitely want to connect to your SharePoint Online site. For this purpose you will use the `Connect-SPOService` cmdlet with the following group of parameters:

- `-Url`: This parameter defines the URL for your SharePoint Online site
- `-Credential`: This parameter defines the logon credentials for the SharePoint Online site administrator who must also be an Office 365 global administrator

The script will be as follows:

```
#Connect to SharePoint Online
Connect-SPOService -Url https://<YOUR_OFFICE365_DOMAIN>-admin.SharePoint.
Com -Credential USER@<YOUR_OFFICE365_DOMAIN>.onmicrosoft.com
```

Let's assume that your SharePoint Online site is `http://PowerShell.SharePoint.com`. So the command should look the following:

```
Connect-SPOService -Url https://PowerShell-admin.SharePoint.com
-Credential admin@PowerShell.onmicrosoft.com
```

Scenario 1 – exporting a list of SharePoint Online sites to CSV

In this scenario, you are a SharePoint Online administrator who wants to generate a file containing the list of all the SharePoint Online site collections and subsites. For this purpose you will use the `Get-SPOSite` cmdlet.

We will be performing the following steps:

1. Get the list of site collections and sites using the `Get-SPOSite` cmdlet with the `-Detailed` switch for detailed information about each site.
2. Use the `Export-Csv` cmdlet to export the list to a CSV file.

The script will be as follows:

```
#Get and Export the list of SharePoint Online site
Get-SPOSite -Detailed | export-csv $home\desktop\SPO-sites.csv
```

Scenario 2 – restoring a deleted SharePoint Online site

In this scenario, you are a SharePoint Online administrator who wants to restore a SharePoint Online site that has been deleted by mistake. The deleted sites of SharePoint Online go to the recycling bin for 30 days before they are permanently deleted. In order to restore the site, you need to get the list of deleted sites to make sure that your site is still retained and then restore it.

We will be performing the following steps:

1. Get the list of the deleted SharePoint Online sites using the `Get-SPODeletedSite` cmdlet.

2. Restore the deleted SharePoint Online sites using the `Restore-SPODeletedSite` cmdlet with the `-NoWait` switch to execute the restored job immediately.

The script will be as follows:

```
#Get and Restore the list of SharePoint Online deleted site
Get-SPODeletedSite | Restore-SPODeletedSite -NoWait
```

Scenario 3 – checking the SharePoint Online site's health status

In this scenario, you are a SharePoint Online administrator who wants to generate a health check report for all the SharePoint Online sites.

We will be performing the following steps:

1. Get the list of SharePoint Online sites using the `Get-SPOSite` cmdlet.

2. Check the site's health using the `Test-SPOSite` cmdlet.

The script will be as follows:

```
#Run health checks on the list of SharePoint Online sites
Get-SPOSite | Test-SPOSite
```

Scenario 4 – setting the SharePoint Online User as Site Collection Administrator

In this scenario, you are a SharePoint Online administrator who wants to assign a "Site Collection Administrator" role to the SharePoint Online User. For this purpose you will use the `Set-SPOUser` cmdlet with the following group of parameters:

- `-Identity`: This parameter defines the URL of the site collection
- `-LoginName`: This parameter is the login name for a SharePoint Online User (an Office 365 user)
- `-IsSiteCollectionAdmin`: This parameter assigns/removes users to/from the role of site collection administrators

The script will be as follows:

```
#Assign site collection admin role to user

Set-SPOUser https://WindowsPowerShell.sharepoint.com/sites/blog
-LoginName Sherif@WindowsPowerShell.onmicrosoft.com
-IsSiteCollectionAdmin $true
```

Windows PowerShell Command Builder for SharePoint and Office 365

Windows PowerShell Command Builder is a simple and nice web-based application that helps you to easily explore, discover, and build PowerShell commands for SharePoint 2010, SharePoint 2013, SharePoint Online, and Office 365.

All you have to do is drag-and-drop the chosen PowerShell cmdlets (Verbs and Nouns) over the **Design Surface** area to show all the required and optional parameters in the form of textboxes. Then, fill the textboxes with your values and click on the **Copy to Clipboard** button to copy it. It also has a list of prebuilt commands for the most common tasks for each product to help you in adopting the Windows PowerShell for these products. For example, for SharePoint 2010 you have tasks such as Create, Back up, and Remove sites. For SharePoint Online, you also have a task such as Connect to SharePoint online site, and the same can be used for each product. The following screenshot gives a peek into the Windows PowerShell Command Builder for SharePoint:

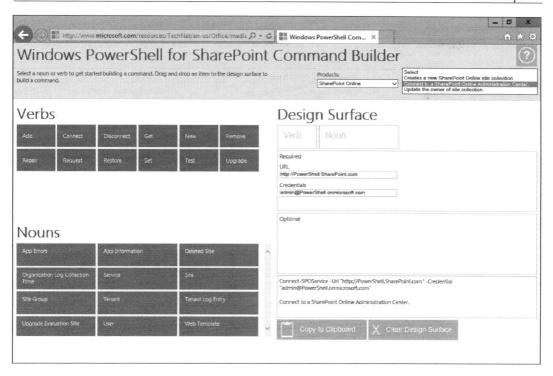

What is SQL Server PowerShell

SQL Server introduced SQL Server PowerShell first in SQL Server 2008 R2 where SQL Server provided a Windows PowerShell module called SQLPS. This module helps SQL Server administrators benefit from the capabilities of Windows PowerShell and T-SQL to perform SQL Server complex administration scripts.

The SQL Server PowerShell module provides a SQL Server Provider PS SQLSERVER :\> that allows to deal with SQL Server instances, databases, tables, and other SQL components as a filesystem driver when you use the traditional commands to navigate, rename, and delete objects.

For more information about the PowerShell provider, refer to http://msdn.microsoft.com/en-us/library/windows/desktop/ee126186(v=vs.85).aspx.

The following screenshot shows how to use the normal `dir` command with the SQL Server provider for listing the available databases as if it is a file or a folder:

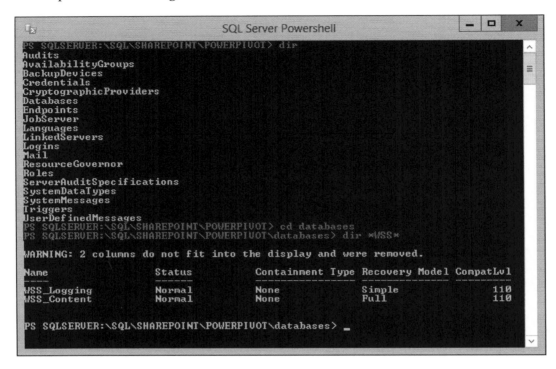

SQL Server PowerShell also provides a set of cmdlets that allows executing T-SQL and XQuery statements.

How to load SQL Server PowerShell

In order to load the SQL Server PowerShell, you can either import the SQL Server PowerShell module directly into the PowerShell session or start it directly from the **SQL Server Management Studio (SSMS)**.

Method 1 – importing the SQL Server PowerShell module

The script for this method will be as follows:

```
#Import SQL Server PowerShell Module
Import-Module SQLPS -DisableNameChecking
```

Method 2 – launching SQL Server PowerShell from SSMS

This method uses the following steps:

1. Open the Microsoft SQL Server Management Studio.

2. Right-click on any item under the **Object Explorer** pane, as shown in the following screenshot:

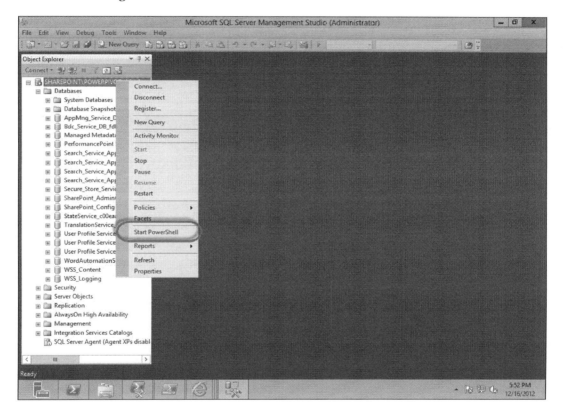

3. Select **Start PowerShell** to launch the SQL PowerShell. Selecting this option will take us to the following window:

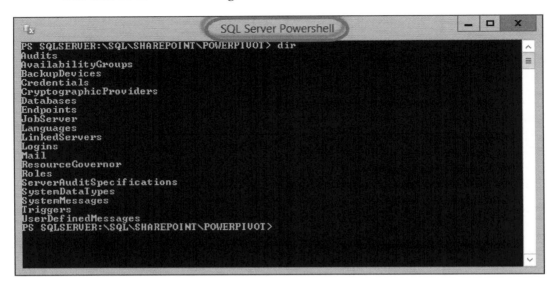

Getting started with SQL Server scripting

In this part we will help you get started with SQL Server scripting and automation using a set of Windows PowerShell scenarios and examples.

Scenario 1 – executing the T-SQL statement

In this scenario, you are a database administrator who is writing a set of SQL Server automation tasks and you want to execute the T-SQL statement via Windows PowerShell. For this purpose you will use the `Invoke-Sqlcmd` cmdlet with the following group of parameters:

- `-ServerInstance`: This parameter defines the SQL Server instance `<SERVER_NAME\INSTANCE_NAME>`

- `-Database`: This parameter is the name of the database

- `-Hostname`: This parameter is the name of the server running the SQL Server

- `-Query`: This parameter defines the T-SQL statement

The script will be as follows:

```
#Invoke SQL Query using PowerShell
Invoke-Sqlcmd -ServerInstance SQL01\SharePoint -Database Master
-Query "SELECT db_name(dbid) as DB,name,filename FROM sysaltfiles"
-HostName SQL01
```

Scenario 2 – backing up the SQL Server database

In this scenario, you are a database administrator who wants to use Windows PowerShell to back up all SQL Server databases hosted under a specific instance. For this purpose you will use the `Backup-SqlDatabase` cmdlet.

We will be using the following steps:

1. Use the `ForEach` loop to iterate over the list of databases under the `SharePoint\PowerPivot` instance.

2. Define variables to store the full file path for each database and database log within the `ForEach` loop defined in the previous step.

3. Use the `Backup-SqlCmdlet` cmdlet to back up each database in the file path defined in the previous step with a filename similar to the database name.

The script will be as follows:

```
ForEach($Database in (Get-ChildItem SQLSERVER:\SQL\SharePoint\PowerPivot\
Databases))
{
    $FilePath = "C:\Backup\" + $Database.Name + ".bak"
    $LogFilePath = "C:\Backup\" + $Database.Name + ".log"


    #Backup Database File
Backup-SqlDatabase -ServerInstance SharePoint\PowerPivot -Database
$Database.Name -BackupAction Database -BackupFile $FilePath


    #backup Database Log File
Backup-SqlDatabase -ServerInstance SharePoint\PowerPivot -Database
$Database.Name -BackupAction Log -BackupFile $LogFilePath
}
```

Scenario 3 – restoring the SQL Server database

In this scenario, you are a database administrator who wants to use Windows PowerShell to restore a SQL Server database. For this purpose you will use the `Restore-SqlDatabase` cmdlet.

We will use the following steps:

1. Use the `ForEach` loop to iterate over the folder that contains the database's backup files.
2. Use the `Restore-SqlCmdlet` cmdlet to restore each database to the file path defined in the previous step with a filename similar to the database name.

The script will be as follows:

```
$BackupFolder = "C:\Backup\"
$ServerInstance = "SharePoint\PowerPivot"


ForEach($File in (Get-ChildItem $BackupFolder))
{
    $DatabaseName = $File.Name.Replace(".bak","")


#Restore Database File
Restore-SqlDatabase -ServerInstance SharePoint\PowerPivot -Database
$DatabaseName -RestoreAction Database -BackupFile $File.FullName
}
```

Scenario 4 – getting server instances and databases properties

In this scenario, you are a database administrator who wants to generate a report that contains the SQL Server instance and underlying database properties. For this purpose, you will use SQL **Server Management object (SMO)** with Windows PowerShell.

The following steps show a step-by-step procedure of how to use SQL SMO in PowerShell:

1. Load the SQL SMO assembly using `[void][System.Reflection.Assembly]::LoadWithPartialName(ASSEMBLY_NAME)`.

2. Create an SMO object `$Server` of the current SQL Server instance.

3. Use the previously created object to get the list of server instance properties and also the list of databases under this instance.

4. Use the `ForEach` loop to iterate over the list of retrieved databases to get the properties of each database.

The script will be as follows:

```
#Server Instance name
$ServerInstance = "SharePoint\PowerPivot"


#Load SQL SMO assembly
[void][System.Reflection.Assembly]::LoadWithPartialName('Microsoft.SqlServer.SMO')
#Create SMO object of SQL Server Instance
$Server = new-object ('Microsoft.SqlServer.Management.Smo.Server') $ServerInstance


Write-Host "$ServerInstance Server Instance Properties" -ForegroundColor Red


#Get the Server Instance Properties
$Server.Properties | Select Name, Value


#Iterate over the list of the databases under the Server Instance
ForEach($Database in $Server.Databases)
{
    Write-Host $Database.Name " Database Properties"
    -ForegroundColor Green

    #Get the Database Properties
    $Database.Properties | Select Name, Value
}
```

Scenario 5 – generating the SQL script for databases, tables, and stored procedures

In this scenario, you are a database administrator who wants to generate an SQL script for a specific database and its tables and stored procedures. For this purpose you will use an SQL SMO with Windows PowerShell.

The following steps show a step-by-step procedure of how to use SQL SMO and PowerShell to generate the SQL scripts:

1. Load the SQL SMO assembly using [void] [System.Reflection.Assembly]::LoadWithPartialName(ASSEMBLY_NAME).
2. Create an SMO object $Server of the current SQL Server instance.
3. Use the previously created object to get the list of server instance properties and also the list of databases under this instance.
4. Use the ForEach loop to iterate over the list of retrieved databases to get the properties of each database.
5. Create a folder for each database, and then export the database script file to it.
6. For each database, use the ForEach loop to iterate over the list of tables and stored procedures, and then export them to the SQL scripts.

The script will be as follows:

```
$ServerInstance = "SharePoint\PowerPivot"

$ExportFolder = "C:\SqlScripts"


#Load SQL SMO assembly

[void] [System.Reflection.Assembly]::LoadWithPartialName('Microsoft.SqlServer.SMO')

#Create SMO object of SQL Server Instance

$Server = new-object ('Microsoft.SqlServer.Management.Smo.Server')
$ServerInstance


#Iterate over the list of the databases under the Server Instance

ForEach($Database in $Server.Databases)
{
```

```
#Create Folder for each Database
New-Item -ItemType Directory -Path ("$ExportFolder\" +
$Database.Name + "\") | Out-Null
#Create folder for tables under each database folder
New-Item -ItemType Directory -Path ("$ExportFolder\" +
$Database.Name + "\Tables\") | Out-Null
#Create folder for stored procedures under each database folder
New-Item -ItemType Directory -Path ("$ExportFolder\" +
$Database.Name + "\StoredProcedures\") | Out-Null


#Generate and Export Database Script
$Database.Script() | Out-File ("$ExportFolder\" +
$Database.Name + "\" + $Database.Name + ".sql")


#Iterate over the list of the tables under each database
ForEach($table in $Database.Tables)
{
    #Generate and Export Tables Scripts
    $table.Script() | Out-File ("$ExportFolder\" +
    $Database.Name + "\Tables\" + $table.Name + ".sql")
}


#Iterate over the list of the stored procedures under each database
ForEach($SP in $Database.StoredProcedures)
{
    #Generate and Export Stored Procedures Scripts
    $SP.Script() | Out-File ("$ExportFolder\" + $Database.Name + "\
StoredProcedures\" + $SP.Name + ".sql")
}
}
```

Summary

In this chapter, we have seen the capabilities of Windows PowerShell with SharePoint Server, SharePoint Online, and SQL Server and the real value of using it to manage and administer such complex technologies.

As part of your job as an IT administrator or a helpdesk executive, you need to make sure that your environment is in control and the end users are working fine with minimal problems. In any environment using a computer, the most painful part is dealing with desktops and client operating systems. You have to deal with many desktops and notebooks on a daily basis to fix and solve their problems, which is almost the same problem for everyone. Hence the virtualization concept has been invented to deliver another kind of solution called **Desktop Virtualization**.

In the next chapter, we will learn what is Desktop Virtualization, and Microsoft implementation for this concept in Windows Server 2012. We will also learn how to use Windows PowerShell to install, configure, and manage the **Remote Desktop Services (RDS)**.

10
Managing Microsoft Desktop Virtualization with PowerShell

Nowadays, one of the biggest sources of pain to any member of an IT department is the problems that the end user faces. You may be receiving many requests daily from many users complaining about the performance of their devices, asking for extra permission, wanting to install software, and so on.

As an IT administrator, you are always inside the loop, trying to balance between users' needs and business requirements that by nature of the situation require investment in tools, hardware resources, and manpower. That is why, the concept of Desktop Virtualization has been introduced to solve this formula and help the administrator satisfy users' needs, while keeping the environment secure and in control with a centralized management solution and, moreover, saving the money spent on devices such as CAPEX and OPEX.

In this chapter we will cover:

- What Desktop Virtualization is
- What the different types of Desktop Virtualization solutions are
- How to manage Microsoft Remote Desktop Services using PowerShell

What Desktop Virtualization is

Desktop Virtualization is an architecture model where the client operating system is separated from the physical hardware layer that is the end users' device.

There are two types of Desktop Virtualization solutions:

- **Virtual Desktop Infrastructure (VDI)**: This solution provides the user with a virtual desktop that is a completely isolated operating system hosted on the data center
- **Session Virtualization**: This solution provides the user with just a session on the shared Session Host server

Desktop Virtualization gives you the following advantages:

- **Centralized management**: Manages all the desktops from a single console
- **Enhanced security**: Data is always locked inside the data center; no more vulnerability can be caused because if a device is stolen or lost, no one can take something out without proper permissions
- **Anywhere access**: The user can get connected any time, anywhere, from desktops, notebooks, thin clients, tablet devices, and smartphones
- **Business continuity**: The desktop's failure recovery and problem resolution is faster than physical desktops

Understanding Desktop Virtualization components

In order to build any Desktop Virtualization environment, you should have the following components:

- **Virtualization platform**: This component is the hypervisor layer responsible for providing virtualization capabilities in order to host the virtual desktops.
- **Connection broker**: This is the core component of any Desktop Virtualization solution. This layer is responsible for the communication between end users and the virtual desktop; it manages who can access what, and how. Also, it is responsible for features, such as optimizing virtual desktop performance over a WAN connection, redirecting local resources such as printers and USB devices to the virtual desktop, and providing a physical desktop such as user experience in terms of multimedia and graphics.
- **Application delivery**: This component is responsible for delivering the application to the end users' desktop on demand, using the concept of application virtualization, where the application is running on the desktop locally without being installed.

- **User profile and data**: This technology is responsible for separating a user's profile and data from the operating system and ensuring that it is saved in a central store so that users can access their profiles, settings, and data anywhere, regardless of the desktop and operating system.
- **Client access device**: This is the device where the users can access their virtual desktops or sessions. The device could be a normal desktop, notebook, thin-client, tablet, or smartphone.

The following diagram shows the common Desktop Virtualization architecture:

What Remote Desktop Services is

Remote Desktop Services (RDS) is a Microsoft implementation of the Desktop Virtualization concept. Remote Desktop Services is a Windows Server role that allows you to build VDI, session-based virtualization, and RemoteApp.

Managing RDS using PowerShell

In order to manage RDS using Windows PowerShell, you have the Windows PowerShell module called `RemoteDesktop` that provides many RDS-related cmdlets that help you perform all the tasks available on the GUI wizards. You do not need to install any prerequisites in order to get the `RemoteDesktop` module; the module available by default in Windows Server 2012 so you can use it directly to implement the RDS itself.

```
#Import Remote Desktop Services Module PowerShell module
PS> Import-Module RemoteDesktop
```

Getting started with RDS scripting

In this part we will help you get started with RDS scripting and automation using a set of Windows PowerShell scenarios and examples.

In the following scenarios, we will build a hybrid Desktop Virtualization environment with the six RDS roles described later in this chapter in order to provide both VM-based and Session-based Desktop Virtualization scenarios. Also, we will build two nodes of the **Remote Desktop Connection Broker (RDCB)** for high-availability purposes.

Scenario 1 – creating new RDS deployments

In this scenario, you are a Desktop Virtualization administrator who wants to install RDS in order to implement a Desktop Virtualization solution for your organization.

In the previous version of Windows Server, we used to install RDS roles using the **Server Manager** wizard to install Windows Server roles and features. However in Windows Server 2012, if you want to install Windows roles or features, you will get a couple of options asking you what kind of installation you want to perform, either **Role-based or feature-based installation** or **Remote Desktop Services installation**, as shown in the following screenshot:

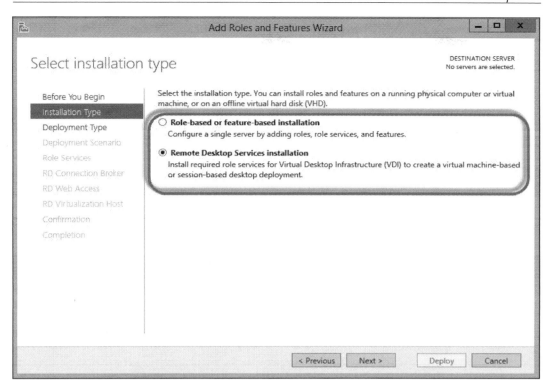

By design, RDS has six different server roles that should be installed on at least three separate servers. So the second option—**Remote Desktop Services installation**—exists to help you deploy different RDS roles on different servers in one installation step from a central location.

Well, does it make any difference while installing RDS from Windows PowerShell? Yes, indeed. You will not be able to use the `Install-WindowsFeature` cmdlet to install it. Instead, you will have to use the deployment cmdlet that comes with the `RemoteDesktop` PowerShell module.

An RDS installation provides two deployment scenarios, namely **Virtual machine-based desktop deployment** and **Session-based desktop deployment** as shown in the following screenshot:

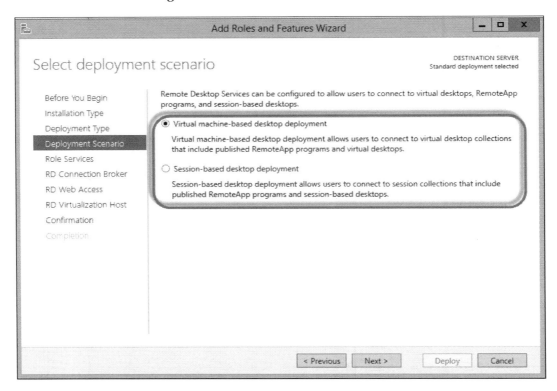

Task 1.1 – creating a new virtual-machine-based deployment

In this type of deployment, you create an RDS environment capable of hosting VDI scenarios. This deployment requires three RDS roles: **Remote Desktop Virtualization Host (RDVH)**, **Remote Desktop Session Broker (RDCB)**, and **Remote Desktop Web Access (RDWeb)**. For this purpose, you will use the New-RDVirtualDesktopDeployment cmdlet with the following parameters:

- -ConnectionBroker: This parameter defines the FQDN of the server to hold the Connection Broker role

- -WebAccessServer: This parameter defines the FQDN of the web server to hold the Web Access role

- `-VirtualizationHost`: This parameter defines the FQDN of the Hyper-V server to host the Virtualization Host role
- `-CreateVirtualSwitch`: This parameter creates a virtual network switch on the Hyper-V server to be used by the virtual machine created by RDS

The script will be as follows:

```
#Remote Desktop Virtualization Host
$RDVH = 'RDVH-01.Contoso.local'


#Remote Desktop Connection Broker
$RDCB = 'RDCB-01.Contoso.local'


#Remote Desktop Web Access
$RDWeb = 'RDWeb-01.Contoso.local'
#Creating new Virtual Machine-based deployment
New-RDVirtualDesktopDeployment -ConnectionBroker $RDCB -WebAccessServer
$RDWeb -VirtualizationHost $RDVH -CreateVirtualSwitch
```

Task 1.2 – creating a new session-based deployment

In this type of deployment, you create an RDS environment capable of hosting Session Virtualization scenarios. This deployment requires three RDS roles: **Remote Desktop Session Host (RDSH)**, RDCB, and RDWeb. For this purpose, you will use the `New-SessionDeployment` cmdlet with the following parameters:

- `-ConnectionBroker`: This parameter defines the FQDN of the server to hold the Connection Broker role
- `-WebAccessServer`: This parameter defines the FQDN of the web server to hold the Web Access role
- `-SessionHost`: This parameter defines the FQDN of the server to host the Session Host role

The script will be as follows:

```
#Remote Desktop Session Host
$RDSH = 'RDSH-01.Contoso.local'


#Remote Desktop Connection Broker
$RDCB = 'RDCB-01.Contoso.local'
```

```
#Remote Desktop Web Access
$RDWeb = 'RDWeb-01.Contoso.local'


#Creating new Session-based deployment
New-SessionDeployment -SessionHost $RDSH -ConnectionBroker $RDCB
-WebAccessServer $RDWeb
```

Scenario 2 – adding a Remote Desktop Server to an existing deployment

In the previous scenarios, you have created a Remote Desktop deployment twice, one for a VM-based environment and the other for a session-based environment. Each of those scenarios installed three RDS roles out of a total of six. So, what if you want to add other roles to the deployment? Or you want to combine the two kinds of deployment into a hybrid RD deployment?

In this scenario, you are a Desktop Virtualization administrator who has an existing RD deployment and wants to make it hybrid by adding either the RDSH role to the VM-based deployment or the RDVH role to the session-based deployment. For this purpose, you will use the Add-RDServer cmdlet with the following parameters:

- -ConnectionBroker: This parameter defines the FQDN of the server that holds the Connection Broker role for the existing deployment.
- -Server: This parameter defines the FQDN of the server to add to the deployment.
- -Role: This parameter defines which RD role the server will hold. The following values can be used with the -Role parameter:
    - ○ RDS-RD-Server to add an RD session host
    - ○ RDS-Virtualization to add an RD virtualization host
    - ○ RDS-Connection-Broker to add an RD connection broker
    - ○ RDS-Web-Access to add RD web access
    - ○ RDS-Gateway to add an RD gateway
    - ○ RDS-Licensing to add an RD licensing server

The script will be as follows:

```
$RDCB = 'RDCB-01.Contoso.local'


#Adding Virtualization Host to Session-based deployment
Add-RDServer -Server 'RDVH-01.Contoso.local' -ConnectionBroker $RDCB
-Role RDS-Virtualization -CreateVirtualSwitch $true


#Adding Session Host to VM-based deployment
Add-RDServer -Server 'RDSH-01.Contoso.local' -ConnectionBroker $RDCB
-Role RDS-RD-Server
```

Scenario 3 – adding and configuring an RD Gateway

In this scenario, you are a Desktop Virtualization administrator who wants to expose the current deployment to the Internet in order to make the environment accessible to remote users. So, you have to add the **Remote Desktop Gateway (RDG)** role to the existing deployment. For this purpose, you will use the Add-RDServer cmdlet to add the gateway to the existing deployment and then use the Set-RDDeploymentGatewayConfiguration cmdlet to configure the RD gateway settings using the following group of parameters:

- -ConnectionBroker: This parameter defines the FQDN of the server that holds the Connection Broker role for the existing deployment.

- -BypassLocal: This parameter allows the user to bypass the RD gateway by providing him/her with internal access.

- -LogonMethod: This parameter defines which logon method is to be used by the user. It could be either AllowUserToSelectDuringConnection, Smartcard, or Password.

- -GatewayMode: This parameter defines whether the RD gateway is used or not and how it will be configured, either by auto detect or manually.

- -GatewayExternalFqdn: This parameter defines the external FQDN for RDG to be accessible remotely over the Internet.

This script will be as follows:

```
$RDCB = 'RDCB-01.Contoso.local'
$RDG = 'RDG01.contoso.local'


#Adding RD Gateway Server
Add-RDServer -Server $RDG -ConnectionBroker $RDCB -Role RDS-GATEWAY
-GatewayExternalFqdn RDG.Contoso.com


#Configuring RD Gateway
Set-RDDeploymentGatewayConfiguration -ConnectionBroker $RDCB -BypassLocal
$true -LogonMethod AllowUserToSelectDuringConnection -GatewayMode Custom
-GatewayExternalFqdn RDG.Contoso.com
```

Scenario 4 – adding and configuring RD Licensing Server

Remote Desktop Licensing (RDL) is the legal role of RDS. It has no technical impact on the environment or the deployment, however it is required to make sure that your RDS licenses are properly configured. In this scenario, you will learn how to add and configure the RDL role. For this purpose, you will use the Add-RDServer cmdlet to add the gateway to the existing deployment and then use the Set-RDLicenseConfiguration cmdlet to configure the RD gateway settings.

The Set-RDLicenseConfiguration cmdlet will be used with the following group of parameters:

- -ConnectionBroker: This parameter defines the FQDN of the server that holds the Connection Broker role for the existing deployment.

- -LicenseServer: This parameter defines the name of the server to hold the RDL role.

- -Mode: This parameter defines the license mode of the RDS. It could be PerUser or PerDevice.

The script will be as follows:

```
$RDCB = 'RDCB-01.Contoso.local'
$RDL = 'RDL01.contoso.local'


#Adding RD Licensing Server
Add-RDServer -Server $RDL -Role RDS-LICENSING -ConnectionBroker $RDCB
```

```
#Configuring RD Licensing

Set-RDLicenseConfiguration -Mode PerUser -LicenseServer $RDL
-ConnectionBroker $RDCB
```

Scenario 5 – creating new RDS collections

Now after completing the RDS deployments for the VM-based and session-based environments, it is the time to create a collection for each deployment. RDS collections are a way to define the settings of your environments, such as how the users will connect to it, which groups are authorized to access it, and which servers will be used for this collection. You can also consider RDS collections as a logical group for your Virtualization Desktop environment.

Task 5.1 – creating new session-based collections

In this scenario, you will need to create a collection for the session-based deployment created previously. For this purpose, you will use the `New-RDSessionCollection` cmdlet with the following parameters:

- `-CollectionName`: This parameter defines a name for the RDS collection
- `-ConnectionBroker`: This parameter defines the FQDN of the server currently holding the Connection Broker role
- `-SessionHost`: This parameter defines the FQDN of the RDSH server(s) to server to host the Session Host role

The script will be as follows:

```
#Remote Desktop Connection Broker

$RDCB = 'RDCB-01.Contoso.local'


#Remote Desktop Session Host(s)

$RDSH = @('RDSH-01.Contoso.local','RDSH-02.Contoso.local')


#Creating new Session-based Collection

New-RDSessionCollection -CollectionName "mySessions"
-CollectionDescription "RDS - Session Virtualization Collection"
-ConnectionBroker $RDCB -SessionHost $RDSH
```

Task 5.2 – creating new VM-based collections

A VM-based collection provides the authorized user with a complete operating system on a dedicated virtual desktop. The VM-based collection can be defined either as a Pooled or Personal VM collection.

- **Pooled collection**: In this type of collection, you create a group of virtual desktops and assign them to a users or groups. Assignment of the virtual desktop is automatic and random so the user will connect to a different machine every time. Moreover, the machine will roll back to the default state once the user logs off.

- **Personal collection**: In this type of collection, the virtual desktop is assigned manually so that the user connects to the same machine every time and changes are stored on the machine even after the user logs off and the machine restarts.

>
> A Pooled or Personal VM collection could both be created as either a Managed collection, where virtual desktops are created using a single master template, or as an Unmanaged collection, where the virtual desktops are created manually or using different templates.
>
> In real-world implementations, it is recommended to have Managed Pooled and Unmanaged Personal collections.

Task 5.2.A – creating a Managed Pooled collection

In this scenario, you will use the `New-RDVirtualDesktopCollection` cmdlet, and also the `Grant-RDOUAccess` cmdlet to grant the RDS permission on the OU that will host the VDI computer accounts and also with the following parameters:

- `-CollectionName`: This parameter defines the name of the RDS collection

- `-ConnectionBroker`: This parameter defines the FQDN of the server holding the Connection Broker role

- `-PooledManaged`: This parameter defines the Managed Pooled VM-based collection

- `-UserGroups`: This parameter defines the users and groups authorized to access this collection

- `-Domain`: This parameter defines the Managed Pooled VM-based collection

- `-VirtualDesktopTemplateHostServer`: This parameter defines the FQDN of the server hosting the new virtual desktop template

- `-VirtualDesktopTemplateName`: This parameter defines the name of the new virtual desktop template
- `-VirtualDesktopNamePrefix`: This parameter defines the VM name prefix
- `-VirtualDesktopTemplateStorgePath`: This parameter defines the path for the storage hosting the template
- `-StorageType`: This parameter defines the type of storage, either Local, SMB Shared, or SAN
- `-VirtualDesktopAllocation`: This parameter defines how the created virtual desktops will be allocated across the different RD virtualization hosts

The script will be as follows:

```
#Remote Desktop Connection Broker
$RDCB = 'RDCB-01.Contoso.local'


#Virtual Server hosting the Virtual Desktop Template
$RDtemplateHost = 'RDVH-01.Contoso.local'


#Domain name
$DomainName = 'Contoso.local'


#AD OU  that will contain the VDI computer accounts
$OU = 'VDI'


#Grant RDS a permission on the selected OU to create/remove computer
accounts for Virtual Desktops
Grant-RDOUAccess -Domain $DomainName -OU $OU -ConnectionBroker $RDCB


#Creating new VM-based Collection
New-VirtualDesktopCollection -CollectionName 'Win 7 SP1' -Description
'RDS - Virtual Desktop Collection' -PooledManaged -UserGroups "Contoso\
Domain Users" -Domain "Contoso.local" -VirtualDesktopTemplateHostServer
$RDtemplateHost -VirtualDesktopTemplateName 'Win7SP1-Temp'
-ConnectionBroker $RDCB -OU $OU -VirtualDesktopNamePrefix
"VD-W7-" -VirtualDesktopTemplateStoragePath "C:\VDs"
 -StorageType LocalStorage -VirtualDesktopAllocation
@{"RDVH-01.Contoso.local"=5;"RDVH-02.Contoso.local"=5}
```

Task 5.2.B – creating an Unmanaged Personal collection

In this scenario, you will use the `Grant-RDOUAccess` cmdlet to grant the RDS permission on the OU that will host the VDI computer accounts, the `New-RDVirtualDesktopCollection` cmdlet to create the VM-based collection, and also the `Set-RDPersonalVirtualDesktopAssignment` cmdlet to assign a virtual desktop to a user.

The `New-RDVirtualDesktopCollection` cmdlet is used with the following parameters:

- `-CollectionName`: This parameter defines the name of the RDS collection
- `-ConnectionBroker`: This parameter defines the FQDN of the server holding the Connection Broker role
- `-PersonalUnmanaged`: This parameter defines the Unmanaged Personal VM-based collection
- `-UserGroups`: This parameter defines the users and groups authorized to access this collection
- `-VirtualDesktopName`: This parameter specifies the name of the virtual machine to be added to the collection
- `-VirtualDesktopTemplateName`: This parameter defines the name of the new virtual desktop template
- `-AutoAssignPersonalVirtualDesktopToUser`: This parameter defines whether a virtual desktop is automatically assigned to the users or not
- `-GrantAdministrativePrivilege`: This parameter grants the user an administrative privilege on the virtual desktop

The `Set-RDPersonalVirtualDesktopAssignment` cmdlet is used with the following parameters:

- `-CollectionName`: This parameter defines the name of the RDS collection
- `-ConnectionBroker`: This parameter defines the FQDN of the server holding the Connection Broker role
- `-VirtualDesktopName`: This parameter defines the name of the VM to be assigned
- `-User`: This parameter defines the user who will get the virtual machine

The script will be as follows:

```
#Remote Desktop Connection Broker
$RDCB = 'RDCB-01.Contoso.local'


#Remote Desktop Virtualization Host(s)
$RDSH = @('RDSH-01.Contoso.local','RDSH-02.Contoso.local')


#Domain name
$DomainName = 'Contoso.local'


#AD OU will contain the VDI computer accounts
$OU = 'VDI'


#Grant RDS a permission on the selected OU to create/remove computer
accounts for Virtual Desktops
Grant-RDOUAccess -Domain $DomainName -OU $OU -ConnectionBroker $RDCB


#Creating new VM-based Collection
New-RDVirtualDesktopCollection -CollectionName 'Win 7 SP1'
-Description 'RDS - Virtual Desktop Collection' -PersonalUnmanaged
-UserGroups "Contoso\Domain Admins" -ConnectionBroker $RDCB
-VirtualDesktopName "XYZ" -AutoAssignPersonalVirtualDesktopToUser
$false -GrantAdministrativePrivilege $true


#Assign Virtual Desktop to a User
Set-RDPersonalVirtualDesktopAssignment -CollectionName 'Win 7 SP1'
-User 'Contoso\Sherif' -VirtualDesktopName 'XYZ' -ConnectionBroker
$RDCB
```

Scenario 6 – setting session-based collection configuration

In this scenario, you will create an RD-session-based collection and set the collection configuration in order to it make ready for end users. For this purpose, you will use the Set-RDSessionCollectionConfiguration cmdlet with the following parameters:

- -CollectionName: This parameter defines the name of the collection to be modified.

- -UserGroup: This parameter defines which user groups are authorized to access this collection

- -ClientDeviceRedirectionOptions: This parameter defines what should be redirected from the client device to the remote session, for example, a clipboard, audio, or drive.

- -ClientPrinterRedirected: This parameter defines whether the user can use the locally installed printer on the remote session or not.

- -BrokenConnectionAction: This parameter defines the action to be taken when the user's session is broken. So the server can disconnect or log off the session to save the resources for other sessions.

- -AutomaticReconnectionEnabled: This parameter defines whether the broken session can be reconnected automatically or not.

- -MaxRedirectedMonitors: This parameter defines the number of monitors that can be redirected per user session.

- -IdleSessionLimitMin: This parameter defines the number of minutes before the idle sessions are disconnected.

- -TemporaryFoldersPerSession: This parameter creates a temporary folder for each session or uses one for all sessions.

- -ConnectionBroker: This parameter defines the FQDN of the server that holds the Connection Broker role for the existing deployment.

The script will be as follows:

```
#Remote Desktop Connection Broker
$RDCB = 'RDCB-01.Contoso.local'


#Setting Session-based Collection Configuration
Set-RDSessionCollectionConfiguration -CollectionName mySessions
-UserGroup "CoEx\Domain Users" -ClientDeviceRedirectionOptions
Drive -ClientPrinterRedirected $true -BrokenConnectionAction
Disconnect -AutomaticReconnectionEnabled $true
-MaxRedirectedMonitors 4 -IdleSessionLimitMin 60
-TemporaryFoldersPerSession $true -MaxRedirectedMonitors 4
-ConnectionBroker $RDCB
```

Scenario 7 – setting VM-based collection configuration

In this scenario, you will create a VM-based collection and set the collection configuration in order to make it ready for end users. For this purpose, you will use the `Set-RDVirtualDesktopCollectionConfiguration` cmdlet with the following parameters:

- `-CollectionName`: This parameter defines the name of the collection to be modified

- `-UserGroups`: This parameter defines which users and groups are authorized to access this collection

- `-RedirectAllMonitors`: This parameter allows the users to redirect all monitors to the virtual desktop

- `-GrantAdministrativePrivilege`: This parameter grants the user an administrative privilege on the virtual desktop

- `-AutoAssignPersonalVirtualDesktopToUser`: This parameter automatically assigns virtual desktops to the user

- `-ConnectionBroker`: This parameter defines the FQDN of the server that holds the Connection Broker role for the existing deployment

The script will be as follows:

```
#Remote Desktop Connection Broker
$RDCB = 'RDCB-01.Contoso.local'


#Setting VM-based Collection Configuration
Set-RDVirtualDesktopCollectionConfiguration "Call-Center Pool"
-UserGroups "Contoso\CallCenter Users" -RedirectAllMonitors
$false -ClientDeviceRedirectionOptions AudioVideoPlayBac
k,PlugAndPlayDevice -GrantAdministrativePrivilege $true
-AutoAssignPersonalVirtualDesktopToUser $true -ConnectionBroker $RDCB
```

Scenario 8 – updating VM-based collections

In this scenario, you have a VM-based collection created using a specified Windows 7 template. For some reason, you made some changes on the master template and you want to apply these changes on the virtual desktops in this collection. For this purpose, you will use the `Update-RDVirtualDesktopCollection` cmdlet with the following parameters:

- `-CollectionName`: This parameter defines the name of the collection to be updated

- `-ConnectionBroker`: This parameter defines the FQDN of the server that holds the Connection Broker role for the existing deployment

- `-VirtualDesktopTemplateHostServer`: This parameter defines the FQDN of the server hosting the new virtual desktop template

- `-VirtualDesktopTemplateName`: This parameter defines the name of the new virtual desktop template

- `-DisableVirtualDesktopRollback`: This parameter defines whether the machine can be rolled back or not after the update

- `-StartTime`: This parameter defines the time at which the update operation will start

- `-ForceLogoffTime`: This parameter defines the time at which the connected user will be forced to log off to perform the update operation

The script will be as follows:

```
#Remote Desktop Connection Broker
$RDCB = 'RDCB-01.Contoso.local'


#Virual Desktop Template Host Server
$VDtemplateHost = 'RDVH-01.Contoso.local'


#Virtual Desktop Template
$VDtemplate = 'Win 7 SP1 Jan 2013 Update'


#Updating VM-based Collection
Update-RDVirtualDesktopCollection -CollectionName "Win 7 SP1"
-ConnectionBroker $RDCB -VirtualDesktopTemplateHostServer $VDtemplateHost
-VirtualDesktopTemplateName $VDtemplate -DisableVirtualDesktopRollback
$false -StartTime (Get-Date) -ForceLogoffTime (Get-Date).AddHours(8)
```

Scenario 9 – assigning Profile Disks to collections

Profile Disks is a new feature introduced in RDS in Windows Server 2012. Profile Disks saves users' profiles on a **Virtual Hard Disk (VHD)** file; this file follows the user everywhere in the collection, so once the user connects to any virtual machine or session, Profile Disks will be attached automatically.

By default, the Profile Disks feature is disabled, and you have to activate it on the desired collection in order to use it. It can be used with the session-based and VM-based collections and configured using the Set-RDSessionCollectionConfiguration and Set-RDVirtualDesktopCollectionConfiguration cmdlets.

I can hear you; you are wondering why we did not do that in the previous scenarios? The answer is the parameters related to Profile Disks must be used exclusively and not with normal configuration parameters.

The following parameters are common for Profile Disks irrespective of whether you are configuring it for a VM-based or session-based collection:

- -CollectionName: This parameter defines the name of the collection to be modified.

- -EnableUserProfileDisk: This parameter enables the Profile Disks feature.

- -DisableUserProfileDisk: This parameter disables the Profile Disks feature.

- -DiskPath: This parameter is the path used to store Profile Disks. It could be a local directory or a shared folder. A shared folder is preferred if you are using multiple servers per collection.

- -MaxUserProfileDiskSizeGB: This parameter defines the maximum size for each Profile Disks feature.

- -IncludeFolderPath: This parameter defines the custom folder to be saved on Profile Disks.

- -ExcludeFolderPath: This parameter defines the default profile folder to be removed from Profile Disks.

- -RedirectAllMonitors: This parameter allows the users to redirect all monitors to the virtual desktop.

The script will be as follows:

```
#Remote Desktop Connection Broker
$RDCB = 'RCCB-01.Contoso.local'


#Enable and Assign Profile Disk to Session-based Collection
Set-RDSessionCollectionConfiguration -CollectionName "mySessions"
-EnableUserProfileDisk -DiskPath '\\FileServer-01\ProfileDisks'
-MaxUserProfileDiskSizeGB 20 -IncludeFolderPath 'C:\myReports'
-ConnectionBroker $RDCB


#Enable and Assign Profile Disk to VM-based Collection
Set-RDVirtualDesktopCollectionConfiguration -CollectionName "Win7SP1"
-EnableUserProfileDisk -DiskPath '\\FileServer-01\ProfileDisks'
-MaxUserProfileDiskSizeGB 20 -ExcludeFolderPath 'C:\Users\Sherif\Desktop\
myVideos' -ConnectionBroker $RDCB
```

Scenario 10 – publishing Remote Desktop RemoteApp to collections

RemoteApp is one of the RDS features that allows you to publish an application through RDS Web Access so that users can launch the application directly without even installing the application on the local machine.

In this scenario, you already have a VM-based collection and you want to set up a RemoteApp and publish it to this collection in order to allow users to use this application. For this purpose, you will use the New-RDRemoteApp cmdlet with the following parameters:

- -CollectionName: This parameter defines the name of the collection to be modified

- -ShowinWebAccess: This parameter chooses whether to show RemoteApp in the web access portal or to hide it

- -UserGroups: This parameter specifies the users and groups with authorized access to this RemoteApp feature

- -DisplayName: This parameter defines the display name of the RemoteApp feature

- -FilePath: This parameter gives the path file of the RemoteApp feature executable file

- -ConnectionBroker: This parameter defines the FQDN of the server that holds the Connection Broker role for the existing deployment

The script will be as follows:

```
#Remote Desktop Connection Broker
$RDCB = 'RDCB-01.Contoso.local'


#Publish Remote Desktop RemoteApp to Collection
New-RDRemoteApp -CollectionName "mySessions" -ShowInWebAccess $true
-UserGroups "Contoso\CallCenter Users" -ConnectionBroker $RDCB
-DisplayName Skype -FilePath "C:\Program Files (x86)\Skype\Phone\Skype.
exe"
```

Scenario 11 – configuring Remote Desktop Connection Broker for high availability

In this scenario, you are a virtualization administrator at Contoso where Desktop Virtualization is one of the important components, and you found that the current implementation has only one **Remote Desktop Connection Broker (RDCB)** that is a single point of failure. So, you have decided to add one more server for high availability to save the environment in case of a disaster.

For this purpose, you will use the `Set-RDConnectionBrokerHighAvailability` cmdlet to configure the High-Availability settings and then the `Add-RDServer` cmdlet to add a new RDCB server to the array.

The `Set-RDConnectionBrokerHighAvailability` cmdlet is used with the following group of parameters:

- `-ConnectionBroker`: This parameter defines the FQDN of the server that holds the Connection Broker role for the existing deployment.

- `-DatabaseConnectionString`: This parameter defines the connection string to be used by the RDS to connect to the configuration database on SQL Server.

- `-ClientAccessName`: This parameter defines the name used by the clients to access Connection Broker. The name should be configured in DNS as a round-robin record.

- `-DatabaseFilePath`: This parameter defines the path that creates the RDCB configuration database file.

Before you start configuring the RDCB high availability, ensure that:
- The RDCB servers have an administrative permissions on SQL Server
- The RDCB servers have SQL Server's native client installed
- The RDCB servers have a DNS round-robin record
- The RDCB servers have a static assigned IP Address

The script will be as follows:

```
#Remote Desktop Connection Broker
$RDCB = 'RDCB-01.Contoso.local'


#SQL Server Instance
$SQLinstance 'SQL-01.Contoso.local'


#RD Connection Broker Database name
$RDCBDB = 'RDCB'


$ConStr = "DRIVER=SQL Server Native Client 10.0;SERVER=$SQLinstan
ce;Trusted_Connection=Yes;APP=Remote Desktop Services Connection
Broker;Database=$RDCBDB"


#Configuring RDCB HA settings
Set-RDConnectionBrokerHighAvailability -ConnectionBroker $RDCB
-DatabaseConnectionString $ConStr -ClientAccessName RDCB.Contoso.Local
-DatabaseFilePath ("C:\$RDCBDB" + '.mdf')


#Adding the second RDCB the HA Array
Add-RDServer -ConnectionBroker $RDCB -Server RDSH-02.Contoso.local -Role
RDS-CONNECTION-BROKER
```

Summary

It is very obvious that virtualization in general has played a major role in changing the shape of the ICT industry. In this chapter, we had a sneak peek at Desktop Virtualization as a concept, its benefits, and the value of using it from a business and technical perspective. Also, we learned how to use Windows PowerShell to install, configure, and manage Microsoft Remote Desktop Services.

In the next chapter, we will continue the Windows PowerShell's journey of knowledge with Microsoft Cloud solutions. The spotlight will be on how Windows PowerShell can help you to build and manage your infrastructure and the platforms hosted on the cloud, with a focus on Microsoft's implementation of **Infrastructure-as-a-Service (IaaS)** represented in Windows Azure and **Platform-as-a-Service (PaaS)** represented in SQL Azure.

11

Managing Microsoft Cloud Platform with PowerShell

Cloud is one of the most popular words in the ICT industry nowadays; we hear it every day, everywhere, and at every occasion. In simple words, **cloud computing** is the concept of using and delivering computing resources to the end user as a service. A computing resource could be software such as web portals and messaging systems, or hardware such as CPU, memory, network, and storage. It could be hosted internally in a corporate's data center "Private Cloud" or externally in a vendor's data center "Public Cloud".

There are different types of cloud computing:

- **Software-as-a-Service (SaaS)**: In SaaS, you get your software (for example, e-mail, web portals, or CRM) as a service hosted in the cloud; you do not have to worry about hardware requirements, software prerequisites, implementation, and maintenance hassles. In simple words, you can get software that is ready to use in a few clicks.

  Popular solution(s): Microsoft Office 365 and Oracle CRM On Demand

- **Platform-as-a-Service (PaaS)**: In PaaS, you get Data Platform such as SQL Server as a service such as SaaS hosted in the cloud. You can also get your SQL Server instance and database ready in no time.

  Popular solution(s): Microsoft SQL Azure and Google App Engine

- **Infrastructure-as-a-Service (IaaS)**: In IaaS, you get the infrastructure (hardware) components as a service. It is similar to the web hosting concept in which you get a specific hardware configuration to host your website; however, in IaaS you get the hardware configuration to build and host your virtual servers.

  Popular solution(s): Microsoft SQL Azure and Amazon Web Services

This chapter will cover how Windows PowerShell helps in administering, managing, and automating a cloud computing platform such as Microsoft Windows Azure.

We will also cover the following topics:

- What is Windows Azure?
- What is Windows Azure PowerShell?
- Managing Windows Azure using PowerShell.

What Windows Azure is

Windows Azure is a cloud-computing concept that is created by Microsoft. Mainly, Windows Azure provides IaaS and PaaS, so you can think about using it in many scenarios, such as hosting a web application, deploying a centralized data store, building a development and testing environment, or even implementing a **disaster recovery (DR)** site for your on-premise environment.

What Windows Azure PowerShell is

Windows Azure comes with a very neat and easy, web-based management interface that allows you to do any task in a few clicks, but unfortunately this interface is a bit limited. For example, you cannot create a couple of virtual machines in one shot; you have to repeat the same steps twice in order to get two virtual machines. The same goes for the rest of the Azure tasks. That is why, Windows Azure provides a powerful scripting environment via Windows PowerShell to make it easier for administrators to automate multiple Azure tasks, such as the provisioning of virtual machines, application deployment, and infrastructure management.

Installing Windows Azure PowerShell

Windows Azure PowerShell is provided with the Windows PowerShell module as part of the Windows Azure Software Development Kit (SDK). In order to install Windows Azure PowerShell:

1. Go to Windows Azure's download page:

   http://www.windowsazure.com/en-us/manage/downloads/

2. In the **Windows** section, click on **Install** to download the web installer EXE file for Windows Azure PowerShell:

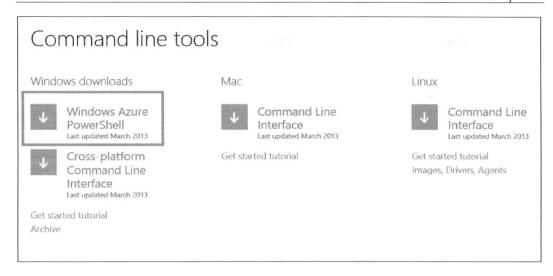

3. Launch the web installer file; click on **Install** to start Windows Azure PowerShell's installation and configuration.

4. Follow the installation wizard to complete the process.

After installing Windows Azure PowerShell, a module called "Azure" should be available in your system.

Making Windows PowerShell understand Windows Azure cmdlets

In order to use Windows Azure cmdlets in Windows PowerShell, you can either directly launch the Windows Azure PowerShell shortcut to quickly jump into the Windows Azure PowerShell environment or launch the import Windows Azure PowerShell module into your Windows PowerShell session using the following command:

```
#Import Windows Azure PowerShell module
PS> Import-Module Azure
```

Connecting to your Windows Azure environment

After downloading, installing, and importing the Windows Azure PowerShell, you are just one step away from managing your Windows Azure environment using PowerShell. The last step is connecting to your Windows Azure subscription.

In order to set up your Windows Azure subscription in your PowerShell, you have to import the `PublishSettings` file that contains your Windows Azure subscription's unique information, such as the subscription ID, name, service endpoint URL, and certificate thumbprint. This information will be used by PowerShell to reach your Windows Azure environment.

You can get the `PublishSettings` file easily by using the `Get-AzurePublishSettingsFile` cmdlet. This cmdlet will take you to the Windows Azure portal. When you enter your credentials, you will be redirected to an instructional page to generate and download your Windows Azure `PublishSettings` file for your subscription.

```
#Generate and download the Windows Azure PublishSettings File
PS> Get-AzurePublishSettingsFile
```

Now you should have the `publishsettings` file called `<AzurePublishSettings>.publishSettings` that contains your Windows Azure subscription. The next step is to import it to PowerShell in order to define your subscription information into Windows PowerShell. To import the `PublishSettings` file, use the `Import-AzurePublishSettingsFile` cmdlet as follows:

```
#Import Windows Azure PublishSettings File
PS> Import-AzurePublishSettingsFile <FileName>.publishsettings
```

Once the `PublishSettings` file is imported successfully, Windows PowerShell will set your subscription as a default subscription; so every time you open Windows PowerShell and use Windows Azure cmdlets, it will automatically connect to Windows Azure using the default subscription. In order to show your subscription information, use the `Get-AzureSubscription` cmdlet.

```
PS C:\Users\v-shta\desktop> Get-AzureSubscription

SubscriptionName      : Windows Azure MSDN - Visual Studio Ultimate
SubscriptionId        : 5c6a                    a149
Certificate           : [Subject]
                          CN=Windows Azure Tools

                        [Issuer]
                          CN=Windows Azure Tools

                        [Serial Number]
                          03674                        D215

                        [Not Before]
                          12/28/2012 2:37:50 AM

                        [Not After]
                          12/28/2013 2:37:50 AM

                        [Thumbprint]
                          6AE6F61                       CB6

ServiceEndpoint       : https://management.core.windows.net/
SqlAzureServiceEndpoint :
CurrentStorageAccount : cnex
IsDefault             : True
```

So at this point, we can say congratulations!! Your Windows PowerShell environment is now ready to manage your Windows Azure.

Getting started with Windows Azure scripting

In this section, we will help you get started with Windows Azure scripting and automation using a set of Windows PowerShell scenarios and examples.

Scenario 1 – creating a new Azure Affinity Group

In this scenario, you are a Windows Azure administrator who wants to get the best performance by making sure that any related cloud components associated with a specific cloud service are placed in the same data center, especially when Microsoft has multiple Azure data centers distributed across the United States, Europe, and Asia. So for this purpose, you need to create an "affinity group" in order to group the related components logically. For this, you will use the New-AzureAffinityGroup cmdlet with the following group of parameters:

- -Name: Defines the name of the new affinity group
- -Location: Defines the location of the affinity group; this will define which data center needs to be used to place the cloud components associated with this affinity group

Use the `Get-AzureLocation` cmdlet to get the list of available locations.

You can use the following code:

```
#Create New Azure Affinity Group
PS> New-AzureAffinityGroup –Name "ContosoAffinityGroup" –Location
"West US"
```

Scenario 2 – creating a new Azure storage account

In this scenario, you will create an Azure storage account in order to allow your services, applications, and infrastructure to utilize Windows Azure storage. For this purpose, you will use the `New-AzureStorageAccount` cmdlet with the following group of parameters:

- `-StorageAccountName`: Defines the name of the new azure storage account
- `-AffinityGroup`: Defines the name of the affinity group that the storage account should be associated with

You can use the following code:

```
#Create New Azure Storage Account
PS> New-AzureStorageAccount -StorageAccountName "contoso"
-AffinityGroup "ContosoAffinityGroup"
```

Scenario 3 – assigning a storage account to an Azure subscription

In this scenario, you will assign a previously created Azure storage account to your Windows Azure subscription in order to make sure that any task created under this subscription will use this storage account by default. For this purpose, you will use the `Set-AzureSubscription` cmdlet to define the Windows Azure subscription's settings with the following group of parameters:

- `-SubscriptionName`: Defines the name of the Azure subscription; use the `Get-AzureSubscription` cmdlet to list all the available subscriptions in Windows PowerShell
- `-CurrentStorageAccount`: Defines the name of the previously created Azure storage account

You can use the following code:

```
#Assign Azure storage account to a specific azure subscription
PS> Set-AzureSubscription -SubscriptionName <Subscription_Name>
-CurrentStorageAccount "Contoso"
```

Scenario 4 – creating a new Azure Cloud Service

In this scenario, you will create a Windows Azure Cloud Service. A cloud service describes the components of each solution you have on Windows Azure. For example, if you have a web application hosted on a web server (IIS) that connects to a database hosted on a database server (SQL Server), these two components should be called "Cloud Service". So, cloud service is an essential requirement for any Azure component you want to create on Windows Azure. For this purpose, you will use the New-AzureService cmdlet with the following group of parameters:

- -ServiceName: Defines the name of the new Azure service
- -AffinityGroup: Defines the affinity group the storage account should be associated with

You can use the following code:

```
#Create new Azure Cloud Service
PS> New-AzureService -ServiceName "myCloudService" -AffinityGroup
"ContosoAffinityGroup"
```

Scenario 5 – creating a new SQL Azure Database Server

In this scenario, you will create a centralized SQL Server database hosted in the cloud, utilizing the SQL Azure capabilities to host your database. So before you create your SQL Server database, you first need to create a SQL Server instance to host this SQL database. For this purpose, you will use the New-AzureSqlDatabaseServer cmdlet with the following group of parameters:

- -AdministratorLogin: Defines the login name for the SQL Azure instance administrator
- -AdministratorLoginPassword: Defines the login and password for the SQL Azure instance administrator
- -Location: Defines the SQL Azure server instance's location

You can use the following code:

```
#Create new SQL Azure Database Server instance
PS> New-AzureSqlDatabaseServer -AdministratorLogin "SherifT"
-AdministratorLoginPassword "P@ssw0rd" -Location "West US"
```

Scenario 6 – creating a new SQL Azure database

In this scenario, you will create a SQL Azure database on a previously created SQL Azure database server instance. For this purpose you will use a couple of cmdlets; the first cmdlet is the `New-AzureSqlDatabaseServerContext` cmdlet that is used to define which server you will connect to, and the second cmdlet is the `New-AzureSqlDatabase` cmdlet that is used to create the SQL Azure database.

Following are the group of parameters:

- `New-AzureSqlDatabaseServerContext`

    ○ `-ServerName`: Defines SQL Azure server name

- `New-AzureSqlDatabase`

    ○ `-Context`: Defines the database context object created using the `New-AzureSqlDatabaseServerContext` cmdlet

    ○ `-DatabaseName`: Defines the name of the new database you want to create

    ○ `-Collation`: Defines the collation of the database

    ○ `-Edition`: Defines the database edition, either "Web" or "Business"

    ○ `-MaxSizeGB`: Defines the maximum size of the database in gigabytes; the maximum size of the database depends on which database edition you are using

You can use the following code:

```
#Create SQL Azure Database Server Context
PS> $context = New-AzureSqlDatabaseServerContext -ServerName <server_
Name>

#Create new SQL Azure Database
PS> New-AzureSqlDatabase –Context $context -DatabaseName "myDatabase"
-Collation SQL_Latin1_General_CP1_CI_AS -Edition "Web" -MaxSizeGB 1
```

Scenario 7 – creating a new SQL Azure Database Server firewall rule

In this scenario, you will create a SQL Azure Database server firewall rule in order to allow communication between your SQL Azure database server and web application that is hosted either somewhere else or on other computers in a specific network range. For this purpose, you will use the `New-AzureSqlDatabaseServerFirewallRule` cmdlet to define the firewall rule settings for SQL Azure Server.

Following are the group of parameters:

- `-ServerName`: Defines SQL Azure server name
- `-RuleName`: Defines the name of the firewall rule
- `-StartIpAddress`: Defines the start IP address
- `-EndIpAddress`: Defines the end IP address

> Use `0.0.0.0` for `-StartIpAddress` and `-EndIpAddress` to allow communication between SQL Azure and Windows Azure.

You can use the following code:

```
#Create SQL Azure Database Server Firewall Rule
PS> New-AzureSqlDatabaseServerFirewallRule –ServerName <Server_Name>
-RuleName "myIntranet" -StartIpAddress 192.168.1.1 -EndIpAddress
192.168.1.254
```

Scenario 8 – provisioning the new Azure VM in Windows (quick mode)

In this scenario, you will create a new Windows Azure virtual machine running a Windows operating system using the quick mode. The quick mode allows you to create a new virtual machine with minimal input from your side; it is good for testing purposes. For the purpose of creating a new virtual machine, you will use the `New-AzureQuickVM` cmdlet with the following group of parameters:

- `-Windows`: Defines that a virtual machine will run a Windows operating system.
- `-ServiceName`: Defines the cloud service that will host the virtual machine.
- `-Name`: Defines the name of the virtual machine.

- -Password: Defines the operating system's administrator password.
- -ImageName: Defines the name of the image that will be used to provision the virtual machine.

 Use the Get-AzureVMImage cmdlet to list all the images available in Windows Azure.

- -InstanceSize: Defines the size of the virtual machine: "ExtraSmall", "Small", "Medium", "Large", or "ExtraLarge". The difference between instance sizes is the number of CPU cores and memory.

You can use the following code:

```
#Create new Windows Azure VM - Windows using Quick Mode
PS > New-AzureQuickVM -Windows -ServiceName "DatabaseService" -Name
"CAI-DC-03" -ImageName "MSFT__Windows-Server-2012-Datacenter-
201210.01-en.us-30GB.vhd" -Password P@ssw0rd -AffinityGroup
"ContosoAffinityGroup" -AffinityGroup "ContosoAffinityGroup"
```

Scenario 9 – provisioning the new Azure VM in Linux (quick mode)

In this scenario, you will create a new Windows Azure virtual machine that is running Linux operating system using the quick mode. For the purpose of creating a new virtual machine, you will use the New-AzureQuickVM cmdlet with the following group of parameters:

- -Linux: Defines that the virtual machine will run a Linux operating system.
- -ServiceName: Defines the cloud service that will host the virtual machine.
- -Name: Defines the name of the virtual machine.
- -LinuxUser: Defines the Linux administrator user.
- -Password: Defines the operating system's administrator password.
- -ImageName: Defines the name of the image that will be used to provision the virtual machine. Use the Get-AzureVMImage cmdlet to list all the available images.
- -InstanceSize: Defines the size of the virtual machine: "ExtraSmall", "Small", "Medium", "Large", or "ExtraLarge". The difference between instance sizes is the number of CPU cores and memory.

You can use the following code:

```
#Create new Windows Azure VM - Linux using Quick Mode
PS> New-AzureQuickVM -Linux -ServiceName "myLinuxEnv" -Name
"SUSE-02" -ImageName "b4590d9e3ed742e4a1d46e5424aa335e__SUSE-Linux-
Enterprise-Server-11-SP2-New" -LinuxUser "root"  -Password P@ssw0rd
-AffinityGroup "CoontosoAffinityGroup"
```

Scenario 10 – provisioning the new Windows Azure VM (advanced mode)

In this scenario, you will create a Windows Azure virtual machine that is running the Windows operating system using the advanced mode in order to add extra configurations that are not available using the quick mode, such as virtual machine disk and endpoint configurations. For this purpose, you will use a combination of the following Azure cmdlets:

- The `New-AzureVMConfig` cmdlet is used to configure a new virtual machine configuration. Its parameters are as follows:
    - ° `-Name`: Defines the name of the virtual machine.
    - ° `-ImageName`: Defines the name of the image that will be used to provision the virtual machine.
    - ° `-InstanceSize`: Defines the size of the virtual machine: "ExtraSmall", "Small", "Medium", "Large", or "ExtraLarge". The difference between instance sizes is the number of CPU cores and memory.

- The `Add-AzureProvisionConfig` cmdlet is used to define the virtual machine's provision configuration, such as the operating system, domain, time zone, and automatic updates. Its parameters are as follows:
    - ° `-Windows`: Defines that the virtual machine will run a Windows operating system
    - ° `-Password`: Defines the operating system's administrator password
    - ° `-DisableAutomaticUpdates`: Disables the automatic update feature on the virtual machine
    - ° `-ResetPasswordOnFirstLogon`: Forces the user to change the password on the first login
    - ° `-TimeZone`: Defines the time zone for the virtual machine
    - ° `-WindowsDomain`: Defines that the virtual machine will join a domain
    - ° `-Domain`: Defines the name of the domain the virtual machine will join

- ° -JoinDomain: Defines the fully qualified domain name (FQDN) of the domain the virtual machine will join

- ° -DomainUserName: Defines the username of the domain account that has permission to join the virtual machine to the domain

- ° -DomainPassword: Defines the password for the domain username

- ° -MachineObjectOU: Defines the fully qualified domain name (FQDN) for the **Organizational Unit (OU)** in which the computer account will be created

- The New-AzureVM cmdlet is used to create a new virtual machine using the previously created virtual machine configuration and provisioning configuration. Its parameters are as follows:

  - ° -ServiceName: Defines the cloud service that will host the virtual machine

  - ° -VMs: Defines the virtual machine configuration object that will be used to create the virtual machine

You can use the following code:

```
#Create Azure VM configuration
PS> $vm1 = New-AzureVMConfig -Name myWeb01 -InstanceSize
Medium -ImageName "a699494373c04fc0bc8f2bb1389d6106__Windows-
Server-2012-Datacenter-201212.01-en.us-30GB.vhd" | Add-
AzureProvisioningConfig -Windows –Password "P@ssw0rd" –WindowsDomain
–Domain "Contoso" –JoinDomain "Contoso.com" –DomainUserName
"Administrator" –DomainPassword "P@ssw0rd" -MachineObjectOU
"OU=Azure,DC=Contoso,DC=com" -DisableAutomaticUpdates –
ResetPasswordOnFirstLogon –TimeZone "Pacific Standard Time"

#Create Azure VM using the previously created VM
PS> New-AzureVM -ServiceName "ContosoWeb" -VMs $vm1
```

Scenario 11 – Adding a new endpoint to Windows Azure VM (NoLB)

In this scenario, you have a secure website running on the Windows Azure virtual machine and you want to make this website accessible to other users. In order to achieve this task, you will have to create an endpoint that is configured to allow communication between users in different networks and the website on your virtual machine. Network Endpoint is similar to the concept of **Network Address Translation (NAT)** or the Port Forward features in network switches and routers.

To make your website accessible to other users, you will use the Add-AzureEndPoint cmdlet with the following parameters to add a new **Not Load-Balanced (NoLB)** endpoint to the secure website-utilizing port 443 for HTTPS:

- -Name: Defines the name of the Endpoint rule
- -Protocol: Defines the protocol of the endpoint, either TCP or UDP
- -LocalPort: Defines the local port of the endpoint that is used for communicating with the application on the virtual machine
- -PublicPort: Defines the public port that the Endpoint will use to listen to incoming requests

You can use the following steps:

1. Get the Windows Azure VM you want to assign the Endpoint rule to, using the Get-AzureVM cmdlet with the –ServiceName and –Name parameters.
2. Use the Add-AzureEndPoint cmdlet to add a new endpoint.
3. Commit the changes on the virtual machine using the Update-AzureVM cmdlet.

You can use the following code:

```
#Add NoLB EndPoint to Windows Azure virtual machine
PS> Get-AzureVM -ServiceName "CorpWebsite" -Name "WebSrv01" | Add-AzureEndpoint -Name "HTTPs" -Protocol tcp -LocalPort 443 -PublicPort 443 | Update-AzureVM
```

Scenario 12 – configuring the Windows Azure Virtual Machines load balancing (LB)

In this scenario, you have cloud services running on the corporate website portal; these cloud services consist of three virtual web servers, and you want to make sure that load balancing is configured for this server. In order to achieve this task, you will have to add a new Load-Balancing Endpoint and assign this endpoint to all those virtual machines that should be members of the load balancing stack.

For this purpose, you will use the `Add-AzureEndPoint` cmdlet with the following parameters to add a new **Load-Balanced (LB)** EndPoint for the server hosting the website portal:

- `-Name`: Defines a name for the EndPoint rule
- `-Protocol`: Defines the protocol for the endpoint, either TCP or UDP
- `-LocalPort`: Defines the local port for the endpoint that is used for communicating with the application on the virtual machine
- `-PublicPort`: Defines the public port that the endpoint will use to listen to incoming requests
- `-LBSetName`: Defines a name for the Load-Balanced EndPoint set
- `-ProbeProtocol`: Defines the protocol for the Load-Balanced EndPoint that is to be probed (tested); it's either HTTP or TCP
- `-ProbePort`: Defines the port to be used by the probes; by default, the public port is used if this parameter is not defined
- `-ProbePath`: Defines the URI to be used by the probes; it's used only with the HTTP probe protocol

You can use the following steps:

1. Get all Windows Azure VMs under the cloud service that you want to assign a Load-Balanced EndPoint to, using the `Get-AzureVM` cmdlet with the `-ServiceName` parameter.
2. Use the `Add-AzureEndPoint` cmdlet to add a new endpoint.
3. Commit the changes on the virtual machine using the `Update-AzureVM` cmdlet.

You can use the following code:

```
#Add Load-Balanced EndPoint to Windows Azure virtual machine
PS> Get-AzureVM -ServiceName CorpWebsite  | Add-AzureEndpoint -Name
"LB-Http" -Protocol tcp -PublicPort 80 -LocalPort 80 -LBSetName "LB-
WebFarm" -ProbePort 80 -ProbeProtocol "http" -ProbePath "/" | Update-
AzureVM
```

Scenario 13 – creating and assigning a data disk to Windows Azure Virtual Machine

In this scenario, you have a Windows Azure virtual machine with only one disk for the operating system, and you want to create a new data disk and attach it to this virtual machine. For this purpose, you will use the `Add-AzureDataDisk` cmdlet with the following group of parameters:

- `-CreateNew`: Creates a new data disk
- `-DiskLabel`: Defines the disk label for the new data disk
- `-DiskSizeInGB`: Defines the data disk size in gigabytes
- `-LUN`: Defines the Logical Unit Number (LUN) location for the data disk in the virtual machine; you can assign LUN from 0 to 15

You can use the following steps:

1. Get the Windows Azure VM to which you want to assign the data disk, using the `Get-AzureVM` cmdlet with the `-ServiceName` and `-Name` parameters.

2. Use the `Add-AzureDataDisk` cmdlet with `-CreateNew` to create a new data disk.

3. Commit the changes on the virtual machine using the `Update-AzureVM` cmdlet.

You can use the following code:

```
#Create and Assign a new data disk to Windows Azure VM
PS> Get-AzureVM -ServiceName "myWebFarm" -Name WebSrv01 |
Add-AzureDataDisk -CreateNew -DiskSizeInGB 30 -DiskLabel
"UserDataDisk" -LUN 0 | Update-AzureVM
```

Scenario 14 – moving the Local VHD to Windows Azure

In this scenario, you want to migrate a virtual machine from your on-premise Hyper-V server to Windows Azure without rebuilding the server from scratch. So you have decided to move the local VHD file for the virtual machine to your storage on Windows Azure. For this purpose, you will use the `Add-AzureVhd` cmdlet with the following group of parameters:

- The `Add-AzureVhd` cmdlet is used to move the VHD file from the local server to Windows Azure. Its parameters are as follows:
    - `-LocalFilePath`: Assigns the file path for the local VHD file

- ○ -Destination: Assigns the URI for the Windows Azure container to which the VHD will upload

- The Add-AzureDisk cmdlet is used to add the VHD to the Windows Azure Disk library. Its parameters are as follows:

  - ○ -OS: Defines that the VHD is an operating system disk; it accepts either Windows or Linux
  - ○ -DiskName: Defines the name of the disk on the library
  - ○ -MediaLocation: Defines the location of the VHD that is to be added to the disk library

You can use the following steps:

1. Define a variable $LocalVHD to store the local path for the VHD file.
2. Define a variable $Destination to store the URI for the Windows Azure container.
3. Use the Add-AzureVhd cmdlet to move the VHD file.
4. Use the Add-AzureDisk cmdlet to convert the VHD to Azure Disk and store it in the disk library.

You can use the following code:

```
#Get the Azure Storage Account for the default Azure Subscription
PS> $StorageAccountName = (Get-AzureSubscription).CurrentStorageAccount

#Define DiskName
PS> $DiskName = "AppVServerDisk"

#Define Local VHD file path
PS > $LocalVHD = 'D:\Hyper-V\Virtual Hard Disks\AppVServer.vhd'

#Define the URI for the Windows Azure Container
PS > $Destination = 'http://' + $StorageAccountName + '.blob.core.
windows.net/vhds/AppVServerDisk.vhd'

#Move VHD file from local server to Windows Azure Storage
PS > Add-AzureVhd -LocalFilePath $LocalVHD -Destination $Destination

#Convert the VHD file to Windows Azure Disk
PS > Add-AzureDisk -OS Windows -DiskName $DiskName -MediaLocation
$Destination
```

Scenario 15 – provisioning a new Windows Azure VM from a Disk

In this scenario, you have a VHD for one of your virtual servers that has recently been moved from the on-premise Hyper-V server to the Windows Azure storage, and you want to create a new Windows Azure virtual machine using this VHD. For this purpose, you will use a combination of the following Azure cmdlets:

- The `New-AzureVMConfig` cmdlet is used to create a new virtual machine configuration. Its parameters are as follows:
    - `-Name`: Defines the name for the new virtual machine.
    - `-DiskName`: Defines the name of the disk that will be attached to the virtual machine to provision it.
    - `-InstanceSize`: Defines the size of the virtual machine: "ExtraSmall", "Small", "Medium", "Large", or "ExtraLarge". The difference between instance sizes is the number of CPU cores and memory.

- The `New-AzureVM` cmdlet is used to create a new virtual machine using the previously created virtual machine configuration and provisioning configuration. Its parameters are as follows:
    - `-ServiceName`: Defines the cloud service that will host the virtual machine
    - `-VMs`: Defines the virtual machine configuration object that will be used to create the virtual machine

You can use the following code:

```
#Create Azure VM Configuration object
PS> $vm1 = New-AzureVMConfig -Name AppVServer -InstanceSize Medium
-DiskName "AppVServerDisk"

#Create new VM from Azure VM Configuration
PS> New-AzureVM -ServiceName "ContosoWeb" -VMs $vm1
```

Scenario 16 – creating Windows Azure Image from a VM

In this scenario, you have a customized Windows Azure virtual machine and you want to use this virtual machine as a base image for the future provisioning of virtual machines. For this purpose, you will use the `Save-AzureVMImage` cmdlet to capture the virtual machine and save it as an image.

The parameters of the `Save-AzureVMImage` cmdlet are as follows:

- `-ServiceName`: Defines the name of the cloud service hosting the virtual machine
- `-Name`: Defines the name of the virtual machine
- `-NewImageName`: Defines a name for the new image

> Make sure to Sysprep your virtual machine before using the `Save-AzureVMImage` cmdlet.

You can use the following code:

```
#Create Azure VM Image
PS> Save-AzureVMImage -ServiceName "CorpWebsite" -Name "myWeb01"
-NewImageName "Corp Website Core Image, Update Jan 2013"
```

Scenario 17 – exporting and importing Windows Azure VM

In this scenario, you have a Windows Azure virtual machine running under a specific cloud service and you want to move it to another cloud service. Unfortunately, there is no option in the Windows Azure portal that allows moving the virtual machine between different cloud services. The workaround is to use a combination of Windows Azure PowerShell cmdlets to achieve this goal. These cmdlets are as follows:

- The `Export-AzureVM` cmdlet is used to export a virtual machine state (configuration) to an XML file. Its parameters are as follows:
  - `-ServiceName`: Defines the name of the cloud service hosting the virtual machine
  - `-Name`: Defines the name of the virtual machine
  - `-Path`: Defines the path in which to export the XML state file

- The `Remove-AzureVM` cmdlet is used to remove the current virtual machine and lease the attached disk. Its parameters are as follows:
    - ° `-ServiceName`: Defines the name of the cloud service hosting the virtual machine
    - ° `-Name`: Defines the name of the virtual machine

 The `Remove-AzureVM` cmdlet removes the virtual machine but not the attached disk.

- The `Import-AzureVM` cmdlet is used to import the virtual machine state file. Its parameter is as follows:
    - ° `-Path`: Defines the path of the XML state file

 The `Import-AzureVM` cmdlet might import the virtual machine with a new IP Address.

- he `New-AzureVM` cmdlet is used to create a new virtual machine using a state (configuration) XML file imported in the last step. Its parameter is as follows:

    - ° `-ServiceName`: Defines the name of the cloud service hosting the virtual machine

You can use the following code:

```
#Export Azure VM configuration
PS> Export-AzureVM -ServiceName CorpWebsite -Name myWeb01 -Path $home\
desktop\myWeb01.xml

#Remove Azure VM
PS> Remove-AzureVM -ServiceName CorpWebsite -Name myWeb01

#Importing Azure VM configuration file, and create new VM using the
import file
PS> Import-AzureVM -Path $home\desktop\myWeb01.xml | New-AzureVM
-ServiceName CorpPortal
```

Scenario 18 – starting, stopping, and restarting the Windows Azure VM

In this scenario, you have a large number of Windows Azure virtual machines and you spend a lot of time starting, restarting, or stopping these using the management portal. Using the management portal, you are doing this task one by one and you want to discover the other possibilities in PowerShell. For this purpose, Windows Azure PowerShell provides a quick and basic task equivalent to this:

- The `Start-AzureVM` cmdlet used to power on a virtual machine
- The `Stop-AzureVM` cmdlet used to shut down a running virtual machine
- The `Restart-AzureVM` cmdlet used to restart a virtual machine

All three cmdlets use the same parameters as follows:

- `-ServiceName`: Defines the name of the cloud service hosting the virtual machine
- `-Name`: Defines the name of the virtual machine

You can use the following code:

```
#Start Azure VM
PS> Start-AzureVM -ServiceName CorpWebsite -Name myWeb01

#Restart Azure VM
PS> Restart-AzureVM -ServiceName CorpWebsite -Name myWeb01

#Shutdown Azure VM
PS> Stop-AzureVM -ServiceName CorpWebsite -Name myWeb01
```

Scenario 19 – uploading the certificate to Windows Azure

In this scenario, you have a **Secure Socket Layer (SSL)** certificate that you want to use for one of the services hosted on Windows Azure. In order to use it, you will have to upload it first to your Windows Azure subscription. For this purpose, you will use the `Add-AzureCertificate` cmdlet with the following group of parameters:

- `-ServiceName`: Defines the cloud service in which you will deploy the certificate

- `-CertToDeploy`: Defines the local path for the certificate files such as CER and PFX certificates

- `-Password`: Defines the certificate password, if any

You can use the following code:

```
#Upload certificate to Windows Azure service
PS> Add-AzureCertificate -ServiceName "myDevEnv" -CertToDeploy
<myCertificate.pfx> -Password abc123
```

Scenario 20 – generating the Azure Virtual Machine RDP file

In this scenario, you will generate a remote desktop file for your Windows Azure virtual machines so you can connect to them directly instead of using the Windows Azure portal. For this purpose, you will use the `Get-AzureRemoteDesktopFile` cmdlet with the following group of parameters:

- `-ServiceName`: Defines the cloud service in which your virtual machine resides

- `-Name`: Defines the name of the virtual machine for which you want to generate the RDP file

- `-LocalPath`: Defines the local path where you want to save the RDP file

- `-Launch`: Launches the remote desktop session for the selected session

You can use the following code:

```
#Generate Remote Desktop File for Windows Azure VM
PS> Get-AzureRemoteDesktopFile -ServiceName "myDevEnv" -Name
"DevTools" -LocalPath $home\Desktop\DevTools.rdp -Launch
```

Summary

It is very obvious that cloud computing is the future of our ICT industry; it is going to be a core component in each and every entity, and this is no secret. There are huge benefits and roadmaps provided by this technology for future growth.

In this chapter, we have seen Microsoft Windows Azure and SQL Azure as a real-life example of a cloud computing implementation, and we have learned how Windows PowerShell can play a major role in operating such a technology easily, as if managing a normal virtualized environment.

In the next chapter, we will talk about IT Process Automation (also known as Runbook automation) and the concept behind it. Also, we will learn how Windows PowerShell and System Center Orchestrator can be integrated together to implement and complete this concept in real life.

12
Integrating Windows PowerShell and System Center Orchestrator

In previous chapters of this book, we had a deeper look at Windows PowerShell and its capabilities as an automation engine. We also had a long tour discovering Windows PowerShell and its capabilities with different products and technologies. The fact is that PowerShell is not only a command-line interface (for products such as Exchange Server or Windows Server) that allows a better and easier configuration and management, but it also plays a major role in areas such as **Business Process Automation (BPA)**.

In this chapter we will cover the following topics:

- What is **IT Process Automation (ITPA)**?
- What is **System Center Orchestrator (SCO)**?
- Windows PowerShell and System Center Orchestrator are better together.

Completing your ITPA story with PowerShell and Orchestrator

ITPA, also known as **Run Book Automation (RBA)**, is the concept of delivering an end-to-end automation, integration, and orchestration scenarios between people, processes, tools, and other different parties in enterprise and complex IT environments.

ITPA is one of the best ways to:

- Increase IT resource utilization and allocation; the resources are either people or equipment
- Reduce the cost of operations as it reduces the human error factor, **Mean Time To Respond/Repair (MTTR)**
- Effectively and efficiently implement IT industry standards and best practices, such as ITIL and **Microsoft Operations Framework (MOF)**

What System Center Orchestrator is

System Center Orchestrator is the Microsoft platform for implementing ITPA. Orchestrator allows you to build workflows that automate and integrate the different tools and software from the same and different vendors together in order to standardize deployment, provisioning, configuring, monitoring, and troubleshooting of the different components in your IT environment.

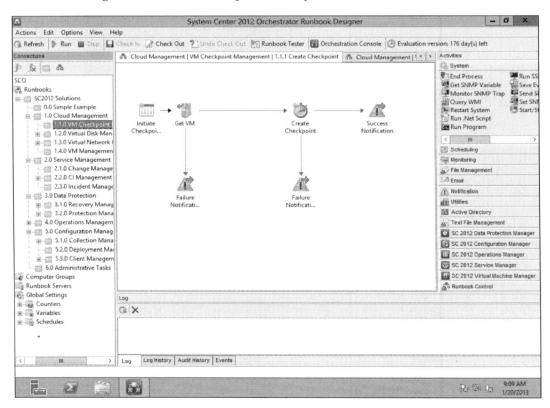

Understanding Orchestrator workflows

As mentioned earlier in this book, the workflow term represents a set of objects, tasks, and activities that are connected together and are running concurrently or sequentially. In Orchestrator, the workflow activity represents a task such as creating a new domain user or creating a new mailbox, and each group of activities is wrapped together in a package called **Integration Pack (IP)**, where each Integration Pack contains a set of related tasks. For example, Active Directory Integration Pack contains a set of activities that represents the different Active Directory tasks such as creating security groups, removing organizational units, and resetting computer accounts. The activities in Orchestrator are either .NET activities developed using Orchestrator SDK and C# or are activities created by Command Line Activity Wizard using command line tools such as Windows PowerShell or SSH.

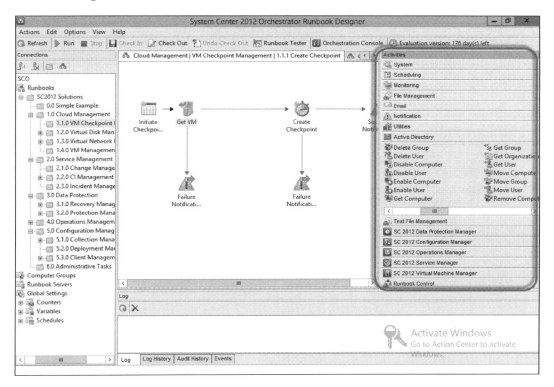

If you had the time to play with **System Center Operations Manager (SCOM)**, you definitely know that SCOM requires a **Management Pack (MP)** for the different software and hardware in order to be capable to monitor these products. The concept applies to SCO, where vendors provide the Integration Pack for their products in order to automate and integrate them with each other.

Orchestrator and PowerShell are better together

The great thing about Orchestrator and PowerShell is that they complement the missing parts in each other. In this section you will find how this can happen by covering the following points:

- Using PowerShell in Orchestrator workflow
- Using PowerShell to build Orchestrator Integration Packs

Using PowerShell in Orchestrator workflow

Although Orchestrator provides a variety of Integration Packs for different products across different vendors, you may sometimes need an activity that is not available or is has a limited functionality. That is why Orchestrator has a standard activity called *Run .Net Script*, which allows you to write your own PowerShell code to be executed as an activity within your workflow.

The following steps show how you can achieve this task:

1. Launch **Runbook Designer** in System Center Orchestrator.

2. Under the **Connections** pane on the left-hand side, select **Runbook Server**, and then right-click on **Runbooks** folder and go to **New | Runbook** to create a new Runbook, as shown in the following screenshot:

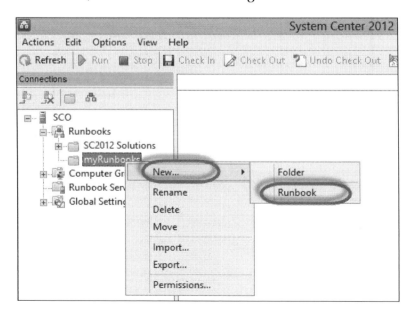

3. Under the **Activities** pane on the right-hand side, select **System | Run .NET Script**, and then drag-and-drop the activity to the Runbook design area as shown in the following screenshot:

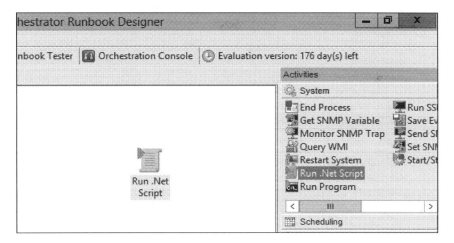

4. Open the **Run .NET Script** activity to select the language type and script code, as shown in the following screenshot:

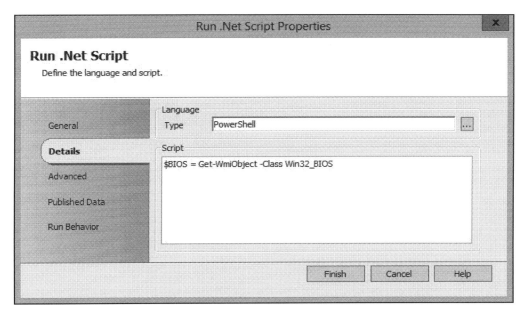

5. If you want to load specific *Namespaces* or *Assembly References*, go to **Advanced**, and then add the binaries you want.

6. If you want to retrieve the results of the script in a variable that can be passed to another workflow activity, go to **Published Data**, and click on **Add** to add new published data, and then enter the following details:

    1. **Name**: Name of the published data that will be used be Orchestrator

    2. **Type**: Data type of the data populated from PowerShell

    3. **Variable name**: PowerShell variable name that stores the results

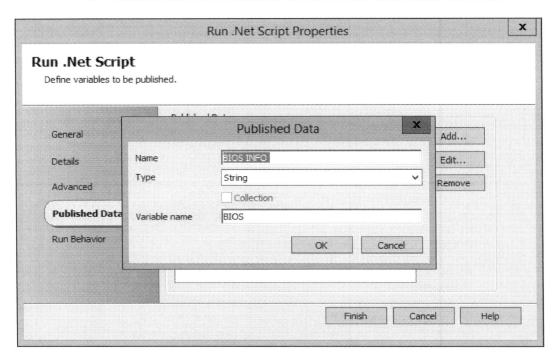

7. Click on **OK** to add the new published data, and then click on **Finish** to close the activity properties wizard.

8. Launch **Runbook Tester** to test the workflow activities.

9. In the **Runbook Tester** window, click on **Run** to start workflow testing and monitor the testing logs in the bottom-center pane, as shown in the following screenshot:

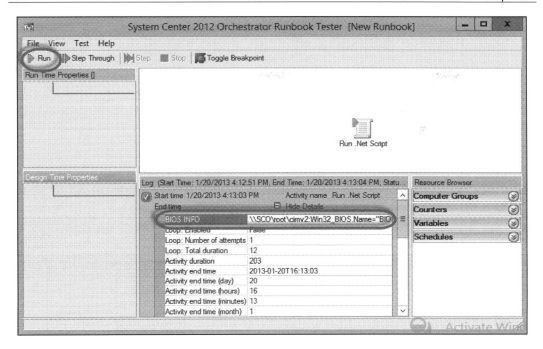

Using PowerShell to build Orchestrator Integration Packs

Usually, enterprises do not rely only on ready-made software and solutions from software vendors but might also develop their own **Line-of-Business (LoB)** applications. In order to automate such an application, you have to build your own custom activities and IPs.

For the purpose of achieving this task, Orchestrator already comes with the Orchestrator Integration toolkit that helps you to extend Orchestrator's capabilities by developing different types of custom activities and IPs.

Orchestrator Integration Toolkit contains:

- **Integration Toolkit SDK**: This is a **Software Development Kit (SDK)** for System Center Orchestrator that allows building custom activities using C#.
- **Command Line Activity Wizard**: This wizard allows building custom activities using command line tools such as Windows `cmd`, Windows PowerShell, and SSH.
- **Integration Pack Wizard**: This utility allows wrapping the custom activities' assemblies generated by either Integration Toolkit SDK or Command-Line Activity Wizard in Integration Pack format.

Orchestrator Integration Toolkit can be downloaded at: `http://www.microsoft.com/en-us/download/details.aspx?id=28725`

After downloading and installing Orchestrator Integration Toolkit, it is now time to start building your first custom activity and Integration Pack. In order to build a custom activity using PowerShell, you need to use the Command-Line Activity Wizard.

In the following example, you will create a custom activity that accepts the *Computer Name* as a parameter to retrieve its operating system information using the `Win32_OperatingSystem` WMI class.

Step 1 – creating the assembly file (.dll)

In this step you will learn how the assembly file that contains the commands and activities will be used later to build the Integration Pack.

1. Launch **Orchestrator Command-Line Activity Wizard**, and then click on **Next** to create a new custom activity assembly file.

 This wizard allows you to either create a new assembly for the custom activity or modify an existing assembly.

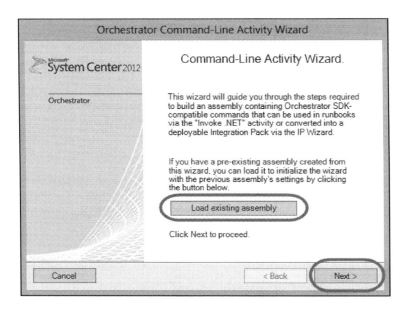

2. Enter the assembly file's name and the path to create and save the assembly file, and then click on **Next** to move to the commands step.

 Use the **Assembly Information** button to add more details about the assembly, such as description, company, and version.

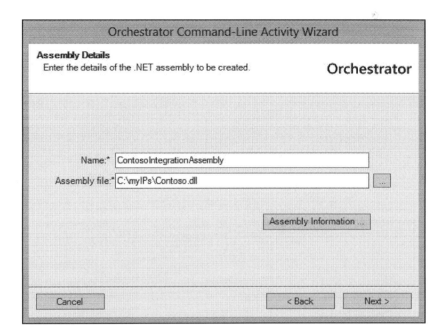

3. Now it is time to define the commands that will be used by the custom activity. In this case, define the command that will retrieve the operating system information for a specific computer. Click on the **Add** button to define your command.

   Under the **General** tab, define:

   1. **Name**: Name of the command

   2. **Mode**: Command mode such as Windows Command, PowerShell, SSH, or Run a Program

   3. **Program**: select a program if the command's **Mode** is Run a Program

4. **Description**: Description of the command

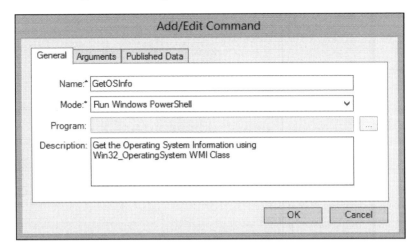

Under the **Arguments** tab, define:

1. The parameters that will be passed to the command line:

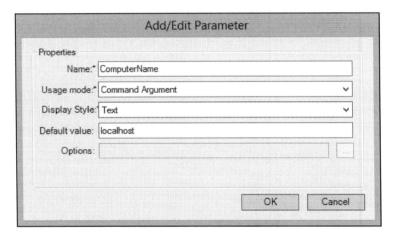

2. The command line that will be executed:

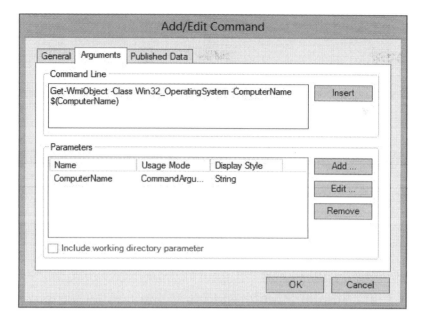

Under the **Published Data** tab, define:

1. The results of command-line execution and how they will be displayed in Orchestrator.

2. You need to create a published data record for each property you want to show.

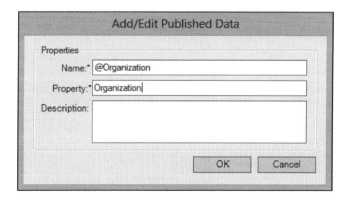

The @ symbol is for published data record names for the sake of better sorting when displaying the results.

4. Click on **Next** to build and create the assembly file.

Now, after building the assembly file for the command-line custom activity, it is time to use it, either by loading it to the Runbook using the `Invoke.Net` activity or wrapping the assembly in an Integration Pack.

Step 2 – creating the Integration Pack

In this step you will learn how to use the assembly file created in the previous step and the Integration Pack Wizard to build your first integration pack.

1. Launch **Orchestrator Integration Pack Wizard**, and then click on **Next** to create a new IP file.

 This wizard allows you to either create an IP or modify an existing IP.

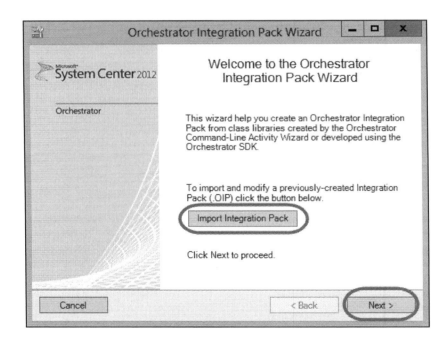

2. Enter the new Integration Pack details and then click on **Next**

3. Now it is time to define the activities that will be part of this IP by selecting the custom assembly files created in the previous step. Each command in the assembly file represents a single activity in the Integration Pack.

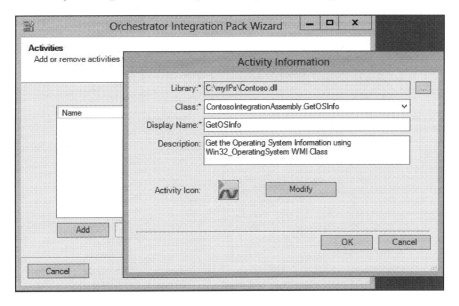

4. Define the Integration Pack dependencies and the files to be deployed with the Integration Pack, such as documentations, scripts, and the assembly file.

5. Finally, define the path to create and save the Integration Pack file, and then click on **Next** to start building the file, as shown in the following screenshot:

Step 3 – importing the Integration Pack into Orchestrator

In this step you will learn how to import the Integration Pack created in the previous step into System Center Orchestrator.

1. Launch **Orchestrator Deployment Manager**.

2. Choose Orchestrator Management Server on which you want to deploy the Integration Pack if you have more than one server.

3. Right-click on the **Integration Packs** folder, select **Register IP with the Orchestrator Management Server**, and then follow the wizard to select the Contoso.OIP IP file to register it with the server.

4. Right-click on the **Integration Packs** folder, select **Deploy IP to Runbook Server or Runbook Designer**, and then follow the wizard to select the IP that has been registered in the previous step, Contoso IP, and choose the server to deploy on it.

Step 4 – testing and using the new Integration Pack

In this step you will learn how to test and use the Integration Pack created and imported in steps 2 and 3.

1. Launch **System Center Orchestrator Runbook Designer**.

2. Under the **Activities** pane on the right-hand side, you will find a new tab called **Contoso Basic Automation** with a single activity, **GetOSInfo**; select it and then drag-and-drop the activity to Runbook's design area.

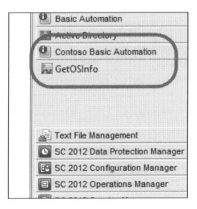

3. Open the **GetOSInfo** activity to modify the **ComputerName** property, which was defined as a parameter in the Command-Line Activity Wizard:

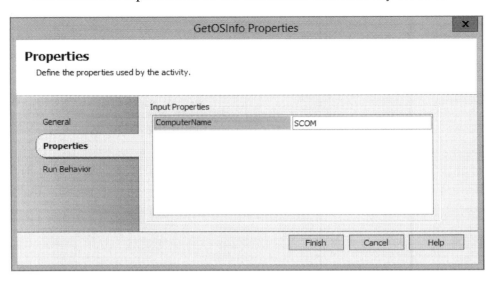

4. Launch the **Runbook Tester** application to test the workflow activities.

5. In the **Runbook Tester** window, click on **Run** to start workflow testing and monitor the testing logs in the bottom-center pane. In the first few records in the log section, you will notice that the published data starts with the "@" symbol reflecting the results from PowerShell execution:

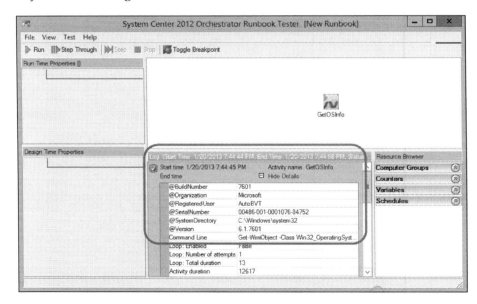

Summary

Windows PowerShell is not just a command-line tool or a scripting engine; it provides different capabilities and usage scenarios depending on the area you are using Windows PowerShell in and for.

In this chapter, we have seen how enterprises and entities with complex IT environments can use Windows PowerShell with another component such as System Center Orchestrator to define a new meaning for automation and provide more benefits and values via IT Process Automation.

Now, having reached the final destination together in this book, it is your turn to take the lead and continue sailing the Windows PowerShell sea with your own ship and the tools you have learned in this book to gain more, build your own scripting Arsenal, and become ready for any challenge. Just remember that PowerShell is the future, so be ready for more to learn.

Index

Symbols

Thank you for buying
PowerShell 3.0 Advanced Administration Handbook

About Packt Publishing

Packt, pronounced 'packed', published its first book "Mastering phpMyAdmin for Effective MySQL Management" in April 2004 and subsequently continued to specialize in publishing highly focused books on specific technologies and solutions.

Our books and publications share the experiences of your fellow IT professionals in adapting and customizing today's systems, applications, and frameworks. Our solution based books give you the knowledge and power to customize the software and technologies you're using to get the job done. Packt books are more specific and less general than the IT books you have seen in the past. Our unique business model allows us to bring you more focused information, giving you more of what you need to know, and less of what you don't.

Packt is a modern, yet unique publishing company, which focuses on producing quality, cutting-edge books for communities of developers, administrators, and newbies alike. For more information, please visit our website: www.packtpub.com.

About Packt Enterprise

In 2010, Packt launched two new brands, Packt Enterprise and Packt Open Source, in order to continue its focus on specialization. This book is part of the Packt Enterprise brand, home to books published on enterprise software – software created by major vendors, including (but not limited to) IBM, Microsoft and Oracle, often for use in other corporations. Its titles will offer information relevant to a range of users of this software, including administrators, developers, architects, and end users.

Writing for Packt

We welcome all inquiries from people who are interested in authoring. Book proposals should be sent to author@packtpub.com. If your book idea is still at an early stage and you would like to discuss it first before writing a formal book proposal, contact us; one of our commissioning editors will get in touch with you.

We're not just looking for published authors; if you have strong technical skills but no writing experience, our experienced editors can help you develop a writing career, or simply get some additional reward for your expertise.

SQL Server 2012 with PowerShell V3 Cookbook

ISBN: 978-1-84968-646-4   Paperback: 634 pages

Increase your productivity as a DBA, developer, or IT Pro, by using PowerShell with SQL Server to simplify database management and automate repetitive, mundane tasks

1. Provides over a hundred practical recipes that utilize PowerShell to automate, integrate and simplify SQL Server tasks

2. Offers easy to follow, step-by-step guide to getting the most out of SQL Server and PowerShell

3. Covers numerous guidelines, tips, and explanations on how and when to use PowerShell cmdlets, WMI, SMO, .NET classes or other components

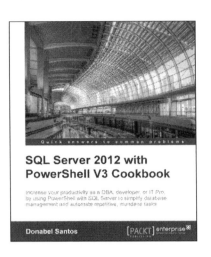

Microsoft Exchange 2010 PowerShell Cookbook

ISBN: 978-1-84968-246-6   Paperback: 480 pages

Manage and maintain your Microsoft Exchange 2010 environment with Windows PowerShell 2.0 and the Exchange Management Shell

1. Step-by-step instructions on how to write scripts for nearly every aspect of Exchange 2010 including the Client Access Server, Mailbox, and Transport server roles

2. Understand the core concepts of Windows PowerShell 2.0 that will allow you to write sophisticated scripts and one-liners used with the Exchange Management Shel

Please check **www.PacktPub.com** for information on our titles

Microsoft Windows PowerShell 3.0 First Look

A quick, succinct guide to the new and exciting features in PowerShell 3.0

Adam Driscoll

Microsoft Windows PowerShell 3.0 First Look

ISBN: 978-1-84968-644-0   Paperback: 200 pages

A quick, succinct guide to the new and exciting features in PowerShell 3.0

1. Explore and experience the new features found in PowerShell 3.0

2. Understand the changes to the language and the reasons why they were implemented

3. Discover new cmdlets and modules available in Windows 8 and Server 8

4. Quickly get up to date with the latest version of Powershell with concise descriptions and simple examples

Microsoft SharePoint 2010 and Windows PowerShell 2.0: Expert Cookbook

50 advanced recipes for administrators and IT Pros to master Microsoft SharePoint 2010 and Microsoft PowerShell 2.0 automation

Yaroslav Pentsarskyy

Microsoft SharePoint 2010 and Windows PowerShell 2.0: Expert Cookbook

ISBN: 978-1-84968-410-1   Paperback: 310 pages

50 advanced recipes for administrators and IT Pros to master Microsoft SharePoint 2010 and Microsoft PowerShell 2.0 automation

1. Dive straight into expert recipes for SharePoint and PowerShell administration without dwelling on the basics

2. Master how to administer BCS in SharePoint, automate the configuration of records management features, create custom PowerShell cmdlets

3. A hands-on cookbook focusing on only the most high level tips and tricks for mastering SharePoint and PowerShell administration

Please check **www.PacktPub.com** for information on our titles

37470790R00209

Made in the USA
Lexington, KY
03 December 2014